By Hilaire Belloc

Cautionary Verses
The Bad Child's Book of Beasts
More Beasts for Worse Children

These are Borzoi Books
published in New York by Alfred A. Knopf

BELLOC

BELLOC

A Biographical Anthology

Edited by

HERBERT VAN THAL

Alfred A. Knopf   New York   1970

When I am dead, I hope it may be said:
His sins were scarlet, but his books were read.

HILAIRE BELLOC

'Belloc will probably be "edited" in a hundred years'
time, when his propagandism has become archaic,
and when his extraordinary ability will shine like the
jewel it is.'

FRANK SWINNERTON:
The Georgian Literary Scene 1935 (p. 10)

'Belloc's own magnificent English should be less read
about than read; and preferably read aloud. It is not
only a flexible and sensitive and precise instrument
for conveying meaning. It can give to the listener a
shock of auditory pleasure like that shock of visual
delight with which unerring draughtsmanship is seen.'

RENÉE HAYNES:
Hilaire Belloc, pp. 21–2, 1953.

ACKNOWLEDGMENTS

*The editor expresses his thanks to
the following for permission to include
the extracts from the following works of Belloc.*

Messrs Duckworth & Co for
Sonnets and Verse and *Cautionary Tales.*

Messrs Allen & Unwin for *The Path to Rome.*

The Oxford University Press for *The French Revolution.*

Messrs Constable & Co for *The Cruise of the Nona.*

CONTENTS

FOREWORD

When my old friend, Bertie van Thal, invited me to write a Foreword to this book, it gave me the chance of doing two things. One was to do a very small service for a selfless, loyal and devoted servant of literature and of every author whose work he has ever sponsored. The other was to testify to the genius of one of the greatest and most versatile English writers of our age.

The controversial, not to say belligerent, character of some of Belloc's opinions, has tended to obscure for contemporaries the noble purity of his prose and poetry. So has the astonishing range of his genius in a country where versatility is always suspect. Mr van Thal's anthology will enable readers hitherto unacquainted with Belloc's work to appreciate his many-sided genius. Here is graphic historical narrative and imaginative, yet realistic, re-creation of the past as in his wonderful account of Louis XI's final triumph over Charles the Bold of Burgundy; character-drawing in the brilliant sketches of Mirabeau and Danton; satirical and comic verse of a laconic perfection seldom surpassed in our own or any other language; criticism like the scholarly Taylorian Lecture on Translation; topographical portraiture and much else beside; inspired poetry like those three marvellous, apocalyptic verses called 'Ha'nacker Mill'. For all his furious tilting at windmills, the man was a prophet; witness the sentence on our present rigid Party system written in 1911; 'We are in for one of those evil spaces, subject to foreign insults and domestic misfortune, which invariably attach to nations when, for a period, they lose grip over their destiny.'

The sheer magnitude of Belloc's contribution to English literature can be seen from the list of more than a hundred and fifty published works given in the Appendix. That from a new anthology of less than 400 pages much of high excellence has had to be omitted is inevitable; among so much writing that is superlative it has not been possible to include even the exquisite poem at the end

of *The Four Men* or these haunting verses—often reprinted—from
the Dedicatory Ode which picture

> *the tender Evenlode that makes*
> *Her meadows hush to hear the sound*
> *Of waters mingling in the brakes,*
> *And binds my heart to English ground.*

Yet there is one of Belloc's later poems so beautiful that, though
omitted from the main body of the book, I cannot refrain from
adding to the Foreword:

> *Lady, when your lovely head*
> *Droops to sink among the dead,*
> *And the quiet places keep*
> *You that so divinely sleep*
> *Then the dead shall blessed be*
> *With a new solemnity;*
> *For such Beauty, so descending*
> *Pledges them that Death is ending.*
> *Sleep your fill—but when you wake*
> *Dawn shall over Lethe break.*

ARTHUR BRYANT

PREFACE

Hilaire Belloc published over one hundred works, and at the time of writing this, most of these volumes are out of print, with the exception of his comic verse and two of his more famed books *The Path to Rome* and *The Cruise of the Nona*. To sample, now, his rich variety, one would have to turn to Mr J. B. Morton's admirable anthology in the *Everyman Library*. Previously an anthology had been compiled by that Belloc enthusiast, W. N. Roughead, but this is now out of print.

To celebrate the centenary of Belloc's birth, I felt that he deserved a new hearing, and we have thus devised this book on different lines from the existing and previous anthologies.

There is today, doubtless, an entirely new generation which knows little or nothing either of Belloc's life or of his works. To remedy this a little I have given an appropriate brief note linked to each selection from his writings.

Any author who lived as long as Belloc did, and who wrote as much as he did, would give an anthologist a difficult task of selection. My main objective has been to give representation to the differing facets of the man and his genius.

The reader seeking the 'best of Belloc' should certainly find it if he links this book with Mr Morton's.

I wish to thank Mr A. D. Peters for his considerable advice; Mr Robert Speaight's biography *Hilaire Belloc* and *Letters from Hilaire Belloc* were of inestimable value; Mr Frank Swinnerton came up to the Reform Club to talk to me about Belloc; Miss Joan Bailey of the London Library found every book I asked for; Mrs Mackay deciphered my illegible writing.

B.V.T.

BELLOC

I

The First Day's March
(From *Hills and the Sea*, 1906)
1891

*When Belloc was twenty-one years of age he enlisted in the French
Army, joining the 10th Battery of the 8th Regiment of Artillery at
Toul (the garrison town from whence he was to set forth on his famous
walk to Rome ten years later). 'He was described in the service book as
1.74 metres tall, chestnut-brown hair in colouring, with blue eyes, high
forehead, nose fort. He was placed in the second class for revolver
shooting and fencing, and in the third for gymnastics. It was noted that
he was an excellent swimmer, and that he could read, write and add up.'[1]*

*His life in the army was to prove very hard as his essay, 'The First
Day's March' from* Hills and the Sea *(1906) depicts. Yet it obviously
toughened him for his subsequent ability to become such a magnificent
walker, and it fostered his life-long interest in military matters. He
also learned to sing French songs, a lasting habit, and acquired a hatred
of the Prussian.*

[1] R. Speaight: *Hilaire Belloc*, p. 64.

3

The First Day's March

I very well remember the spring breaking ten years ago in Lorraine. I remember it better far than I shall ever remember another spring, because one of those petty summits of emotion that seem in boyhood like the peaks of the world was before me. We were going off to camp.

Since every man that fires guns or drives them in France—that is, some hundred thousand and more at any one time, and taking in reserves, half a million—must go to camp in his time, and that more than once, it seems monstrous that a boy should make so much of it; but then to a boy six months is a little lifetime, and for six months I had passed through that great annealing fire of drill which stamps and moulds the French people today, putting too much knowledge and bitterness into their eyes, but a great determination into their gestures and a trained tenacity into the methods of their thought.

To me also this fire seemed fiercer and more transforming because, until the day when they had marched me up to barracks in the dark and the rain with the batch of recruits, I had known nothing but the easy illusions and the comfort of an English village, and had had but journeys or short visits to teach me that enduring mystery of Europe, the French temper: whose aims and reticence, whose hidden enthusiasms, great range of effort, divisions, defeats, and resurrections must now remain the principal problem before my mind; for the few who had seen this sight know that the French mind is the pivot on which Europe turns.

I had come into the regiment faulty in my grammar and doubtful in accent, ignorant especially of those things which in every civilization are taken for granted but never explained in full; I was ignorant, therefore, of the key which alone can open that civilization to a stranger. Things irksome or a heavy burden to the young men of my age, born and brought up in the French air, were to me, brought up with Englishmen an Englishman, odious and bewildering. Orders that I but half comprehended; simple phrases that seemed charged with menace; boasting (a habit of which I knew little), coupled with a fierce and, as it were, expected courage that

4

seemed ill-suited to boasting—and certainly unknown outside this army; enormous powers of endurance in men whose stature my English training had taught me to despise; a habit of fighting with the fists, coupled with a curious contempt for the accident of individual superiority—all these things amazed me and put me into a topsy-turvy world where I was weeks in finding my feet.

But strangest of all, and (as I now especially believe) most pregnant with meaning for the future, was to find the inherited experience in me of so much teaching and careful habit—instinct of command, if you will—all that goes to make what we call in Western Europe a 'gentleman', put at the orders and the occasional insult of a hierarchy of office, many of whose functionaries were peasants and artisans. Stripes on the arm, symbols suddenly, became of overwhelming value; what I had been made with so much care in an English public school was here thought nothing but a hindrance and an absurdity. This had seemed to me first a miracle, then a grievous injustice, then most unpractical, and at last, like one that sees the answer to a riddle, I saw (when I had long lost my manners and ceased to care for refinements) that the French were attempting, a generation before any others in the world, to establish an army that should be a mere army, and in which a living man counted only as one numbered man.

Whether that experiment will hold or not I cannot tell; it shocks the refinement of the whole West of Europe; it seems monstrous to the aristocratic organization of Germany; it jars in France also with the traditions of that decent elder class of whom so many still remain to guide the Republic, and in whose social philosophy the segregation of a 'directing class' has been hitherto a dogma. But soon I cared little whether that experiment was to succeed or no in its final effort, or whether the French were to perfect a democracy where wealth has one vast experience of its own artificiality, or to fail. The intellectual interest of such an experiment, when once I seized it, drove out every other feeling.

I became like a man who has thoroughly awaked from a long sleep and finds that in sleep he has been taken overseas. I merged into the great system whose wheels and grindings had at first astonished or disgusted me, and I found that they had made of me what they meant to make. I cared more for guns than for books; I now obeyed by instinct not men, but symbols of authority. No comfortable fallacy remained; it no longer seemed strange that my captain was a man promoted from the ranks; that one of my lieutenants was an Alsation charity boy and the other a rich fellow mixed up with sugar-broking; that the sergeant of my piece should be a poor young noble, the wheeler of No. 5 a wealthy and very vulgar chemist's son, the man in the next bed (my 'ancient', as they say in that service) a cook of some skill, and my bombardier a mild young farmer. I thought only in terms of the artillery; I could judge men for their aptitude alone, and in me, I suppose, were accomplished many things—one of Danton's dreams, one of St Just's prophecies, the fulfilment also of what a hundred brains had silently determined twenty years before when the staff gave up their swords outside Metz; the army and the kind of army of which Chanzy had said in the first breath of the armistice, 'A man who forgets it should be hanged, but a man who speaks of it before its time should be shot with the honours of his rank.'

All this had happened to me in especial in that melting-pot up in the eastern hills, and to thirty thousand others that year in their separate crucibles.

In this process things had passed which would seem to you incredible if I wrote them all down. I cared little in what vessel I ate, or whether I had to tear meat with my fingers. I could march in reserve more than twenty miles a day for day upon day. I knew all about my horses; I could sweep, wash, make a bed, clean kit, cook a little, tidy a stable, turn to entrenching for emplacement, take a place at lifting a gun or changing a wheel. I took change with a gunner, and could point well. And all this was not learnt save under a grinding pressure of authority and harshness, without which in one's whole life I suppose one would never properly have learnt a half of these things—at least, not to do them so readily, or in such unison, or on so definite a plan. But (what will seem astonishing to our critics and verbalists) with all this there increased the power, or perhaps it was but the desire, to express the greatest thoughts— newer and keener things. I began to understand De Vigny when he wrote, 'If a man despairs of becoming a poet, let him carry his pack and march in the ranks.'

Thus the great hills that border the Moselle, the distant frontier, the vast plain which is (they say) to be a battlefield, and which lay five hundred feet sheer below me; the far guns when they were practising at Metz, the awful strength of columns on the march moved me. The sky also grew more wonderful, and I noticed living things. The Middle Ages, of which till then I had had but troubling visions, rose up and took flesh in the old town, on the rare winter evenings when I had purchased the leisure to leave quarters by some excessive toil. A man could feel France going by.

It was at the end of these six months, when there was no more darkness at roll-call, and when the bitter cold (that had frozen us all winter) was half forgotten, that the spring brought me this excellent news, earlier than I had dared to expect it—the news that sounds to a recruit half as good as active service. We were going to march and go off right away westward over half a dozen horizons, till we could see the real thing at Chalons, and with this news the world seemed recreated.

Seven times that winter we had been mobilized; four times in the dead of the night, once at mid-day, once at evening, and once at dawn. Seven times we had started down the wide Metz road, hoping in some vague way that they would do something with us and give us at least some manoeuvres, and seven times we had marched back to barracks to undo all that serious packing and to return to routine.

Once, for a week in February, the French and German Governments, or, more probably, two minor permanent officials, took it into their silly heads that there was some danger of war. We packed our campaign saddles every night and put them on the pegs behind the stalls; we had the emergency rations served out, and for two days in the middle of that time we had slept ready. But nothing came of it. Now at least we were off to play a little at the game whose theory we had learnt so wearily.

And the way I first knew it would easily fill a book if it were told as it should be, with every detail and its meaning unrolled and with every joy described: as it is, I must put it in ten lines. Garnon (a sergeant), three others, and I were sent out (one patrol out of fifty) to go round and see the reserve horses on the farms. That was delight enough, to have a vigorous windy morning with the clouds large and white and in a clear sky, and to mix with the first grain of the year, 'out of the loose-box'.

We took the round they gave us along the base of the high hills, we got our papers signed at the different stables, we noted the

7

hoofs of the horses and their numbers; a good woman at a large farm gave us food of eggs and onions, and at noon we turned to get back to quarters for the grooming. Everything then was very well— to have ridden out alone without the second horse and with no horrible great pole to crush one's leg, and be free—though we missed it—of the clank of the guns. We felt like gentlemen at ease, and were speaking grandly to each other, when I heard Garnon say to the senior of us a word that made things seem better still, for he pointed out to a long blue line beyond Domremy and overhanging the house of Joan of Arc, saying that the town lay there. 'What town?' said I to my Ancient; and my Ancient, instead of answering simply, took five minutes to explain to me how a recruit could not know that the round of the reserve horses came next before camp, and that this town away on the western ridge was the first halting-place upon the road. Then my mind filled with distances, and I was overjoyed, saving for this one thing, that I had but two francs and a few coppers left, and that I was not in reach of more.

When we had ridden in, saluted and reported at the guard, we saw the guns drawn up in line at the end of the yard, and we went into grooming and ate and slept, hardly waiting for the morning and the long regimental call before the réveillé; the notes that always mean the high road for an army, and that are as old as Fontenoy.

That next morning they woke us all before dawn—long before dawn. The sky was still keen, and there was not even a promise of morning in the air, nor the least faintness in the eastern stars. They twinkled right on the edges of the world over the far woods of Lorraine, beyond the hollow wherein lay the town; it was even cold like winter as we harnessed; and I remember the night air catching me in the face as I staggered from the harness-room, with my campaign saddle and the traces and the girths and the saddle cloth, and all the great weight that I had to put upon my horses.

We stood in the long stables all together, very hurriedly saddling and bridling and knotting up the traces behind. A few lanterns gave us an imperfect light. We hurried because it was a pride to be the first battery, and in the French service, rightly or wrongly, every-thing in the artillery is made for speed, and to speed everything is sacrificed. So we made ready in the stable and brought our horses

8

out in order before the guns in the open square of quarters. The high plateau on which the barracks stood was touched with a last late frost, and the horses coming out of the warm stables bore the change ill, lifting their heads and stamping. A man could not leave the leaders for a moment, and, while the chains were hooked on, even my middle horses were restive and had to be held. My hands stiffened at the reins, and I tried to soothe both my beasts, as the lantern went up and down wherever the work was being done. They quieted when the light was taken round behind by the tumbrils, where two men were tying on the great sack of oats exactly as though we were going on campaign.

These two horses of mine were called Pacte and Basilique. Basilique was saddled: a slow beast, full of strength and sympathy, but stupid and given to sudden fears. Pacte was the led horse, and had never heard guns. It was prophesied that when first I should have to hold him in camp when we were practising he would break everything near him, and either kill me or get me cells. But I did not believe these prophecies, having found my Ancient and all third-year men too often to be liars, fond of frightening the younger recruits. Meanwhile Pacte stood in the sharp night, impatient, and shook his harness. Everything had been quickly ordered.

We filed out of quarters, passed the lamp of the guard, and saw huddled there the dozen or so that were left behind while we were off to better things. Then a drawn-out cry at the head of the column was caught up all along its length, and we trotted; the metal of shoes and wheel-rims rang upon the road, and I felt as a man feels on a ship when it leaves harbour for great discoveries.

We had climbed the steep bank above St Martin, and were on the highest ridge of land dominating the plain, when the sky first felt the approach of the sun. Our backs were to the east, but the horizon before us caught a reflection of the dawn; the woods lost their mystery, and one found oneself marching in a partly cultivated open space with a forest all around. The road ran straight for miles like an arrow, and stretched swarmingly along it was the interminable line of guns. But with the full daylight, and after the sun had risen in a mist, they deployed us out of column into a wide front on a great heath in the forest, and we halted. There we brewed coffee, not by batteries, but gun by gun.

Warmed by this little meal, mere coffee without sugar or milk,

but with a hunk left over from yesterday's bread and drawn stale
from one's haversack (the armies of the Republic and of Napoleon
often fought all day upon such sustenance, and even now, as you
will see, the French do not really eat till a march is over—and this
may be a great advantage in warfare)—warmed, I say, by this little
meal, and very much refreshed by the sun and the increasing merri-
ment of morning, we heard first the trumpet-call and then the
shouted order to mount.

We did not form one column again. We went off at intervals by
batteries; and the reason of this was soon clear, for on getting to a
place where four roads met, some took one and some took another,
the object being to split up the unwieldy train of thirty-six guns,
with all their wagons and forges, into a number of smaller groups,
marching by ways more or less parallel towards the same goal; and
my battery was left separate, and went at last along a lane that ran
through pasture land in a valley.

The villages were already awake, and the mist was all but lifted
from the meadows when we heard men singing in chorus in front
of us some way off. These were the gunners that had left long
before us and had gone on forward afoot. For in the French artillery
it is a maximum (for all I know, common to all others—if other
artilleries are wise) that you should weight your limber (and therefore your horses) with useful things alone; and as gunners are
useful only to fire guns, they are not carried, save into action, or
when some great rapidity of movement is desired. I do, indeed,
remember one case when it was thought necessary to send a group
of batteries during the manoeuvres right over from the left to the
right of a very long position which our division was occupying on
the crest of the Argonne. There was the greatest need for haste,
and we packed the gunners on to the limber (there were no seats on
the gun in the old type—there are now) and galloped all the way
down the road, and put the guns in action with the horses still panting and exhausted by that extra weight carried at such a speed and
for such a distance. But on the march, I say again, we send the
gunners forward, and not only the gunners, but, as you shall hear
when we come to Commercy, a reserve of drivers also. We send
them forward an hour or two before the guns start; we catch them
up with the guns on the road; they file up to let us pass, and commonly salute us by way of formality and ceremony. Then they

come into the town of the halt an hour or two after we have reached it.

So here in this silent and delightful valley, through which ran a river, which may have been the Meuse or may have been a tributary only, we caught up our gunners. Their song ceased, they were lined up along the road, and not till we were passed were they given a little halt and repose. But when we had gone past with a huge clattering and dust, the bombardier of my piece, who was a very kindly man, a young farmer, and who happened to be riding abreast of my horses, pointed them out to me behind us at a turning in the road. They were taking that five minutes rest which the French have borrowed from the Germans, and which comes at the end of every hour on the march. They had thrown down their knapsacks and were lying flat taking their ease. I could not long look back-wards, but a very little time after, when we had already gained nearly half a mile upon them, we again heard the noise of their singing, and knew that they had re-shouldered the heavy packs. And this pack is the same in every unmounted branch of the service, and is the heaviest thing, I believe, that has been carried by infantry since the Romans.

It was not yet noon, and extremely hot for the time of year and for the coldness of the preceding night, when they halted us at a place where the road bent round in a curve and went down a little hollow. There we dismounted and cleaned things up a little before getting into the town, where we were to find what the French call an *étape*; that is, the town at which one halts at the end of one's march, and the word is also used for the length of a march itself. It is not in general orders to clean up in this way before coming in, and there were some commanders who were never more pleased than when they could bring their battery into town covered with dust and horses steaming and the men haggard, for this they thought to be evidence of a workmanlike spirit. But our colonel had given very contrary orders, to the annoyance of our captain, a man risen from the ranks who loved the guns and hated finery.

Then we went at a walk, the two trumpets of the battery sound-ing the call which is known among French gunners as 'the eighty hunters', because the words to it are, '*quatre-vingt, quatre-vingt, quatre-vingt, quatre-vingt, quatre-vingt, quatre-vingt, quatre-vingt, chasseurs*', which words, by their metallic noise and monotony, exactly express the long call that announces the approach of guns. We went right through the town, the name of which is Commercy, and the boys looked at us with pride, not knowing how hateful they would find the service when once they were in for its grind and hopelessness. But then, for that matter, I did not know myself with what great pleasure I should look back upon it ten years after. Moreover, nobody knows beforehand whether he will like a thing or not; and there is the end of it.

We formed a park in the principal place of the town; there were appointed two sentinels to do duty until the arrival of the gunners who should relieve them and mount a proper guard, and then we were marched off to be shown our various quarters. For before a French regiment arrives at a town others have ridden forward and have marked in chalk upon the doors how many men and how many horses are to be quartered here or there, and my quarters were in a great barn with a very high roof; but my Ancient, upon whom I depended for advice, was quartered in a house, and I was therefore lonely.

We groomed our horses, ate our great mid-day meal, and were free for a couple of hours to wander about the place. It is a garrison, and, at that time, it was full of cavalry, with whom we fraternized; but the experiment was a trifle dangerous, for there is always a risk of a quarrel when regiments meet as there is with two dogs, or two of any other kind of lively things.

Then came the evening, and very early, before it was dark, I was asleep in my clothes in some straw, very warm; but I was so lazy that I had not even taken off my belt or sword. And that was the end of the first day's marching.

II

The Bad Child's Book of Beasts
1896

Belloc went up to Oxford in 1892, winning an open scholarship to Balliol, when Benjamin Jowett was Master. He also won the Bracken-bury Scholarship for History and obtained a First from his Schools, but he failed to gain a Fellowship to All Souls, the disappointment rankling all his life.

His oratory captivated all who heard him and he was soon a prominent figure on the platform of the Union, becoming Secretary in 1893 and President in 1894; he was also elected Librarian. He stood well to the left of Liberalism.

The Bad Child's Book of Beasts *was his first book of nonsense verse and was an immediate success, the first edition being sold out in four days. His illustrator, Lord Basil Blackwood, was among his close friends, and he and Belloc had been on holiday together in Scandinavia in the year (1895) previous to publication.*

George

*Who played with a Dangerous Toy, and suffered a
Catastrophe of considerable Dimensions.*

When George's Grandmamma was told

That George had been as good as Gold,
She Promised in the Afternoon
To buy him an *Immense BALLOON.*

And

so she did; but when it came,

It got into the candle flame,
And being of a dangerous sort
Exploded

with a loud report!

The Lights went out! The Windows broke!
The Room was filled with reeking smoke.
And in the darkness shrieks and yells
Were mingled with Electric Bells,
And falling masonry and groans,
And crunching, as of broken bones,
And dreadful shrieks, when, worst of all,
The House itself began to fall!
It tottered, shuddering to and fro,
Then crashed into the street below—
Which happened to be Savile Row.

When Help arrived, among the Dead

Were

Cousin Mary,

Little Fred,

 The Footmen

(both of them),

The Groom,

The man that cleaned the Billiard Room,

The Chaplain, and

The Still-Room Maid.

And I am dreadfully afraid
That Monsieur Champignon, the Chef,
Will now be

permanently deaf—

And both his

Aides

are much the same;
While George, who was in part to blame,
Received, you will regret to hear,
A nasty lump

behind the ear.

MORAL

The moral is that little Boys
Should not be given dangerous Toys.

III

A Letter to Maurice Baring
1897

*This was the year that Belloc met Maurice Baring. 'That summer,'
records Baring, 'I made friends with Hilary[1] Belloc, who lived at
Oxford in Holywell and was coaching pupils. I had met him once
before with Basil Blackwood, but all he had said to me was that I would
most certainly go to hell, and so I had thought it unlikely that we
should ever make friends, although I recognized the first moment I saw
him that he was a remarkable man.'[2] They were to remain close friends
all their lives.*

[1] All his friends called him Hilary.
[2] M. Baring: *The Puppet Show of Memory*, pp. 170–1.

18

To Maurice Baring

BALINTORE, KIRRIEMUIR, N.B.
Monday, July 5th, 1897

Maurice, the pride and wonder of our times,
Master of dear, if somewhat morbid, rhymes,
These from the northern lands that stretch more far
Than Thule herself to th'Aquilonian Star,
Girt high with hills, and diademed with cloud
And rich in living waters wide and loud,
From Caledonia, from the Grampian Hills,
Receive these letters from the Prince of Squills.
What is a 'squill'? You ask (and well you may
For this, like other words, had had its day).
A squill, dear friend, is any one whose fate
Makes him a stranger at the Oaken Gate,
A squill is one whose birth or fortune mean
Condemn him to those paltry dens obscene,
Magdalen or Balliol or St John's or New;
A squill is one beside those happy few
Who dwell in Christ Church and who know a Lord.
A squill is something wretched and abhorred,
Beyond conception of you Cambridge men,
Whose rules (I've heard it whispered now and then)
All class divisions and class prides annul,
A just and equal polity—but Dull.
Well then, the poet of the squills receives
A missive from the Beefsteak club: and grieves.
Grieves to be thought recalcitrant: grieves more
To know he should have written long before.
Grieves most of all to think that cruel chance
Should lead his pen so singular a dance.
Why not write slowly in a laboured prose:
Why not in subtle phrases tell my woes,
Why not with Irony, the master style,
Praise, bless, condemn, grow warm, but always smile.

19

Why not declaim, in slow delightful course
Of Highland Lawers[1] and Heather and the gorse
Of Balintore and of the Burn that fills
With tiny tinkling falls the Caledonian Hills?
Why not? Because I haven't got the time,
My day is burdened so I take to Rhyme,
As people in a hurry take a cab
(Instead of walking like Architorab
Whose story in the epic you may read
Which tells of Ogier's Journey on the mead),
As men that wish to write in furious haste
Use a typewriter, careless of good taste,
And all oblivious of her shapely waist,
So I in haste, in hurry, in the need
Of writing that which lends itself to speed
Write you this letter in heroic feet
Pentameters Iambic all complete.
Decasyllabic. And for ending write
'Si Vales Valeo', all of us indite
Some special ending to their letters. Mine is.
'Si Vales Valeo'
                    Imprimatur.
                              Finis
Tomorrow morning at the break of day
I shall arise from chaste and thin repose,
Take me a pen as swiftly as I may
And write you fully in a laboured prose
And sign myself 'Hilaire Belloc' B.A.
And only *after that* put on my clothes.
Such is the debt my pen your friendship owes
Such is the coin wherein such debt to pay.

---

[1] Pronounced 'Laws' = Hills.

IV

From *The Modern Traveller*
1898

In 1897 Belloc returned from America, with his wife Elodie Hogan, whom he had married on June 16, 1896, at Napa, her birthplace. The marriage was an exceedingly happy one, though her family scarcely welcomed him with open arms, for it was naturally thought that a penniless and struggling author was hardly 'a catch'. Belloc never got over her untimely death at the early age of forty-two in 1914. On this second visit he had lectured so extensively that he returned to England exhausted. On September 23rd of that year their first son, Louis John, was born. (He was killed in the first world war in a flying accident on August 26, 1918).

The Modern Traveller *followed* More Beasts For Worse Children, *and it has been adjudged to be one of his most considerable efforts in comic and satirical verse. The* Spectator *compared him with Lear and Sir Arthur Quiller-Couch ('Q') fully praised the work, though the press was not as unanimously enthusiastic.*

The first third of it follows.

The Modern Traveller

The *Daily Menace*, I presume?
Forgive the litter in the room.
I can't explain to you
How out of place a man like me
Would be without the things you see—
The Shields and Assegais and odds
And ends of little savage gods.
Be seated; take a pew.
(Excuse the phrase. I'm rather rough,
And—pardon me!—but have you got
A pencil? I've another here:
The one that you have brought, I fear,
Will not be long enough.)
And so the Public want to hear
About the expedition
From which I recently returned:
Of how the Fetish Tree was burned;
Of how we struggled to the coast,
And lost our ammunition;
How we retreated, side by side;
And how, like Englishmen, we died.
Well, as you know, I hate to boast,
And, what is more, I can't abide
A popular position.
I told the Duke the other day
The way I felt about it.
He answered courteously—'Oh!'
An Editor (who had an air
Of what the Dutch call *savoir faire*)
Said, 'Mr Rooter, you are right,
And nobody can doubt it.'
The Duchess murmured, 'Very true.'
Her comments may be brief and true,

But very seldom trite.
Still, representing as you do
A public and a point of view,
I'll give you leave to jot
A few remarks—a very few—
But understand that this is not
A formal interview.
And first of all, I will begin
By talking of Commander Sin.

II

Poor Henry Sin from quite a child,
I fear, was always rather wild;
    But all his faults were due
To something free and unrestrained,
That partly pleased and partly pained
    The people whom he knew.
Untaught (for what our times require),
Lazy, and something of a liar,
    He had a foolish way
Of always swearing (more or less);
    And, lastly, let us say
A little slovenly in dress,
A trifle prone to drunkenness;
A gambler also to excess,
    And never known to pay.
As for his clubs in London, he
Was pilled at ten, expelled from three.
A man Bohemian as could be—
    But really vicious? Oh, no!
When these are mentioned, all is said.
And then—Commander Sin is dead:
    De mortuis cui bono?

Of course, the Public know I mean
To publish in the winter.
I mention the intention in

23

BELLOC

Connection with Commander Sin;
   The book is with the Printer.
And here, among the proofs, I find
The very thing I had in mind—
The portrait upon page thirteen.
Pray pause awhile, and mark
The wiry limbs, the vigorous mien,
The tangled hair and dark;
The glance imperative and hot,
   That takes a world by storm:
All these are in the plate, but what
You chiefly should observe is
The—Did you say his uniform
Betrayed a foreign service?

Of course, it does! He was not born
In little England! No!
Beyond the Cape, beyond the Horn,
Beyond Fernando Po,
In some far Isle he saw the light
That burns the torrid zone,
But where it lay was never quite
Indubitably known.
Himself inclined to Martinique.
His friends to Farralone.
But why of this discussion speak?
The Globe was all his own!
Oh! surely upon such a birth
No petty flag unfurled!
He was a citizen of earth,
A subject of the world!

As for the uniform he bore,
He won it in the recent war
Between Peru and Ecuador,
   And thoroughly he earned it.
Alone of all who at the time
Were serving sentences for crime,
Sin, during his incarceration

Had studied works on navigation;
And when the people learned it,
They promptly let him out of hail,
But on condition he should sail.

It marked an epoch, and you may
Recall the action in
A place called Quaxipotle bay?
Yes, both the navies ran away;
And yet, if Ecuador can say
That on the whole she won the day,
The fact is due to Sin.
The Fleet was hardly ten weeks out,
When somebody descried
The enemy. Sin gave a shout,
The Helmsmen put the ship about;
For, upon either side,
Tactics demanded a retreat.
Due west retired the foreign fleet,
But Sin he steered due east;
He muttered, 'They shall never meet.'
And when, towards the close of day,
The foemen were at least
Fifteen or twenty miles away,
He called his cabin-steward aft,
The boldest of his men;
He grasped them by the hand; he laughed
A fearless laugh, and then,
'Heaven help the right! Full steam a-head,
Fighting for fighting's sake,' he said.

Due west the foe—due east he steered.
Ah, me! the very stokers cheered,
And faces black with coal
And fuzzy with a five days' beard
Popped up, and yelled, and disappeared
Each in its little hole.
Long after they were out of sight,
Long after dark, throughout the night,

Throughout the following day,
He went on fighting all the time!
Not war, perhaps, but how sublime!

Just as he would have stepped ashore,
The President of Ecuador
Came on his quarter-deck;
Embraced him twenty times or more,
And gave him stripes and things galore,
Crosses and medals by the score,
And handed him a cheque—
And then a little speech he read.

'Of twenty years, your sentence said,
That you should serve—another week
(Alas! it shames me as I speak)
Was owing when you quitted.
In recognition of your nerve,
It gives me pleasure to observe
The time you still had got to serve
Is totally remitted.

'Instead of which these friends of mine'—
(And here he pointed to a line
Of Colonels on the Quay)—
'Have changed your sentence to a fine
Made payable to me.
No—do not thank me—not a word!
I am very glad to say
This little cheque is quite a third
Of what you have to pay.'

The crew they cheered and cheered again,
The simple loyal-hearted men!
Such deeds could never fail to be
Renowned throughout the west.
It was our cousins over sea
That loved the Sailor best,—
Our Anglo-Saxon kith and kin,

They doted on Commander Sin,
And gave him a tremendous feast
The week before we started.
O'Hooligan, and Vonderbeast,
And Nicolazzi, and the rest,
Were simply broken-hearted.

They came and ate and cried, 'God speed!'
The Bill was very large indeed,
And paid for by an Anglo-Saxon
Who bore the sterling name of Jackson.
On this occasion Sin was seen
Toasting McKinley and the Queen.
The speech was dull, but not an eye,
Not even the champagne, was dry.

V

From a Letter to
Mrs Wright-Biddulph
1899

Belloc was saddled with added responsibilities in 1899 with the birth of a daughter, Eleanor, on July 14th, at 36 Holywell, Oxford. The following year they were to move to Cheyne Walk, Chelsea. The old-time cri de coeur *of every author is reflected in this letter, and throughout his long life his financial affairs were seldom satisfactory.*

Elodie lies on her back and it *is my fault* that she does not write at once. It is necessary that she should sleep.

I am full of work. It is not lucrative. I earn good wine and sweetbread and caviare by the sweat of my pen, and my pen sweats 'wi' deeficulty' as the Scotchman said of his joking. You will be glad to hear that the publishers ask me for many books but sorry to hear that no man can live on books alone; exactly 30,410 of my books are in the hands of the public and my total earnings therefrom in three years is £500; i.e. £150 to £175 a year.[1]

[1] R. Speaight: *Hilaire Belloc*, p. 120.

VI

Paris

1900

The year 1900 saw the publication of Belloc's first major work. It was a book of which he was proud (he was a considerable critic of his own work). It is a history of Paris, but takes the reader no further than 1789 and more than half the book is devoted to the origins of the city. Paris always stirred Belloc's imagination. 'In spite of modern developments he was aware of the bones of the past underneath every quarter of the city, and for this book, Paris, he made the most careful and extensive researches.'[1]

We have taken two extracts—'The Middle Ages' and 'The Mutilation of Notre Dame during the Terror'.

[1] J. B. Morton: *Belloc. A Memoir*, p. 102.

Paris

Of all definite periods in modern history the early Middle Ages fall most naturally into divisions; for the three centuries which they cover form not only in the outward aspect of civilization, but also in its politics, three different things; and this is especially the case with Paris. For the history of what happened in the city, and the spirit of the times, and at last even the effect of the buildings, change with these three epochs. They are as follows.

The first—when the old society was stirring, when architecture remained what it had been in form but, as it were, more eager, and when Paris, though it seemed in a ferment ready for creation, yet did not increase much nor change its boundaries—ran from the accession of Hugh Capet in 987 to the preaching of the first Crusade in 1095. It was the time when the Normans were sailing out on their great adventures, hammering kingdoms together, and, themselves half-barbarous, showing a half-barbarous Europe how to tax, survey, and centralize. The idea of a new society, of a strict unity, and of a highly-organized Church ran out from Cluny and took shape in the prophetic mouth of Hildebrand. That idea was given a form and became a living thing when the Crusades had startled civilization into being.

The second division is that of the twelfth century, and it may be said, so far as Paris is concerned, to begin with the first Crusade and to end when Philip Augustus started in 1190 for the third. For the twelfth century is, above all, a disordered energy of creation; it is force shapeless, or rather a medley of new things growing. But with that year, 1190, two things appear which are the beginning of form and order: the great wall of Paris is traced out, the University gathers on the hill. This second division in our chapter is Paris finding a definition and a language.

The third is the thirteenth century. It stretches from the building of the wall to the day in 1271 when they brought home the body of St Louis from the place in Barbary where he had died under arms. That long, well-ordered time, of which he was the flower and the type, is the climax and best of the Middle Ages. It had perhaps began to lose the air of freedom, but though St Louis outlived it a little, this good generation had not yet felt intrigue nor the chains of office.

It produced characters not only of such an altitude, but of such a quality, and those secure in such conspicuous and eminent places; it allowed the true leader his place so readily, and even with such insistence, that it seems, for all its incompleteness, a fit type for our society. It had not conquered brutality nor given good laws the machinery of good communications and of a good police, but its ideals were of the noblest, and, what is more, they were sincerely held. Of all the phases through which our race has passed this was surely the least tainted with hypocrisy, and perhaps it was the one in which the more oppressed classes of society were less hopelessly miserable than at any future time.

As to the city, and the king who was its lord, the three hundred years passed in some such stream as this. It entered the Middle Ages a small town, thick in walls and squat in architecture, squalid and rude, barbaric; but there sat in its Palace of the city, under old, grey, round arches, or drinking at long tables in square, unvaulted halls, the beginners of the great dynasty of the Capetians.

They were called Kings of France, and in that name and idea was the seed of a very vigorous plant, but as yet the seed remained unbroken. It was dead, in dead earth. At his crowning the lords of the great provinces came, as it were, to act as symbols; in a vague theory he was superior to any in the space from the Saone Valley and the Rhône Valley to the Atlantic; but in fact he was a crowned noble, given, by the symbolism and the Roman memories of his time, the attributes of central government; allowed to personify that dim, half-formed but gigantic idea of the nation; there his power ended. It all lay in a phrase and a conception. But God has so ordered it that over the French people a phrase or an idea is destined to be of awful weight; and the force of things, the blind, almost unconscious powers of the national spirit, like some organic law, forced the Capetians on a certain path towards the inevitable Latin nationality. Already the epics were singing of the nation in arms, and Roland had been made a patriot saint, for all the world like Hoche or Marceau.

The character of the kings corresponded to this power; and no wonder, for it was a time all of soldiers, when a William of Falaise had only to call for volunteers on the beach of the Caux country and have men from Italy and from Spain coming at his heels. With fate offering such work, it is no wonder that one after the other, with very few exceptions, the early kings are hard fighters; but still, till the great change of the twelfth century, they are only the lords of a little territory which, with change of horse, you might cover in a day's hard riding; here and there a royal town far off, and always the title of King.

At their very gates the castles of their little under-lords defied them. Montlhéry was all but independent, Enghien was a tiny kingdom, and the tower of the one, the hill of the other, are visible from the Mont Ste Geneviève today. As for their great vassals, the peers, the Dukes of Normandy and of Aquitaine, the Count of Champagne and the Lords of the Marches beyond the Loire, they were treaty-making sovereigns, that waged war at their pleasure upon the King of France. William of Normandy, when he held England, or even before that, was a better man in the field. The Duke of Aquitaine let no writs run beyond his boundaries. The Lords of Toulouse would have had difficulty in telling you what their relation was to the distant successor of Charlemagne.

So through the eleventh century the Kings of Paris drag on, always fighting, making little headway. The equals, and at time the inferiors or the provincial over-lords, you might have thought that these would end by making minor kingdoms, or even that the lords of separate manors might in time become the aristocracy of a settled community; but behind them all was the infinite aggregation of silent permanent forces, the national traditions, the feeling of unity, the old Roman memory, and, though it was centuries before the provincial over-lord disappeared for ever, and even centuries more before the lord of the village succumbed, still, a future history was making very slowly all the while the central government and the king.

It is with the close of the eleventh century that the flow of the tide begins. The great crusading march shook Europe out of its routine and torpor. The 'Dust of Villages', already somewhat united by the Hildebrandine reform, was taught the folly of disintegration as each community watched strange men, with a hundred foreign dialects, and with the habits, the laws, the necessities of a hundred varying places, all passing on with the common purpose of Christendom. Trade was opened between towns that had hardly known each other by name; the Mediterranean began to reassume its old place in the western civilization; the necessity of interchange, both social and material, grew in the experiences of that vast emigration; and when, with the last years of the old century, the teaching of the law at Bologna began, Europe was ready for the changes which the pandects were to produce.

This discovery must certainly be made the starting-point for observing the effects of the new development in European life. As I have said, all Europe was awake. The code alone would never have revolutionized society, but the Roman law, falling upon a society already alert, vigorous, attentive, and awaiting new things, had a most prodigious effect.

It gave to what would have been in any case a period of great forces a particular direction, to which we owe the character of all the succeeding centuries. At Paris the king of the eleventh century is a great noble; he is conscious, vaguely, that he stands for government, but government is little more than an idea. As it was, the law which handed down to the Middle Ages, across a gap of many centuries, the spirit of absolute and central authority came with an immense moral force to the help of governments, and therefore of civilization. The code took a century to leaven the whole of society, but when this work was done it produced a very marvellous world, for the thirteenth century is a little gem in the story of mankind. It produced this effect because its logic, its sense of order, its basis of government were combined with those elements of tribal loyalty and of individual action which had emerged in the decline of the Empire, and whose excess had caused many of the harsh and picturesque features of the Dark Ages. Later on, the Roman law became all powerful, and in its too great preponderance the localities and the individuals decayed till the crown grew too heavy for the nation.

While the first three Crusades were being fought Paris was growing in numbers as well as in light. The rough suburbs to the north and south of the island became larger than the parent city. The one climbed up and covered the hill of Ste Geneviève; the other, in a semicircle of nearly half a mile in depth, densely filled the surroundings of the Châtelet and the Place de Grève. Meanwhile, doubtless, as in other parts of France, the rude and debased architecture was struggling to an improvement. The spirit that made the Abbaye aux Dames in Caen must have been present in Paris; but nothing remains of its work, for the Gothic came immediately and transformed the city.

This great change (and the greatest change—to the eye—that ever passed over our European cities) marks the middle and end of the twelfth century, and there goes side by side with it a startling development of learning and of inquiry. That central twelfth century, shaken and startled by the marching of the second Crusade, is the lifetime of Abelard and of St Bernard. Upon every side the human intellect, which had, so to speak, lain fallow for these hundreds of years, arises and begins again the endless task of questions in which it delights. Religion is illuminated with philosophy as the stained glass of a church, unperceived in darkness, may shine out when the sun rises. As though in sympathy with this movement and stirring of the mind, the houses and the churches change. The low, clear, routine method of the Romanesque, the round arch and wide, the flat roof, the square tower and low walls which have corresponded with an unquestioning period, suddenly take on the anxiety and the mystery of the new time. It was the East that did this. The pointed archies; the long, fine pillars; the high-pitched gable roofs, and at last the spires—all that we call 'the Gothic'—appeared, and was the mark of the great epoch upon which we are entering. Already the first stones of Notre Dame were laid, and already its sister thing, the University of Paris, was born. Its earliest buildings were to rise with the first years of the thirteenth century, in the fourteenth its numerous colleges were to gather on the hill of Ste Geneviève.

When the full tide of this movement was being felt there arose, to the singular good fortune of the French people, the personality of Philip the Conqueror.

It was he who turned the King of Paris truly into the King of France. Not Montlhéry nor Enghien were the prizes of his adventures, but Normandy, Poitou, Aquitaine. The centre of what was now a kingdom, the town of Paris, became, with the close of his reign in the early thirteenth century, a changed town. He had paved its streets and surrounded it with a great wall of many towers; outside this wall to the west stood his own new stronghold of the

Louvre, a square castle of stone; within was the group of new churches, the rising walls of Notre Dame, the rapid growth of the town itself; so that St Louis inherited a capital worthy of the perfect chapel which he built at its centre, and almost worthy of his own admirable spirit. He and the century which he fills are the crown and perfection, and also the close of this great epoch in the history of the town.

THE EIGHTEENTH CENTURY

Louis XIV died on September 1, 1715; the mob which took the Bastille rose on the 12th, and inaugurated the new government of Paris on the 13th of July 1789. We have therefore to deal with a period of all but seventy-four years.

What was the character of France and of the capital during these seventy-four years?

We shall see some of the most beautiful monuments of the city destroyed, others mutilated, and things of a frank ugliness substituted without reason; the Louvre treated as a stable, the roof falling in above the palaces, the porch of Notre Dame cut into quaint patterns, the stained glass sold, the old tombs defaced. The Pantheon will be a monument of what the age mistook for grandeur, and Soufflot will be the type of the official architect. We shall be permitted, as an epitome of so much degradation, to hear a Capetian debating the destruction of the Louvre.

Now, as a type of what the reign was, let me begin with the misfortunes of Notre Dame.

It was natural that the eighteenth century should have seen little in the Gothic glories of the thirteenth. There lay between the opening of our period and the last of the Gothic two hundred years—the space between the Tour St Jacques and the Invalides—and these two hundred years were completely ignorant of the spirit which had built Notre Dame. The first of these centuries had indeed retained the old gables and deep lanes of mediaeval Paris, studding them here and there with the vast palaces of the Medicean Valois; but the second . . . rebuilt Paris so completely that it destroyed even the outward example of a thing whose idea had long disappeared. Therefore the reign of Louis XIV had treated the Cathedral carelessly; had put in, just before the king's death, that huge, ugly high altar, and had destroyed the reverend flooring of tombs to make way for the chess-board pattern of black and white that still displeases us. But throughout its action it left the shell and mass of Notre Dame the same. With the reign of Louis XV a very much worse spirit came upon the architects, for they were no longer content to neglect the old work, they were bent upon improving it; and of their many deplorable ventures I will choose three especially to illustrate their spirit.

In the first place, they destroyed the old windows. It is written somewhere that the destruction began with the desire to let a shaft of white light come down upon the new high altar; even this insufficient excuse will hardly hold, for all the glass seems to have been taken away bodily and at one time, in 1741. We lost in that act the fullness and the spirit of Notre Dame, and the loss can never be made good. This is so true that men who all their lives have known the great cathedral, yet, when they first see Rheims or Amiens find for the first time something whose absence in Paris had left an ill-ease. The stained glass gives to the Gothic a sense of completion that is like clothing, and by an accident that has never been made clear it is a thing which cannot be restored. There needs in Notre Dame only one thing, and that is a quality of light which shall be to the common light of the outer city what music is to speech. That thing was given it by the builders, who knew their own harmony so thoroughly, and was taken away quite wantonly by men who lacked the humility of their ignorance. To see how enormous was their folly one has but to go to Chartres, where the blessings of poverty and of a provincial isolation preserved all the Middle Ages decaying but untouched.

The canons replaced the old windows by white glass, excellently arranged in symmetrical lozenges, and in every lozenge a yellow fleur-de-lis, and what they did with the thousand escutcheons of so many donors, no one knows. They left intact—perhaps in fear of the great expense of changing such spaces—the three rose windows of the two transepts and the West front. But one cannot reconstruct the old effect by their example; on the contrary, they jar upon the modern Lorraine work which has replaced the inept glazing of

1741. But one can learn from them, if not the general value, at least the symbolism in design of the old windows; and for such a purpose the principal one, that of the West front, is the best; for, with Our Lady and the Child Jesus in the midst of the prophets, with the two circles of the zodiac and of the works of the year, it is like a book in which the dedication of the church and all that it was meant to do is written.

This, then, was the first great error of the time in its treatment of Notre Dame; the second was in the destruction of the interior monuments. Whether the crowding of so much grotesque or incongruous matter in our cathedrals would have pleased their architects is a very doubtful matter, but time, which has handed down these churches to us, has also filled them with all the changing tastes of their six centuries. So long as this did not encroach upon the body of the building, and so long as the Gothic spirit remained in the whole, no harm was done; and in a Catholic country the habit of such accumulation had this further advantage, that every corner and addition had its use in custom; each statue had attached to it some story or some popular habit, like Our Lady of the Candle or the Children's Basket; so that, when this or that was taken away from the floor of the Cathedral, there went with it the regret and the affection of many; and the loss of so much detail must have been a consternation to the humble and small people who carried even into the eighteenth century the virtues of an earlier time. Of all this the canons new nothing; for them the Philippe le Bel was an ugly medieval thing, the Virgin of the Candle a mere distortion, the great St Christopher a grotesque. To their passion for emptiness they sacrificed all these pleasant incongruities. Not only within but without the church they followed the same policy, and any sign of weakness or age in a thing they made a reason, not for its restoration, but for its removal. Thus (among many examples that one might give) there is the statue that marked the northern of the three porches, the door of the Virgin. Here, on the pier of the doorway, was a figure that was as necessarily the centre of all that carving as the miniature in the great wheel above was, of necessity, the centre of its pictures; for there was carved on the door, as there was painted in the window, the life of a man in the different seasons of the year and also the signs of the zodiac. But there was this about the signs—that only eleven were carved, and for the sign 'Virgo',

Our Lady stood in the centre, holding the Child Jesus, who was blessing the world of men and the months. The figure . . . stood upon a little symbolical tree, carved in stone, which tree was the tree of the Garden of Eden, and had two apples on it, and Our Lady's foot was on the head of the serpent. It is clear that such a thing had no meaning save as the necessary centre of its surroundings, and that, without it, these surroundings also were empty. Nevertheless, when a flaw came in, they destroyed it. And with all this destruction of excellent things—the statues and dedications within, the old carvings without—they could not see that the stories of Notre Dame were ill suited to fine oil-paintings in great gilt frames, and these hung round the nave piteously till our own time.

The third example of the evil done to Notre Dame was the action of Soufflot. I do not mean that heavy, great sacristy that he built, and that many men can still remember; I mean his curious restoration of the central door. Here was the chief glory of the West front . . . its carvings . . . were designed to symbolize the kernel of Christianity, and to make, as it were, a continual Credo for the people who passed beneath. It was very worthy of the first detail that would appear to a man as he came into the great church, and worthy also of a position which has always been the chief place of ornament. Now . . . this door especially laid stress upon the end of man (which it showed in the Last Judgment carefully carved on the tympanum), and it had, on either side of the doorway, the twelve apostles listening to the teaching of Our Lord, whose statue stood in the central pier, as we have just seen Our Lady's did in the northern door. So, if the door was to have any meaning at all, the statue of Our Lord was its natural centre, the apostles whom He was teaching made the bulk of the design; and then, as a result and pendant to this, came the ogival tympanum above, with that subject of the Last Judgment which is the favourite theme of medieval Paris. The canopy carried over the Sacrament during processions was, in the Middle Ages in France (and is still in most countries), a flexible cloth, with four poles to support it. This, when a procession passed through a door, could be partly folded together if it was too wide to go through at its full stretch. Now it so happened that the canopy in the Church of France had been, of late times, made with a stiff framework; there was therefore a certain inconvenience and difficulty in passing through the main door on feast days, because the central pier divided it into two narrow portions. With this little pretext, the canons did not hesitate to ruin the principal door of their church. It was in 1771, thirty years after the misfortune of the stained glass, that this was done. Soufflot, who was then the chief architect of the Government, whom we shall see building the Pantheon, and from whom a miracle preserved the Louvre, set about this folly.

Since the main object was to widen the door, his first act was to throw down the central pier, and to destroy the teaching Christ, for which, we may say, the whole porch existed. But even with this he was not content; for, looking at the heavy, triangular tympanum overhanging this broadened space, he thought to himself that it looked top heavy, and might even fall, now that it lacked its old support. He therefore, very quietly and without comment, cut through the relief and the carving, brought his chisel just where a fine sweeping curve might be traced, dividing kings in the middle, cutting saints slantwise and removing angels, till he had opened a small ogive of his own within the greater one. Then he finished off the whole with a neat moulding. It was as though he had said, 'Mind you, I do not like Gothic; but since the whole place is Gothic, we may as well keep to it, and (incidentally) I will show you how the men of the thirteenth century should have designed this door.' For it seemed to him as natural that a great ogive should have a little one inside, as it did that a dome should have a colonnade; and as for the symbolical carvings of the Middle Ages, he thought they were like the flutings of his false Renaissance pillars.

This hideous thing remained throughout the first part of our century, till Montalembert, in a fine speech, opened the reform, and saw the restoration of the Cathedral begun; and though, in that restoration, most of what was done was in reparation of what the Revolution destroyed, yet it is well to remember that the energy and the great schemes of the generation to which Montalembert and Viollet le Duc belonged were due to the Revolutionary movement, and that the sack and ruin of 1793 had been long prepared by the apathy and ignorance and forgetfulness of the generation preceding it. If Soufflot and the canons could see no beauty in, and could destroy the statuary of Notre Dame, it is not wonderful that the populace should deliberately throw down the memorials of a spirit of which they knew nothing, save that its heirs were then fighting the nation.

All this was the action of the century upon the most perfect of medieval buildings.

VII

Chesterton first meets Belloc

1900

'*When I first met Belloc he remarked to the friend who introduced us that he was in low spirits. His low spirits were and are much more uproarious and enlivening than anybody else's high spirits. He talked into the night, and left behind in it a glowing track of good things. When I have said that I mean things that are good, and certainly not merely* bons mots, *I have said all that can be said in the most serious aspect about the man who has made the greatest fight for good things of all men of my time.*

We met between a little Soho paper shop and a little Soho restaurant his arms and pockets were stuffed with French Nationalist and French Atheist newspapers. He wore a straw hat shading his eyes, which are like a sailor's, and emphasizing his Napoleonic chin . . . The little restaurant to which we went had already become a haunt for three or four of us who held strong but unfashionable views about the South African War, which was then in its earliest prestige. Most of us were writing on the Speaker *. . .*

. . . What he brought into our dream was this Roman appetite for reality and reason for action, and when he came into the door there entered with him the smell of danger.'[1]

[1] Mansell C. C. and Shanks E. *Introduction to Hilaire Belloc: The Man and His Work.*

41

VIII

The New Century

1901

Belloc's career was rapidly shaping into that of historian. He had by now published his Danton *(1899) and* Robespierre *was to appear during this year. 'He had', as Robert Speaight says,[1] 'in equal measure, an attachment to dogma and to fact. This is not to say that he was infallible in reading the fact or in interpreting the dogma, but he knew that belief must be confirmed by experience. The historian must understand the ideas that have moved men to action, but he must also understand the stuff of which men are made. He must recover their physique, their temperament, their idiosyncrasies. He must see them in their time and place and circumstance. In a word, he must bring them to life; and here Michelet was at hand with his doctrine that "History should be a resurrection of the flesh".'*

We have not given here any extract from his three great biographies of the Revolution (the third being Marie Antoinette), *preferring to use the complete essays (the form of prose in which Belloc excelled) on these figures which appeared in his* French Revolution *(1911).*

[1] R. Speaight: *Hilaire Belloc*, p. 134.

IX

The Path to Rome

1902

Belloc was thirty-one years of age, married, with two children, when he decided to embark on a walk from Toul (his old garrison town in France) to Rome. The walk, in reality a pilgrimage of his faith, was a stupendous feat of endurance and courage, as those who have read what is perhaps Belloc's masterpiece, will know.

He was dressed in a thin suit and carried no change of clothing; at one point his heavy boots had worn so thin that the soles flapped along as he trudged through Switzerland. His daily sustenance was bread and ham—and sometimes not even the ham—and wine, and one wonders at his stamina. To save the cost of a night's lodging (generally about one franc) he would sleep under a tree or in a barn. His rate of progress greatly exceeded the four miles an hour of the average walker, and this was through territory which was unfamiliar, mountainous and with alarmingly steep valleys, while temperatures varied enormously.

The spirit of the man shines through this book with starlike quality and had Belloc written no other work than this his name would be secure in the literary firmament.

The Path to Rome

I was on a high plateau, yet I felt myself to be alone with the immensity that properly belongs to plains alone. I saw the stars, and remembered how I had looked up at them on just such a night when I was close to the Pacific, bereft of friends and possessed with solitude. There was no noise; it was full darkness. The woods before and behind me made a square frame of silence, and I was enchased here in the clearing, thinking of all things.

Then a little wind passed over the vast forests of Lorraine. It seemed to wake an indefinite sly life proper to this seclusion, a life to which I was strange, and which thought me an invader. Yet I heard nothing. There were no adders in the long grass, nor any frogs in that dry square of land, nor crickets on the high part of the hill; but I knew that little creatures in league with every nocturnal influence, enemies of the sun, occupied the air and the land about me; nor will I deny that I felt a rebel, knowing well that men were made to work in happy dawns and to sleep in the night, and everything in that short and sacred darkness multiplied my attentiveness and my illusion. Perhaps the instincts of the sentry, the necessities of guard, come back to us out of the ages unawares during such experiments. At any rate the night oppressed and exalted me. Then I suddenly attributed such exaltation to the need of food.

'If we must try this bookish plan of sleeping by day and walking by night,' I thought, 'at least one must arrange night meals to suit it.'

I therefore, with my mind still full of the forest, sat down and lit a match and peered into my sack, taking out therefrom bread and ham and chocolate and Brulé wine. For seat and table there was a heathery bank still full of the warmth and savour of the last daylight, for companions these great inimical influences of the night which I had met and dreaded, and for occasion or excuse there was hunger. Of the Many that debate what shall be done with travellers, it was the best and kindest Spirit that prompted me to this salutary act. For as I drank the wine and dealt with the ham and bread, I felt more and more that I had a right to the road; the stars became familiar and the woods a plaything. It is quite clear that the body

44

must be recognized and the soul kept in its place, since a little refreshing food and drink can do so much to make a man.

On this repast I jumped up merrily, lit a pipe, and began singing, and heard, to my inexpressible joy, some way down the road, the sound of other voices. They were singing that old song of the French infantry which dates from Louis XIV, and is called 'Auprès de ma blonde'. I answered their chorus, so that, by the time we met under the wood, we were already acquainted. They told me they had had a forty-eight hours' leave into Nancy, the four of them, and had to be in by roll-call at a place called Villey the Dry. I remembered it after all those years.

It is a village perched on the brow of one of these high hills above the river, and it found itself one day surrounded by earth-works, and a great fort raised just above the church. Then, before they knew where they were, they learnt that (1) no one could go in or out between sunset and sunrise without leave of the officer in command; (2) that from being a village they had become the 'buildings situate within Fort No. 18'; (3) that they were to be deluged with soldiers; and (4) that they were liable to evacuate their tenements on mobilization. They had become a fort un-wittingly as they slept, and all their streets were blocked with ramparts. A hard fate; but they should not have built their village just on the brow of a round hill. They did this in the old days, when men used stone instead of iron, because the top of a hill was a good place to hold against enemies; and so now, these 73,426 years after, they find the same advantage catching them again to their hurt. And so things go the round.

Anyway Villey the Dry is a fort, and there my four brothers were going. It was miles off, and they had to be in by sunrise, so I offered them a pull of my wine, which, to my great joy, they re-fused, and we parted courteously. Then I found the road beginning to fall, and knew that I had crossed the hills. As the forest ended and the sloping fields began, a dim moon came up late in the east in the bank of fog that masked the river. So by a sloping road, now free from the woods, and at the mouth of a fine untenanted valley under the moon, I came down again to the Moselle, having saved a great elbow by this excursion over the high land. As I swung round the bend of the hills downwards and looked up the sloping dell, I remembered that these heathery hollows were called 'vallons' by the people of Lorraine, and this set me singing the song of the hunters, 'Entends tu dans nos vallons, le Chasseur sonner du clairon', which I sang loudly till I reached the river bank, and lost the exhilaration of the hills.

I had now come some twelve miles from my starting-place, and it was midnight. The plain, the level road (which often rose a little), and the dank air of the river began to oppress me with fatigue. I was not disturbed by this, for I had intended to break these nights of marching by occasional repose, and while I was in the comfort of cities—especially in the false hopes that one got by reading books—I had imagined that it was a light matter to sleep in the open. Indeed, I had often so slept when I had been compelled to it in Manoeuvres, but I had forgotten how essential was a rug of some kind, and what a difference a fire and comradeship could make. Thinking over it all, feeling my tiredness, and shivering a little in the chill under the moon and the clear sky, I was very ready to capitulate and to sleep in bed like a Christian at the next opportunity. But there is some influence in vows or plans that escapes our power of rejudgment. All false calculations must be paid for, and I found, as you will see, that having said I would sleep in the open, I had to keep to it in spite of all my second thoughts.

I passed one village and then another in which everything was dark, and in which I could waken nothing but dogs, who thought me an enemy, till at last I saw a great belt of light in the fog above the Moselle. Here there was a kind of town or large settlement where there were ironworks, and where, as I thought, there would be houses open, even after midnight. I first found the old town, where just two men were awake at some cooking work or other. I found them by a chink of light streaming through their door; but they gave me no hope, only advising me to go across the river and try in the new town where the forges and the ironworks were. 'There,' they said, 'I should certainly find a bed.'

I crossed the bridge, being now much too weary to notice any-thing, even the shadowy hills, and the first thing I found was a lot of wagons that belonged to a caravan or fair. Here some men were awake, but when I suggested that they should let me sleep in their little houses on wheels, they told me it was never done; that it was all they could do to pack in themselves; that they had no straw; that they were guarded by dogs; and generally gave me to understand (though without violence or unpoliteness) that I looked as though I were the man to steal their lions and tigers. They told me, however, that without doubt I should find something open in the centre of the workmen's quarter, where the great electric lamps now made a glare over the factory.

I trudged on unwillingly, and at the very last house of this detestable industrial slavery, a high house with a gable, I saw a window wide open, and a blonde man smoking a cigarette at a balcony. I called to him at once, and asked him to let me a bed. He put to me all the questions he could think of. Why was I there? Where had I come from? Where (if I was honest) had I intended to sleep? How came I at such an hour on foot? and other examinations. I thought a little what excuse to give him, and then, determining that I was too tired to make up anything plausible, I told him the full truth; that I had meant to sleep rough, but had been overcome by fatigue, and that I had walked from Toul, starting at evening. I conjured him by our common Faith to let me in. He told me that it was impossible, as he had but one room in which he and his family slept, and assured me he had asked all these questions out of sympathy and charity alone. Then he wished me goodnight, honestly and kindly, and went in.

By this time I was very much put out, and began to be angry. These straggling French towns give no opportunity for a shelter. I saw that I should have to get out beyond the market gardens, and that it might be a mile or two before I found any rest. A clock struck one. I looked up and saw it was from the belfry of one of those new chapels which the monks are building everywhere, nor did I forget to curse the monks in my heart for building them. I cursed also those who started smelting works in the Moselle valley; those who gave false advice to travellers; those who kept lions and tigers in caravans, and for a small sum I would have cursed the whole human race, when I saw that my bile had hurried me out of the street well into the countryside, and that above me, on a bank, was a patch of orchard and a lane leading up to it. Into this I turned, and, finding a good deal of dry hay lying under the trees, I soon made myself an excellent bed, first building a little mattress, and then piling on hay as warm as a blanket.

I did not lie awake (as when I planned my pilgrimage I had promised myself I would do), looking at the sky through the branches of trees, but I slept at once without dreaming, and woke up to find it was broad daylight, and the sun ready to rise. Then, stiff and but little rested by two hours of exhaustion, I took up my staff and my sack and regained the road.

I should very much like to know what those who have an answer to everything can say about the food requisite to breakfast? Those great men Marlowe and Jonson, Shakespeare, and Spenser before him, drank beer at rising, and tamed it with a little bread. In the regiment we used to drink black coffee without sugar, and cut off a great hunk of stale crust, and eat nothing more till the halt: for the matter of that, the great victories of '93 were fought upon such unsubstantial meals; for the Republicans fought first and ate afterwards, being in this quite unlike the Ten Thousand. Sailors I know eat nothing for some hours—I mean those who turn out at four in the morning; I could give the name of the watch, but that I forget it and will not be plagued to look up technicalities. Dogs eat the first thing they come across, cats take a little milk, and gentlemen are accustomed to get up at nine and eat eggs, bacon, kidneys, ham, cold pheasant, toast, coffee, tea, scones, and honey, after which they will boast that their race is the hardiest in the world and ready to bear every fatigue in the pursuit of Empire. But what rule governs all this? Why is breakfast different from all other things, so that the Greeks called it the best thing in the world, and so that each of us in a vague way knows that he would eat at breakfast nothing but one special kind of food, and that he could not imagine breakfast at any other hour in the day?

The provocation to this inquiry (which I have here no time to pursue) lies in the extraordinary distaste that I conceived that morning for Brulé wine. My ham and bread and chocolate I had consumed overnight. I thought, in my folly, that I could break my fast on a swig of what had seemed to me, only the night before, the best revivifier and sustenance possible. In the harsh dawn it turned out to be nothing but a bitter and intolerable vinegar. I make no attempt to explain this, nor to say why the very same wine that had seemed so good in the forest (and was to seem so good again later on by the canal) should now repel me. I can only tell you that this heavy disappointment convinced me of a great truth that a Politician once let slip in my hearing, and that I have never since forgotten.

'*Man,*' said the Director of the State, '*man is but the creature of circumstance.*'

As it was, I lit a pipe of tobacco and hobbled blindly along for miles under and towards the brightening east. Just before the sun rose I turned and looked backward from a high bridge that re-crossed the river. The long effort of the night had taken me well on my way. I was out of the familiar region of the garrison. The great forest-hills that I had traversed stood up opposite the dawn, catching the new light; heavy, drifting but white clouds, rare at such an hour, sailed above them. The valley of the Moselle, which I had never thought of save as a half mountainous region, had fallen, to become a kind of long garden, whose walls were regular, low, and cultivated slopes. The main waterway of the valley was now not the river but the canal that fed from it.

The tall grasses, the leaves, and poplars bordering the river and the canal seemed dark close to me, but the valley as a whole was vague, a mass of trees with one Lorraine church-tower showing, and the delicate slopes bounding it on either side.

Descending from this bridge I found a sign-post, that told me I had walked thirty-two kilometres—which is twenty miles—from Toul; that it was one kilometre to Flavigny, and heaven knows how much to a place called Charmes. The sun rose in the mist that lay up the long even trends of the vale, between the low and level hills, and I pushed on my thousand yards towards Flavigny. There, by a special providence, I found the entertainment and companion-ship whose lack had left me wrecked all these early hours.

As I came into Flavigny I saw at once that it was a place on which a book might easily be written, for it had a church built in the seventeenth century, when few churches were built outside great towns, a convent, and a general air of importance that made of it that grand and noble thing, that primary cell of the organism of Europe, that best of all Christian associations—a large village.

I say a book might be written upon it, and there is no doubt that a great many articles and pamphlets must have been written upon it, for the French are furiously given to local research and re-views, and to glorifying their native places; and when they cannot discover folk-lore they enrich their beloved homes by inventing it.

There was even a man (I forget his name) who wrote a delightful book called 'Popular and Traditional Songs of my Province', which book, after he was dead, was discovered to be entirely his own invention, and not a word of it familiar to the inhabitants of the soil. He was a large, laughing man that smoked enormously, had great masses of hair, and worked by night; also he delighted in the society of friends, and talked continuously. I wish he had a statue somewhere, and that they would pull down to make room for it any one of those useless bronzes that are to be found even in the little villages, and that commemorate solemn, whiskered men, pillars of the state. For surely this is the habit of the true poet, and marks the vigour and recurrent origin of poetry, that a man should get his head full of rhythms and catches, and that they should jumble up somehow into short songs of his own. What could more suggest (for instance) a whole troop of dancing words and lovely thoughts than this refrain from the Tourdenoise—

> . . . *Son beau corps est en terre*
> *Son âme en Paradis*
> *Tu ris?*
> *Et ris, tu ris, ma Bergére,*
> *Ris, ma Bergére, tu ris.*

That was the way they set to work in England before the Puritans came, when men were not afraid to steal verses from one another, and when no one imagined that he could live by letters, but when every poet took a patron, or begged or robbed the churches. So much for the poets.

Flavigny then, I say (for I seem to be digressing), is a long street of houses all built together as animals build their communities. They are all very old, but the people have worked hard since the Revolution, and none of them are poor, nor are any of them very rich. I saw but one gentleman's house, and that, I am glad to say, was in disrepair. Most of the peasant's houses had, for a ground floor, cavernous great barns out of which came a delightful smell of morning—that is, of hay, litter, oxen, and stored grains and old wood; which is the true breath of morning, because it is the scent that all the human race worth calling human first meets when it rises, and is the association of sunrise in the minds of those who keep the world alive: but not in the wretched minds of townsmen, and least of all in the minds of journalists, who know nothing of morning save that it is a time of jaded emptiness when you have just done prophesying (for the hundredth time) the approaching end of the world, when the floors are beginning to tremble with machinery, and when, in a weary kind of way, one feels hungry and alone: a nasty life and usually a short one.

To return to Flavigny. This way of stretching a village all along one street is Roman, and is the mark of civilization. When I was at college I was compelled to read a work by the crabbed Tacitus on the Germans, where, in the midst of a deal that is vague and fantastic nonsense and much that is wilful lying, comes this excellent truth, that barbarians build their houses separate, but civilized men together. So whenever you see a lot of red roofs nestling, as the phrase goes, in the woods of a hillside in south England, remember that all that is savagery; but when you see a hundred whitewashed houses in a row along a dead straight road, lift up your hearts, for you are in civilization again.

But I continue to wander from Flavigny. The first thing I saw as I came into the street and noted how the level sun stood in a haze beyond, and how it shadowed and brought out the slight irregularities of the road, was a cart drawn by a galloping donkey, which came at and passed me with a prodigious clatter as I dragged myself forward. In the cart were two nuns, each with a scythe; they were going out mowing, and were up the first in the village, as Religious always are. Cheered by this happy omen, but not yet heartened, I next met a very old man leading out a horse, and asked him if there was anywhere where I could find coffee and bread at that hour; but he shook his head mournfully and wished me good-morning in a strong accent, for he was deaf and probably thought I was begging. So I went on still more despondent till I came to a really merry man of about middle age who was going to the fields, singing, with a very large rake over his shoulder. When I had asked him the same question he stared at me a little and said of course coffee and bread could be had at the baker's, and when I asked him how I should know the baker's he was still more surprised at my ignorance, and said, 'By the smoke coming from the large chimney.' This I saw rising a short way off on my right, so I thanked him and went and found there a youth of about nineteen, who sat at a fine oak table and had coffee, rum, and a loaf before him. He was waiting for the bread in the oven to be ready; and meanwhile he was very courteous poured out coffee and rum for me and offered me bread.

It is a matter often discussed why bakers are such excellent citizens and good men. For while it is admitted in every country I was ever in that cobblers are argumentative and atheists (I except the cobbler under Plinlimmon, concerning whom would to heaven I had the space to tell you all here, for he knows the legends of the mountain), while it is public that barbers are garrulous and servile, that millers are cheats (we say in Sussex that every honest miller has a large tuft of hair on the palm of his hand), yet—with every trade in the world having some bad quality attached to it—bakers alone are exempt, and every one takes it for granted that they are sterling: indeed, there are some societies in which, no matter how gloomy and churlish the conversation may have become, you have but to mention bakers for voices to brighten suddenly and for a good influence to pervade every one. I say this is known for a fact, but not usually explained; the explanation is, that bakers are always up early in the morning and can watch the dawn, and that in this occupation they live in lonely contemplation enjoying the early hours.

So it was with this baker of mine in Flavigny, who was a boy. When he heard that I had served at Toul he was delighted beyond measure; he told me of a brother of his that had been in the same regiment, and he assured me that he was himself going into the artillery by special enlistment, having got his father's leave. You know very little if you think I missed the opportunity of making the guns seem terrible and glorious in his eyes. I told him stories enough to waken a sentry of reserve, and if it had been possible (with my youth so obvious) I would have woven in a few anecdotes of active service, and described great shells bursting under my horses and the teams shot down, and the gunners all the while impassive; but as I saw I should not be believed I did not speak of such things, but confined myself to what he would see and hear when he joined.

Meanwhile the good warm food and the rising morning had done two things; they had put much more vigour into me than I had had when I slunk in half an hour before, but at the same time (and this is a thing that often comes with food and with rest) they had made me feel the fatigue of so long a night. I rose up, therefore, determined to find some place where I could sleep. I asked this friend of mine how much there was to pay, and he said 'fourpence.' Then we exchanged ritual salutations, and I took the road. I did not leave the town or village without noticing one extraordinary thing at the far end of it, which was that, whereas most places in France are proud of their town-hall and make a great show of it, here in Flavigny they had taken a great house and written over it ECOLE COMMUNALE in great letters, and then they had written over a kind of lean-to or out-house of this big place the words 'Hôtel de ville' in very small letters, so small that I had a doubt for a moment if the citizens here were good republicans—a treasonable thought on all this frontier.

Then, a mile onward, I saw the road cross the canal and run parallel to it. I saw the canal run another mile or so under a fine bank of deep woods. I saw an old bridge leading over it to that inviting shade, and as it was now nearly six and the sun was gathering strength, I went, with slumber overpowering me and my feet turning heavy beneath me, along the tow-path, over the bridge, and lay down on the moss under these delightful trees. Forgetful of the penalty that such an early repose would bring, and of the great heat that was to follow at midday, I quickly became part of the life of that forest and fell asleep.

The Aar was a shallow brawling torrent, thick with melting ice and snow and mud. Coarse grass grew on the rocks sparsely; there were no flowers. The mist overhead was now quite near, and I still went on and steadily up through the half-light. It was as lonely as a calm at sea, except for the noise of the river. I had overworn myself, and that sustaining surface which hides from us in our health the abysses below the mind—I felt it growing weak and thin. My fatigue bewildered me. The occasional steeps beside the road, one especially beneath a high bridge where a tributary falls into the Aar in a cascade, terrified me. They were like the emptiness of dreams. At last it being now dark, and I having long since entered the upper mist, or rather cloud (for I was now as high as the clouds), I saw a light gleaming through the fog, just off the road, through pine-trees. It was time. I could not have gone much further.

To this I turned and found there one of those new hotels, not very large, but very expensive. They knew me at once for what I was, and welcomed me with joy. They gave me hot rum and sugar, a fine warm bed, told me I was the first that had yet stopped there that year, and left me to sleep very deep and yet in pain, as men sleep who are stunned. But twice that night I woke suddenly, staring at darkness. I had outworn the physical network upon which the soul depends, and I was full of terrors.

Next morning I had fine coffee and bread and butter and the rest, like a rich man; in a gilded dining-room all set out for the rich, and served by a fellow that bowed and scraped. Also they made me pay a great deal, and kept their eyes off my boots, and were still courteous to me, and I to them. Then I brought wine of them—the first wine not of the country that I had drunk on this march, a Burgundy—and putting it in my haversack with a nice white roll, left them to wait for the next man whom the hills might send them.

The clouds, the mist, were denser than ever in that early morning; one could only see the immediate road. The cold was very great; my clothes were not quite dried, but my heart was high, and I pushed along well enough, though stiffly, till I came to what they call the Hospice, which was once a monk-house, I suppose, but is now an inn. I had brandy there, and on going out I found that it stood at the foot of a sharp ridge which was the true Grimsel Pass, the neck which joins the Bernese Oberland to the eastern group of high mountains. This ridge or neck was steep like a pitched roof— very high I found it, and all of black glassy rock, with here and there snow in sharp, even, sloping sheets just holding to it. I could see but little of it at a time on account of the mist.

Hitherto for all these miles the Aar had been my companion, and the road, though rising always, had risen evenly and not steeply. Now the Aar was left behind in the icy glen where it rises, and the road went in an artificial and carefully built set of zigzags up the face of the cliff. There is a short cut, but I could not find it in the mist. It is the old mule-path. Here and there, however, it was possible to cut off long corners by scrambling over the steep black rock and smooth ice, and all the while the cold, soft mist wisped in and out around me. After a thousand feet of this I came to the top of the Grimsel, but not before I had passed a place where an avalanche had destroyed the road and where planks were laid. Also before one got to the very summit, no short cuts or climbing were possible. The road ran deep in a cutting like a Devonshire lane. Only here the high banks were solid snow.

Some little way past the summit, on the first zigzag down, I passed the Lake of the Dead in its mournful hollow. The mist still enveloped all the ridge-side, and moved like a press of spirits over the frozen water, then—as suddenly as on the much lower Brienzer Grat, and (as on the Brienzer Grat) to the southward and the sun, the clouds lifted and wreathed up backward and were gone, and where there had just been fulness was only an immensity of empty air and a sudden sight of clear hills beyond and of little strange distant things thousands and thousands of feet below.

LECTOR. Pray are we to have any more of that fine writing?

AUCTOR. I saw there as in a cup things that I had thought (when I first studied the map at home) far too spacious and spread apart to go into the view. Yet here they were all quite contained and close together, on so vast a scale was the whole place conceived. It was the comb of mountains of which I have written; the meeting of all the valleys.

There, from the height of a steep bank, as it were (but a bank many thousands of feet high), one looked down into a whole district or little world. On the map, I say, it had seemed so great that I had thought one would command but this or that portion of it; as it was, one saw it all.

And this is a peculiar thing I have noticed in all mountains, and have never been able to understand—namely, that if you draw a plan or section to scale, your mountain does not seem a very important thing. One should not, in theory, be able to dominate from its height, nor to feel the world small below one, nor to hold a whole countryside in one's hand—yet one does. The mountains from their heights reveal to us two truths. They suddenly make us feel our insignificance, and at the same time they free the imortal Mind, and let it feel its greatness, and they release it from the earth. But I say again, in theory, when one considers the exact relation of their height to the distances one views from them, they ought to claim no such effect, and that they can produce that effect is related to another thing—the way in which they exaggerate their own steepness.

For instance, those noble hills, my downs in Sussex, when you are upon them overlooking the weald, from Chanctonbury say, feel like this—

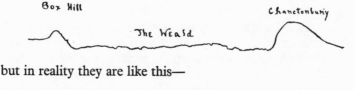

but in reality they are like this—

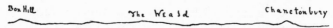

or even lower. Indeed, it is impossible to give them truly, so insignificant are they; if the stretch of the Weald were made nearly a yard long. Chanctonbury would not, in proportion, be more than a fifth of an inch high! And yet, from the top of Chanctonbury, how one seems to overlook it and possess it all!

Well, so it was here from the Grimsel when I overlooked the springs of the Rhone. In true proportion the valley I gazed into and over must have been somewhat like this—

It felt for all the world as deep and utterly below me as this other—

Moreover, where there was no mist, the air was so surprisingly clear that I could see everything clean and sharp wherever I turned my eyes. The mountains forbade any very far horizons to the view, and all that I could see was as neat and vivid as those coloured photographs they sell with bright green grass and bright white snow, and blue glaciers like precious stones.

I scrambled down the mountain, for here, on the south side of the pass, there was no snow or ice, and it was quite easy to leave the road and take the old path cutting off the zigzags. As the air got heavier, I became hungry, and at the very end of my descent, two hundred feet or so above the young Rhone, I saw a great hotel. I went round to their front door and asked them whether I could eat, and at what price. 'Four francs,' they said.

'What!' said I, 'four francs for a meal! Come let me eat in the kitchen, and charge me one.' But they became rude and obstinate, being used only to deal with rich people, so I cursed them, and went down the road. But I was very hungry.

The road falls quite steeply, and the Rhone, which it accompanies in that valley, leaps in little falls. On a bridge I passed a sad Englishman reading a book, and a little lower down, two American women in a carriage, and after that a priest (it was lucky I did not see him first. Anyhow, I touched iron at once, to wit, a key in my pocket), and after that a child minding a goat. Altogether, I felt myself in the world again, and as I was on a good road, all down hill, I thought myself capable of pushing on to the next village. But my hunger was really excessive, my right boot almost gone, and my left boot nothing to exhibit or boast of, when I came to a point where at last one looked down the Rhone valley for miles. It is like a straight trench, and at intervals there are little villages, built of most filthy châlets, the said châlets raised on great stones. There are pine-trees up, up on either slope, into the clouds, and beyond the clouds I could not see. I left on my left a village called 'Between the Waters'. I passed through another called 'Ehringen', but it has no inn. At last, two miles farther, faint from lack of food, I got into Ulrichen, a village a little larger than the rest, and the place where I believed one should start to go either over the Gries or Nufenen Pass. In Ulrichen was a warm, wooden, deep-eaved frousty, comfortable, ramshackle, dark, anyhow kind of a little inn called 'The Bear'. And entering I saw one of the women whom God loves.

She was of middle age, very honest and simple in the face, kindly and good. She was messing about with cooking and stuff, and she came up to me stooping a little, her eyes wide and innocent, and a great spoon in her hand. Her face was extremely broad and flat, and I had never seen eyes set so far apart. Her whole gait, manner, and accent proved her to be extremely good, and on the straight road to heaven. I saluted her in the French tongue. She answered me in the same, but very broken and rustic, for her natural speech was a kind of mountain German. She spoke very slowly, and had a nice soft voice, and she did what only good people do, I mean, looked you in the eyes as she spoke to you.

Beware of shifty-eyed people. It is not only nervousness, it is also a kind of wickedness. Such people come to no good. I have three of them now in mind as I write. One is a Professor.

And, by the way, would you know why universities suffer from this curse of nervous disease? Why the greatest personages stammer or have St Vitus' dance, or jabber at the lips, or hop in their walk, or have their heads screwed round, or tremble in the fingers, or go through life with great goggles like a motor car? Eh? I will tell you. It is the punishment of their *intellectual pride*, than which no sin is more offensive to the angels.

What! here are we with the jolly world of God all round us, able to sing, to draw, to paint, to hammer and build, to sail, to ride horses, to run, to leap; having for our splendid inheritance love in youth and memory in old age, and we are to take one miserable little faculty, our one-legged, knock-kneed, gimcrack, purblind, rough-skinned, underfed, and perpetually irritated and grumpy intellect, or analytical curiosity rather (a diseased appetite), and let it swell till it eats up every other function? Away with such foolery.

LECTOR. When shall we get on to . . .

AUCTOR. Wait a moment. I say, away with such foolery. Note that pedants lose all proportion. They never can keep sane in a discussion. They will go wild on matters they are wholly unable to judge, such as Armenian Religion or the Politics of Paris or what not. Never do they use one of those three phrases which keep a man steady and balance his mind, I mean the words (1) *After all it is not my business.* (2) *Tut! tut! You don't say so!* and (3) *Credo in Unum Deum Patrem Omnipotentem, Factorem omnium visibilium atque invisibilium;* in which last there is a power of synthesis that can jam all their analytical dust-heap into such a fine, tight, and compact body as would make them stare to see. I understand that they need six months' holiday a year. Had I my way they should take twelve, and an extra day on leap years.

LECTOR. Pray, pray return to the woman at the inn.

AUCTOR. I will, and by this road: to say that on the day of Judgment, when St Michael weighs souls in his scales, and the wicked are led off by the Devil with a great rope, as you may see them over the main porch of Notre Dame (I will heave a stone after them myself I hope), all the souls of the pedants together will not weigh as heavy and sound as the one soul of this good woman at the inn.

She put food before me and wine. The wine was good, but in the food was some fearful herb or other I had never tasted before—a pure spice or scent, and a nasty one. One could taste nothing else, and it was revolting; but I ate it for her sake.

Then, very much refreshed, I rose, seized my great staff, shook myself and said, 'Now it is about noon, and I am off for the frontier'.

At this she made a most fearful clamour, saying that it was madness, and imploring me not to think of it, and running out fetched from the stable a tall, sad, pale-eyed man who saluted me profoundly and told me that he knew more of the mountains than any one for miles. And this by asking many afterwards I found out to be true. He said that he had crossed the Nufenen and the Gries whenever they could be crossed since he was a child, and that if I attempted it that day I should sleep that night in Paradise. The clouds on the mountain, the soft snow recently fallen, the rain that now occupied the valleys, the glacier on the Gries, and the pathless snow in the mist on the Nufenen would make it sheer suicide for him, an experienced guide, and for me a worse madness. Also he spoke of my boots and wondered at my poor cotton coat and trousers, and threatened me with intolerable cold.

It seems that the books I had read at home, when they said that the Nufenen had no snow on it, spoke of a later season of the year; it was all snow now, and soft snow, and hidden by a full mist in such a day from the first third of the ascent. As for the Gries, there was a glacier on the top which needed some kind of clearness in the weather. Hearing all this I said I would remain—but it was with a heavy heart. Already I felt a shadow of defeat over me. The loss of time was a thorn. I was already short of cash, and my next money was at Milan. My return to England was fixed for a certain date, and stronger than either of these motives against delay was a burning restlessness that always takes men when they are on the way to great adventures.

I made him promise to wake me next morning at three o'clock, and, short of a tempest, to try and get me across the Gries. As for the Nufenen and Crystalline passes which I had desired to attempt, and which were (as I have said) the straight line to Rome, he said (and he was right), that let alone the impassability of the Nufenen just then, to climb the Crystal Mountain in that season would be as easy as flying to the moon. Now, to cross the Nufenen alone, would simply land me in the upper valley of the Ticino, and take me a great bend out of my way by Bellinzona. Hence my bargain that at least he should show me over the Gries Pass, and this he said, if man could do it, he would do the next day; and I, sending my boots to be cobbled (and thereby breaking another vow), crept up to bed, and all afternoon read the school-books of the children. They were in French, from lower down the valley, and very Genevese and heretical for so devout a household. But the Genevese civilization is the standard for these people, and they combat the Calvinism of it with missions, and have statues in their rooms, not to speak of holy water stoups.

The rain beat on my window, the clouds came lower still down the mountain. Then (as is finely written in the Song of Roland), 'the day passed and the night came, and I slept'. But with the coming of the small hours, and with my waking, prepare yourselves for the most extraordinary and terrible adventure that befell me out of all the marvels and perils of this pilgrimage, the most momentous and the most worthy of perpetual record, I think, of all that has ever happened since the beginning of the world.

At three o'clock the guide knocked at my door, and I rose and came out to him. We drank coffee and ate bread. We put into our sacks ham and bread, and he white wine and I brandy. Then we set out. The rain had dropped to a drizzle, and there was no wind. The sky was obscured for the most part, but here and there was a star. The hills hung awfully above us in the night as we crossed the spongy valley. A little wooden bridge took us over the young Rhone, here only a stream, and we followed a path up into the tributary

ravine which leads to the Nufenen and the Gries. In a mile or two
it was a little lighter, and this was as well, for some weeks before a
great avalanche had fallen, and we had to cross it gingerly. Beneath
the wide cap of frozen snow ran a torrent roaring. I remembered
Colorado, and how I had crossed the Arkansaw on such a bridge as
a boy. We went on in the uneasy dawn. The woods began to show,
and there was a cross where a man had slipped from above that very
April and been killed. Then, most ominous and disturbing, the
drizzle changed to a rain, and the guide shook his head and said it
would be snowing higher up. We went on, and it grew lighter.
Before it was really day (or else the weather confused and darkened
the sky), we crossed a good bridge, built long ago, and we halted at
a shed where the cattle lie in the late summer when the snow is
melted. There we rested a moment.

But on leaving its shelter we noticed many disquieting things.
The place was a hollow, the end of the ravine—a bowl, as it were;
one way out of which is the Nufenen, and the other the Gries.

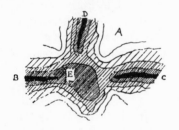

Here it is in a sketch map. The heights are marked lighter and
lighter, from black in the valleys to white in the impassable mountains. E is where we stood, in a great cup or basin, having just come
up the ravine B. C is the Italian valley of the Tosa, and the neck
between it and E is the Gries. D is the valley of the Ticino, and the
neck between E and it is the Nufenen. A is the Crystal Mountain.
You may take the necks or passes to be about 8,000, and the
mountains 10,000 or 11,000 feet above the sea.

We noticed, I say, many disquieting things. First, all that bowl
or cup below the passes was a carpet of snow, save where patches of
black water showed, and all the passes and mountains, from top to
bottom, were covered with very thick snow; the deep surface of it
soft and fresh fallen. Secondly, the rain had turned into snow. It

was falling thickly all around. Nowhere have I perceived the immediate presence of great Death. Thirdly, it was far colder, and we
felt the beginning of a wind. Fourthly, the clouds had come quite
low down.

The guide said it could not be done, but I said we must attempt
it. I was eager, and had not yet felt the awful grip of the cold. We
left the Nufenen on our left, a hopeless steep of new snow buried in
fog, and we attacked the Gries. For half an hour we plunged on
through snow above our knees, and my thin cotton clothes were
soaked. So far the guide knew we were more or less on the path,
and he went on and I panted after him. Neither of us spoke, but
occasionally he looked back to make sure I had not dropped out.

The snow began to fall more thickly, and the wind had risen
somewhat. I was afraid of another protest from the guide, but he
stuck to it well, and I after him, continually plunging through soft
snow and making yard after yard upwards. The snow fell more
thickly and the wind still rose.

We came to a place which is, in the warm season, an alp; that is,
a slope of grass, very steep but not terrifying; having here and there
sharp little precipices of rock breaking it into steps, but by no means
(in summer) a matter to make one draw back. Now, however, when
everything was still Arctic it was a very different matter. A sheer
steep of snow whose downward plunge ran into the driving storm
and was lost, whose head was lost in the same mass of thick cloud
above, a slope somewhat hollowed and bent inwards, had to be
crossed if we were to go any farther; and I was terrified, for I knew
nothing of climbing. The guide said there was little danger, only if
one slipped one might slide down to safety, or one might (much less
probably) get over rocks and be killed. I was chattering a little with
cold; but as he did not propose a return, I followed him. The
surface alternately slabs of frozen snow and patches of soft new
snow. In the first he cut steps, in the second we plunged, and once
I went right in and a mass of snow broke off beneath me and went
careering down the slope. He showed me how to hold my staff
backwards as he did his alpenstock, and use it as a kind of brake in
case I slipped.

We had been about twenty minutes crawling over that wall of
snow and ice; and it was more and more apparent that we were in
for danger. Before we had quite reached the far side, the wind was

blowing a very full gale and roared past our ears. The surface snow was whirring furiously like dust before it: past our faces and against them drove the snow-flakes, cutting the air: not falling, but making straight darts and streaks. They seemed like the form of the whistling wind; they blinded us. The rocks on the far side of the slope, rocks which had been our goal when we set out to cross it, had long ago disappeared in the increasing rush of the blizzard. Suddenly as we were still painfully moving on, stooping against the mad wind, these rocks loomed up over as large as houses, and we saw them through the swarming snow-flakes as great hulls are seen through a fog at sea. The guide crouched under the lee of the nearest; I came up close to him and he put his hands to my ear and shouted to me that nothing further could be done—he had so to shout because in among the rocks the hurricane made a roaring sound, swamping the voice.

I asked how far we were from the summit. He said he did not know where we were exactly, but that we could not be more than 800 feet from it. I was but that from Italy and I would not admit defeat. I offered him all I had in money to go on, but it was folly in me, because if I had had enough to tempt him and if he had yielded we should both have died. Luckily it was but a little sum. He shook his head. He would not go on, he broke out, for all the money there was in the world. He shouted me to eat and drink, and so we both did.

Then I understood his wisdom, for in a little while the cold began to seize me in my thin clothes. My hands were numb, my face already gave me intolerable pain, and my legs suffered and felt heavy. I learnt another thing (which had I been used to mountains I should have known), that it was not a simple thing to return. The guide was hesitating whether to stay in this rough shelter, or to face the chances of descent. This terror had not crossed my mind, and I thought as little of it as I could, needing my courage, and being near to breaking down from the intensity of the cold.

It seems that in a *tourmente* (for by that excellent name do the mountain people call such a storm) it is always a matter of doubt whether to halt or to go back. If you go back through it and lose your way, you are done for. If you halt in some shelter, it may go on for two days or three days, and then there is an end of you.

After a little he decided for a return, but he told me honestly what the chances were, and my suffering from cold mercifully mitigated my fear. But even in that moment, I felt in a confused but very conscious way that I was defeated. I had crossed so many great hills and rivers, and pressed so well on my undeviating arrow-line to Rome, and I had charged this one great barrier manfully where the straight path of my pilgrimage crossed the Alps—and I had failed! Even in that fearful cold I felt it, and it ran through my doubt of return like another and deeper current of pain. Italy was there, just above, right to my hand. A lifting of a cloud, a little respite, and every downward step would have been towards the sunlight. As it was, I was being driven back northward, in retreat and ashamed. The Alps had conquered me.

Let us always after this combat their immensity and their will, and always hate the inhuman guards that hold the gates of Italy, and the powers that lie in wait for men on those high places. But now I know that Italy will always stand apart. She is cut off by no ordinary wall, and Death has all his army on her frontiers.

Well, we returned. Twice the guide rubbed my hands with brandy, and once I had to halt and recover for a moment, failing and losing my hold. Believe it or not, the deep footsteps of our ascent were already quite lost and covered by the new snow since our halt, and even had they been visible, the guide would not have retraced them. He did what I did not at first understand, but what I soon saw to be wise. He took a steep slant downward over the face of the snow-slope, and though such a pitch of descent a little un-nerved me, it was well in the end. For when we had gone down perhaps 900 feet, or a thousand, in perpendicular distance, even I, half numb and fainting, could feel that the storm was less violent. Another two hundred, and the flakes could be seen not driving in flashes past, but separately falling. Then in some few minutes we could see the slope for a very long way downwards quite clearly; then, soon after, we saw far below us the place where the mountain-side merged easily into the plain of that cup or basin whence we had started.

When we saw this, the guide said to me, 'Hold your stick thus, if you are strong enough, and let yourself slide.' I could just hold it, in spite of the cold. Life was returning to me with intolerable pain. We shot down the slope almost as quickly as falling, but it was evidently safe to do so, as the end was clearly visible, and had no break or rock in it.

So we reached the plain below, and entered the little shed, and thence looking up, we saw the storm above us; but no one could have told it for what it was. Here, below, was silence, and the terror and raging above seemed only a great trembling cloud occupying the mountain. Then we set our faces down the ravine by which we had come up, and so came down to where the snow changed to rain. When we got right down into the valley of the Rhone, we found it all roofed with cloud, and the higher trees were white with snow, making a line like a tide mark on the slopes of the hills.

I re-entered 'The Bear', silent and angered, and not accepting the humiliation of that failure. Then, having eaten, I determined in equal silence to take the road like any other fool; to cross the Furka by a fine highroad, like any tourist, and to cross the St Gothard by another fine highroad, as millions had done before me, and not to look heaven in the face again till I was back after my long detour, on the straight road again for Rome.

But to think of it! I who had all that planned out, and had so nearly done it! I who had cut a path across Europe like a shaft, and seen so many strange places!—now to have to recite all the litany of the vulgar; Bellinzona, Lugano, and this and that, which any railway travelling fellow can tell you. Not till Como should I feel a man again. . . .

Indeed it is a bitter thing to have to give up one's sword.

All you that have loved passionately and have torn your hearts asunder in disillusions, do not imagine that things broken cannot be mended by the good angels. There is a kind of splice called 'the long splice' which makes a cut rope seem what it was before; it is even stronger than before, and can pass through a block. There will descend upon you a blessed hour when you will be convinced as by a miracle, and you will suddenly understand the *redintegratio amoris* (*amoris redintegratio*, a Latin phrase). But this hour you will not receive in the rain on the Emilian Way.

Here, then, next day, just outside a town called Borgo, past the middle of morning, the rain ceased.

Its effect was still upon the slippery and shining road, the sky was still fast and leaden, when, in a distaste for their towns, I skirted the place by a lane that runs westward of the houses, and sitting upon a low wall, I looked up at the Apennines, which were now plain above me, and thought over my approaching passage through those hills.

But here I must make clear by a map the mass of mountains which I was about to attempt, and in which I forded so many rivers, met so many strange men and beasts, saw such unaccountable sights, was imprisoned, starved, frozen, haunted, delighted, burnt up, and finally refreshed in Tuscany—in a word, where I had the most extraordinary and unheard-of adventures that ever diversified the life of man.

The straight line to Rome runs from Milan not quite through Piacenza, but within a mile or two of that city. Then it runs across the first folds of the Apennines, and gradually diverges from the Emilian Way. It was not possible to follow this part of the line exactly, for there was no kind of track. But by following the Emilian Way for several miles (as I had done), and by leaving it at the right moment, it was possible to strike the straight line again near a village called Medesano.

Now on the far side of the Apennines, beyond their main crest, there happens, most providentially, to be a river called the Serchio, whose valley is fairly straight and points down directly to Rome. To follow this valley would be practically to follow the line to Rome, and it struck the Tuscan plain not far from Lucca.

But to get from the Emilian Way over the eastern slope of the Apennines main ridge and crest, to where the Serchio rises on the western side, is a very difficult matter. The few roads across the Apennines cut my track at right angles, and were therefore useless. In order to strike the watershed at the sources of the Serchio it was necessary to go obliquely across a torrent and four rivers (the Taro, the Parma, the Enza, and the Secchia), and to climb the four spurs that divided them; crossing each nearer to the principal chain as I advanced until, after the Secchia, the next climb would be that of the central crest itself, on the far side of which I should find the Serchio valley.

Perhaps in places roads might correspond to this track. Certainly the bulk of it would be mule-paths or rough gullies—how much I could not tell. The only way I could work it with my wretched map was to note the names of towns or hamlets more or less on the line, and to pick my way from one to another. I wrote them down as follows: Fornovo, Calestano, Tizzano, Colagna—the last at the foot of the final pass. The distance to that pass as the crow flies was only a little more than thirty miles. So exceedingly difficult was the task that it took me over two days. Till I reached Fornovo beyond the Taro, I was not really in the hills.

By country roads, picking my way, I made that afternoon for Medesano. The lanes were tortuous; they crossed continual streams that ran from the hills above, full and foaming after the rain, and frothing with the waste of the mountains. I had not gone two miles when the sky broke; not four when a new warmth began to steal over the air and a sense of summer to appear in the earth about me. With the greatest rapidity the unusual weather that had accompanied me from Milan was changing into the normal brilliancy of the south; but it was too late for the sun to tell, though he shone through clouds that were now moving eastwards more perceptibly and shredding as they moved.

Quite tired and desiring food, keen also for rest after those dispiriting days, I stopped, before reaching Medesano, at an inn where three ways met; and there I purposed to eat and spend the night, for the next day, it was easy to see, would be tropical, and I should rise before dawn if I was to save the heat. I entered.

The room within was of red wood. It had two tables, a little counter with a vast array of bottles, a woman behind the counter, and a small, nervous man in a strange hat serving. And all the little place was filled and crammed with a crowd of perhaps twenty men, gesticulating, shouting, laughing, quarrelling, and one very big man was explaining to another the virtues of his knife; and all were already amply satisfied with wine. For in this part men do not own, but are paid wages, so that they waste the little they have.

I saluted the company, and walking up to the counter was about to call for wine. They had all become silent, when one man asked me a question in Italian. I did not understand it, and attempted to say so, when another asked the same question; then six or seven—and there was a hubbub. And out of the hubbub I heard a similar sentence rising all the time. To this day I do not know what it meant, but I thought (and think) it meant 'He is a Venetian', or 'He is the Venetian'. Something in my broken language had made them think this, and evidently the Venetians (or a Venetian) were (or was) gravely unpopular here. Why, I cannot tell. Perhaps the Venetians were blacklegs. But evidently a Venetian, or the whole Venetian nation, had recently done them a wrong.

At any rate one very dark-haired man put his face close up to mine, unlipped his teeth, and began a great noise of cursing and threatening, and this so angered me that it overmastered my fear, which had till then been considerable. I remembered also a rule which a wise man once told me for guidance, and it is this: 'God disposes of victory, but, as the world is made, when men smile, smile; when men laugh, laugh; when men hit, hit; when men shout, shout; and when men curse, curse you also, my son, and in doubt let them always take the first move.'

I say my fear had been considerable, especially of the man with the knife, but I got too angry to remember it, and advancing my face also to this insulter's I shouted, '*Dio Ladro! Dios di mi alma! Sanguinamento! Nombre di Dios! Che? Chevole? Non sono da Venezia io! Sono de Francia! Je m'en fiche da vestra Venezia! Non se vede che non parlar vestra lingua? Che sono forestiere?*' and so forth. At this they evidently divided into two parties, and all began raging amongst themselves, and some at me, while the others argued louder and louder that there was an error.

The little innkeeper caught my arm over the counter, and I

turned round sharply, thinking he was doing me wrong, but I saw him nodding and winking at me, and he was on my side. This was probably because he was responsible if anything happened, and he alone could not fly from the police.

He made them a speech which, for all I know, may have been to the effect that he had known and loved me from childhood, or may have been that he knew me for one Jacques of Turin, or may have been any other lie. Whatever, lie it was it appeased them. Their anger went down to a murmur, just like soda-water settling down into a glass.

I stood wine; we drank. I showed them my book, and as my pencil needed sharpening the large man lent me his knife for courtesy. When I got it in my hand I saw plainly that it was no knife for stabbing with; it was a pruning-knife, and would have bit the hand that cherished it (as they say of serpents). On the other hand, it would have been a good knife for ripping, and passable at a slash. You must not expect too much of one article.

I took food, but I saw that in this parish it was safer to sleep out of doors than in; so in the falling evening, but not yet sunset, I wandered on, not at a pace but looking for shelter, and I found at last just what I wanted: a little shed, with dried ferns (as it seemed) strewed in a corner, a few old sacks, and a broken piece of machinery —though this last was of no use to me.

I thought: 'It will be safe here, for I shall rise before day, and the owner, if there is one, will not disturb me.'

The air was fairly warm. The place quite dry. The open side looked westward and a little south.

The sun had now set behind the Apennines, and there was a deep effulgence in the sky. I drank a little wine, lit a pipe, and watched the west in silence.

Whatever was left of the great pall from which all that rain had fallen, now was banked up on the further side of heaven in toppling great clouds that caught the full glow of evening.

The great clouds stood up in heaven, separate, like persons; and no wind blew; but everything was full of evening. I worshipped them so far as it is permitted to worship inanimate things.

They domed into the pure light of the higher air, inviolable. They seemed halted in the presence of a commanding majesty who ranked them all in order.

This vision filled me with a large calm which a travelled man may find on coming to his home, or a learner in the communion of wise men. Repose, certitude, and, as it were, a premonition of glory occupied my spirit. Before it was yet quite dark I had made a bed out of the dry bracken, covered myself with the sacks and cloths, and very soon I fell asleep, still thinking of the shapes of clouds and of the power of God.

Next morning it was as I had thought. Going out before it was fully light, a dense mist all round and a clear sky showed what the day was to be. As I reached Medesano the sun rose. and in half an hour the air was instinct with heat; within an hour it was blinding. An early Mass in the church below the village prepared my day, but as I took coffee afterwards in a little inn, and asked about crossing the Taro to Fornovo—my first point—to my astonishment they shook their heads. The Taro was impassable.

Why could it not be crossed? My very broken language made it difficult for me to understand. They talked of *rami*, which I thought meant oars; but *rami*, had I known it, meant the separate branches or streams whereby these torrential rivers of Italy flow through their arid beds.

I drew a boat and asked if one could not cross in that (for I was a northerner, and my idea of a river was a river with banks and water in between), but they laughed and said 'No'. Then I made the motion of swimming. They said it was impossible, and one man hung his head to indicate drowning. It was serious. They said tomorrow, or rather next day, one might do it.

Finally, a boy that stood by said he remembered a man who knew the river better than anyone, and he, if anyone could, would get me across. So I took the boy with me up the road, and as we went I saw, parallel to the road, a wide plain of dazzling rocks and sand, and beyond it, shining and silhouetted like an Arab village, the group of houses that was Fornovo. This plain was their sort of river in these hills. The boy said that sometimes it was full and a mile wide, sometimes it dwindled into dirty pools. Now, as I looked, a few thin streams seemed to wind through it, and I could not understand the danger.

After a mile or two we came to a spot in the road where a patch of brushwood only separated us from the river-bed. Here the boy bade me wait, and asked a group of peasants whether the guide was in; they said they thought so, and some went up into the hillside with the boy to fetch him, others remained with me, looking at the river-bed and at Fornovo beyond, shaking their heads, and saying it had not been done for days. But I did not understand whether the rain-freshet had passed and was draining away, or whether it had not yet come down from beyond, and I waited for the guide.

They brought him at last down from his hut among the hills. He came with great strides, a kindly-looking man, extremely tall and thin, and with very pale eyes. He smiled. They pointed me out to him, and we struck the bargain by holding up three fingers each for three lira, and nodding. Then he grasped his long staff and I mine, we bade farewell to the party, and together we went in silence through thick brushwood down towards the broad river-bed. The stones of it glared like the sands of Africa; Fornovo baked under the sun all white and black; between us was this broad plain of parched shingle and rocks that could, in a night, become one enormous river, or dwindle to a chain of stagnant ponds. Today some seven narrow streams wandered in the expanse, and again they seemed so easy to cross that again I wondered at the need of a guide.

We came to the edge of the first, and I climbed on the guide's back. He went bare-legged into the stream deeper and deeper till my feet, though held up high, just touched the water; then laboriously he climbed the further shore, and I got down upon dry land. It had been but twenty yards or so, and he knew the place well. I had seen, as we crossed, what a torrent this first little stream was, and I now knew the difficulty and understood the warnings of the inn.

The second branch was impassable. We followed it up for nearly a mile to where 'an island' (that is, a mass of high land that must have been an island in flood-time, and that had on it an old brown village) stood above the white bed of the river. Just at this 'island' my guide found a ford. And the way he found it is worth telling. He taught me the trick, and it is most useful to men who wander alone in the mountains.

You take a heavy stone, how heavy you must learn to judge, for a more rapid current needs a heavier stone; but say about ten pounds. This you lob gently into mid-stream. *How*, it is impossible to describe, but when you do it it is quite easy to see that in about four feet of water, or less, the stone splashes quite differently from the way it does in five feet or more. It is a sure test, and one much easier to acquire by practice than to write about. To teach myself this trick I practised it throughout my journey in these wilds.

Having found a ford then, he again took me on his shoulders, but, in mid-stream, the water being up to his breast, his foot slipped on a stone (all the bed beneath was rolling and churning in the torrent), and in a moment we had both fallen. He pulled me up straight by his side, and then indeed, overwhelmed in the rush of water, it was easy to understand how the Taro could drown men, and why the peasants dreaded these little ribbons of water.

The current rushed and foamed past me, coming nearly to my neck; and it was icy cold. One had to lean against it, and the water so took away one's weight that at any moment one might have slipped and been carried away. The guide, a much taller man (indeed he was six foot three or so), supported me, holding my arm; and again in a moment we reached dry land.

After that adventure there was no need for carrying. The third, fourth, fifth, and sixth branches were easily fordable. The seventh was broad and deep, and I found it a heavy matter; nor should I have waded it but for my guide, for the water bore against me like a man wrestling, and it was as cold as Acheron, the river of the dead. Then on the further shore, and warning him (in Lingua Franca) of his peril, I gave him his wage, and he smiled and thanked me, and went back, choosing his plans at leisure.

Thus did I cross the river Taro; a danger for men.

Where I landed was a poor man sunning himself. He rose and walked with me to Fornovo. He knew the guide.

'He is a good man,' he said to me of this friend. 'He is as good as a little piece of bread.'

'E vero,' I answered; 'e San Cristophero.'

This pleased the peasant; and indeed it was true. For the guide's business was exactly that of St Christopher, except that the Saint took no money, and lived, I suppose, on air.

And so to Fornovo; and the heat blinded and confused, and the air was alive with flies. But the sun dried me at once, and I pressed up the road because I needed food. After I had eaten in this old town I was preparing to make for Calestano and to cross the first high spur of the Apennines that separated me from it, when I saw, as I left the place, a very old church; and I stayed a moment and looked at carvings which were in no order, but put in pell-mell, evidently chosen from some older building. They were barbaric, but one could see that they stood for the last judgment of man, and there were the good-looking foolish, and there were the wicked being boiled by devils in a pot, and what was most pleasing was one devil who with great joy was carrying off a rich man's gold in a bag. But now we are too wise to believe in such follies, and when we die we take our wealth with us; in the ninth century they had no way of doing this, for no system of credit yet obtained.

Then leaving the main road which runs to Pontremoli and at last to Spezzia, my lane climbed up into the hills and ceased, little by little, to be even a lane. It became from time to time the bed of a stream, then nothing, then a lane again, and at last, at the head of the glen, I confessed to having lost it; but I noted a great rock or peak above me for a landmark, and I said to myself—

'No matter. The wall of this glen before me is obviously the ridge of the spur; the rock must be left to the north, and I have but to cross the ridge by its guidance.' By this time, however, the heat overcame me, and, as it was already afternoon, and as I had used so much of the preceding night for my journey, I remembered the wise custom of hot countries and lay down to sleep.

I slept but a little while, yet when I woke the air was cooler. I climbed the side of the glen at random, and on the summit I found, to my disgust, a road. What road could it be? To this day I do not know. Perhaps I had missed my way and struck the main highway again. Perhaps (it is often so in the Apennines) it was a road leading nowhere. At any rate I hesitated, and looked back to judge my direction.

It was a happy accident. I was now some 2,000 feet above the Taro. There, before me, stood the high strange rock that I had watched from below: all around it and below me was the glen or cup of bare hills, slabs, and slopes of sand and stone calcined in the sun, and, beyond these near things, all the plain of Lombardy was at my feet.

It was this which made it worth while to have toiled up that steep wall, and even to have lost my way—to see a hundred miles of the great flat stretched out before me: all the kingdoms of the world.

Nor was this all. There were sharp white clouds on the far northern horizon, low down above the uncertain edge of the world. I looked again and found they did not move. Then I knew they were the Alps.

Believe it or not, I was looking back to a place of days before: over how many, many miles of road! The rare, white peaks and edges could not deceive me; they still stood to the sunlight, and sent me from that vast distance the memory of my passage, when their snows had seemed interminable and their height to monstrous; their cold such a cloak of death. Now they were as far off as childhood, and I saw them for the last time.

All this I drew. Then finding a post directing me to a side road for Calestano, I followed it down and down into the valley beyond: and up the walls of this second valley as the evening fell I heard the noise of the water running, as the Taro had run, a net of torrents from the melting snows far off. These streams I soon saw below me, winding (as those of the Taro had wound) through a floor of dry shingle and rock; but the high hills enclosed that trench, and evening had left it in shadow; and when my road ceased suddenly some hundreds of feet above the bed of the river, and when, full of evening, I had scrambled down through trees to the brink of the water, I found I should have to repeat what I had done that morning and to ford these streams. For there was no track of any kind and no bridge, and Calestano stood opposite me, a purple cluster of houses in the dusk against the farther mountain side.

Very warily, lobbing stones as I had been taught, and following up and down each branch to find a place, I forded one by one the six little cold and violent rivers, and reaching the farther shore, I reached also, as I thought, supper, companionship, and a bed.

But it is not in this simple way that human life is arranged. What awaited me in Calestano was ill favour, a prison, release, base flattery, and a very tardy meal.

It is our duty to pity all men. It is our duty to pity those who are in prison. It is our duty to pity those who are not in prison. How much more is it the duty of a Christian man to pity the rich who cannot ever get into prison? These indeed I do now specially pity, and extend to them my commiseration.

What! Never even to have felt the grip of the policeman; to have watched his bold suspicious eye; to have tried to make a good show under examination . . . never to have heard the bolt grinding in the lock, and never to have looked round at the cleanly simplicity of a cell? Then what emotions have you had, unimprisonable rich; or what do you know of active living and of adventure?

It was after drinking some wine and eating macaroni and bread at a poor inn, the only one in the place, and after having to shout at the ill-natured hostess (and to try twenty guesses before I made her understand that I wanted cheese), it was when I had thus eaten and shouted, and had gone over the way to drink coffee and to smoke in a little café, that my adventure befel me.

In the inn there had been a fat jolly-looking man and two official-looking people with white caps dining at another table. I had taken no notice of them at the time. But as I sat smoking and thinking in the little café, which was bright and full of people, I noticed a first danger-signal when I was told sullenly that 'they had no bed; they thought I could get none in the town'; then, suddenly, these two men in white caps came in, and they arrested me with as much ease as you or I would hold a horse.

A moment later there came in two magnificent fellows, gendarmes, with swords and cocked hats, and moustaches *à l'Abd el Kader*, as we used to say in the old days; these four, the two gendarmes and the two policemen, sat down opposite me on chairs and began cross-questioning me in Italian, a language in which I was not proficient. I so far understood them as to know that they were asking for my papers.

'Niente!' said I, and poured out on the table a card-case, a sketch-book, two pencils, a bottle of wine, a cup, a piece of bread, a scrap of French newspaper, an old *Secolo*, a needle, some thread, and a flute—but no passport.

They looked in the card-case and found 73 lira; that is, not quite three pounds. They examined the sketch-book critically, as behoved southerners who are mostly of an artistic bent: but they found no passport. They questioned me again, and as I picked about for words to reply, the smaller (the policeman, a man with a face like a fox) shouted that he had heard me speaking Italian *currently* in the inn, and that my hesitation was a blind.

This lie so annoyed me that I said angrily in French (which I made as southern as possible to suit them):

'You lie: and you can be punished for such lies, since you are an official.' For though the police are the same in all countries, and will swear black is white, and destroy men for a song, yet where there is a *droit administratif*—that is, where the Revolution has made things tolerable—you are much surer of punishing your policeman, and he is much less able to do you a damage than in England or America; for he counts as an official and is under a more public discipline and responsibility if he exceeds his powers.

Then I added, speaking distinctly, 'I can speak French and Latin. Have you a priest in Calestano, and does he know Latin?'

This was a fine touch. They winced, and parried it by saying that the Sindaco knew French. Then they led me away to their barracks while they fetched the Sindaco, and so I was imprisoned.

But not for long. Very soon I was again following up the street, and we came to the house of the Sindaco or Mayor. There he was, an old man with white hair, God bless him, playing cards with his son and daughter. To him therefore, as understanding French, I was bidden address myself. I told him in clear and exact idiom that his policemen were fools, that his town was a rabbit-warren, and his prison the only cleanly thing in it; that half a dozen telegrams to places I could indicate would show where I had passed; that I was a common tourist, not even an artist (as my sketch-book showed), and that my cards gave my exact address and description.

But the Sindaco, the French-speaking Sindaco, understood me not in the least, and it seemed a wicked thing in me to expose him in his old age, so I waited till he spoke. He spoke a word common to all languages, and one he had just caught from my lips.

'Tourist-e?' he said.

I nodded. Then he told them to let me go. It was as simple as that; and to this day, I suppose, he passes for a very bilingual Mayor. He did me a service, and I am willing to believe that in his youth he smacked his lips over the subtle flavour of Voltaire, but I fear today he would have a poor time with Anatole France.

What a contrast was there between the hour when I had gone out of the café a prisoner and that when I returned rejoicing with a crowd about me, proclaiming my innocence, and shouting one to another that I was a tourist and had seventy-three lira on my person! The landlady smiled and bowed: she had before refused me a bed! The men at the tables made me a god! Nor did I think them worse for this, Why should I! A man unknown, unkempt, unshaven, in tatters, covered with weeks of travel and mud, and in a suit that originally cost not ten shillings; having slept in leaves and ferns, and forest places, crosses a river at dusk and enters a town furtively, not by the road. He is a foreigner; he carries a great club. Is it not much wiser to arrest such a man? Why yes, evidently. And when you have arrested him, can you do more than let him go without proof, on his own word? Hardly!

Thus I loved the people of Calestano, especially for this strange adventure they had given me; and next day, having slept in a human room, I went at sunrise up the mountain sides beyond and above their town, and so climbed by a long cleft the *second* spur of the Apennines: the spur that separated me from the *third* river, the Parma. And my goal above the Parma (when I should have crossed it) was a place marked in the map 'Tizzano'. To climb this second spur, to reach and cross the Parma in the vale below, to find Tizzano, I left Calestano on that fragrant morning; and having passed and drawn a little hamlet called Frangi, standing on a crag, I went on up the steep vale and soon reached the top of the ridge, which here dips a little and allows a path to cross over to the southern side.

X

From *Avril (Villon)*

1904

Avril is Belloc's outstanding critical work. Few writers of his time had so close an understanding of early French literature.

In his dedicatory preface to his close friend Professor F. Y. Eccles, he wrote: 'If you ask me why I should myself approach the matter, I can plead some inheritance of French blood, comparable, I believe, to your own; and though I have no sort of claim to that unique and accomplished scholarship which gives you a mastery of the French tongue, unmatched in England, and a complete familiarity with its history, application and genius, yet I can put to my credit a year of active, if eccentric, experience in a French barrack room, a complete segregation during those twelve mammoth months wherein I could study the very soul of this sincere, creative and tenacious people.

'. . . But if you ask me why the Renaissance especially—and why in the Renaissance these six poets alone[1]—should have formed the subject of my first endeavour, I can only tell you that in so vast a province, whereof the most ample leisure could not in a lifetime exhaust a tithe, Chance, that happy Goddess led me at random to their grove.'

[1] Charles of Orléans, Villon, Marot, Ronsard, du Bellay and Malherbe. [Ed.]

Villon

I have said that in Charles of Orléans the Middle Ages are at first more apparent than the advent of the Renaissance. His forms are inherited from an earlier time, his terminology is that of the long allegories which had wearied three generations, his themes recall whatever was theatrical in the empty pageantry of the great war. It is a spirit deeper and more fundamental than the mere framework of his writing which attaches him to the coming time. His clarity is new; it proceeds from natural things; it marks that return to reality which is the beginning of all beneficent revolutions. But this spirit in him needs examination and discovery, and the reader is confused between the medieval phrases and the something new and troubling in the voice that utters them.

With Villon, the next in order, a similar confusion might arise. All about him as he wrote were the Middle Ages: their grotesque, their contrast, their disorder. His youth and his activity of blood forbad him any contact with other than immediate influences. He was wholly Northern; he had not so much as guessed at what Italy might be. The decrepit University had given him, as best she could, the dregs of her palsied philosophy and something of Latin. He grew learned as do those men who grasp quickly the major lines of their study, but who, in details, will only be moved by curiosity or by some special affection. There was nothing patient in him, and nothing applied, and in all this, in the matter of his scholarship as in his acquirement of it, he is of the dying Middle Ages entirely.

His laughter also was theirs: the kind of laughter that saluted the first Dance of Death which as a boy he had seen in new frescoes round the waste graveyard of the Innocents. His friends and enemies and heroes and buffoons were the youth of the narrow tortuous streets, his visions of height were the turrets of the palaces and the precipitate roofs of the town. Distance had never inspired him, for in that age its effect was forgotten. No one straight street displayed the greatness of the city, no wide and ordered spaces enhanced it. He crossed his native river upon bridges all shut in with houses, and houses hid the banks also. The sweep of the Seine no longer existed for his generation, and largeness of all kinds was hidden under the dust and rubble of decay. The majestic, which in sharp separate lines of his verse he certainly possessed, he discovered within his own mind, for no great arch or cornice, nor no colonnade had lifted him with its splendour.

That he could so discover it, that a solemnity and order should be apparent in the midst of his raillery whenever he desires to produce an effect of the grand, leads me to speak of that major quality of his by which he stands up out of his own time, and is clearly an originator of the great renewal. I mean his vigour.

It is all round about him, and through him, like a storm in a wood. It creates, it perceives. It possesses the man himself, and us also as we read him. By it he launches his influence forward and outward rather than receives it from the past. To it his successors turn as to an ancestry, when they had long despised and thrown aside everything else that savoured of the Gothic dead. By it he increased in reputation and meaning from his boyhood on for four hundred years, till now he is secure among the first lyric poets of Christendom. It led to no excess of matter, but to an exuberance of attitude and manner, to an inexhaustibility of special words, to a brilliancy of impression unique even among his own people.

He was poor; he was amative; he was unsatisfied. This vigour, therefore, led in his actions to a mere wildness; clothed in this wildness the rare fragments of his life have descended to us. He professed to teach, but he haunted taverns, and loved the roaring of songs. He lived at random from his twentieth year in one den or another along the waterside. Affection brought him now to his mother, now to his old guardian priest, but not for long; he returned to adventure—such as it was. He killed a man, was arrested, condemned, pardoned, exiled; he wandered and again found Paris, and again—it seems—stumbled down his old lane of violence and dishonour.

Associated also with this wildness is a curious imperfection in our knowledge of him. His very name is not his own—or any other man's. His father, if it were his father, took his name from Mont-Corbier—half noble. Villon is but a little village over beyond the upper Yonne, near the division, within a day of the water-parting where the land falls southward to Burgundy and the sun in what they call 'The Slope of Gold'. From this village a priest, William, had come to Paris in 1423. They gave him a canonry in that little

church called 'St Bennets Askew', which stood in the midst of the
University, near Sorbonne, where the Rue des Ecoles crosses the
Rue St Jacques today. Hither, to his house in the cloister, he
brought the boy, a waif whom he had found much at the time when
Willoughby capitulated and the French recaptured the city. He had
him taught, he designed him for the University, he sheltered him in
his vagaries, he gave him asylum. The young man took his name
and called him 'more than father'. His anxious life led on to 1468,
long after the poet had disappeared.

For it is in 1461, in his thirtieth year, that Villon last writes
down a verse. It is in 1463 that his signature is last discovered. Then
not by death, or, if by death, then by some death unrecorded, he
leaves history abruptly—a most astonishing exit! . . . You may
pursue fantastic legends, you will not find the man himself again.
Some say a final quarrel got him hanged at last—it is improbable:
no record or even tradition of it remains. Rabelais thought him
a wanderer in England. Poitou preserves a story of his later passage
through her fields, of how still he drank and sang with boon companions, and of how, again, he killed a man . . . Maybe, he only
ceased to write; took to teaching soberly in the University, and
lived in a decent inheritance to see new splendours growing upon
Europe. It may very well be, for it is in such characters to desire
in early manhood decency, honour, and repose. But for us the man
ends with his last line. His body that was so very real, his personal
voice, his jargon—tangible and audible things—spread outward
suddenly a vast shadow upon nothingness. It was the end, also, of
a world. The first Presses were creaking, Constantinople had fallen,
Greek was in Italy, Leonardo lived, the stepping stones of the
Azores were held—in that new light he disappears.

Of his greatness nothing can be said; it is like the greatness of
all the chief poets, a thing too individual to seize in words. It is
superior and exterior to the man. Genius of that astounding kind
has all the qualities of an extraneous thing. A man is not answerable
for it. It is nothing to his salvation; it is little even to his general
character. It has been known to come and go, to be put off and on
like a garment, to be lent by Heaven and taken away, a capricious
gift.

But of the manner of that genius it may be noted that, as his vigour prepared the flood of new verse, so in another matter his genius made him an origin. Through him first, the great town— and especially Paris—appeared and became permanent in letters.

Her local spirit and her special quality had shone fitfully here and there for a thousand years—you may find it in Julian, in Abbo, in Joinville. But now, in the fifteenth century, it had been not only a town but a great town for more than a century—a town, that is, in which men live entirely, almost ignorant of the fields, observing only other men, and forgetting the sky. The keen edge of such a life, its bitterness, the mockery and challenge whereby its evils are borne, its extended knowledge, the intensity of its spirit—all these are reflected in Villon, and first reflected in him. Since his pen first wrote, a shining acerbity like the glint of a sword-edge has never deserted the literature of the capital.

It was not only the metropolitan, it was the Parisian spirit which Villon found and fixed. That spirit which is bright over the whole city, but which is not known in the first village outside; the influence that makes Paris Athenian.

The ironical Parisian soul has depths in it. It is so lucid that its luminous profundity escapes one—so with Villon. Religion hangs there. Humility—fatally divorced from simplicity—pervades it. It laughs at itself. There are ardent passions of sincerity, repressed and reacting upon themselves. The virtues, little practised, are commonly comprehended, always appreciated, for the Faith is there permanent. All this you will find in Villon, but it is too great a matter for so short an essay as this.

XI

From *Esto Perpetua (Timgad)*
1906

Belloc had been elected a member of the Reform Club in March 1905, and his club was to become a second home to him. In January of 1906 he became Liberal Member of Parliament for South Salford. Notwithstanding such activities he published not one, but several major works as well as contributions to newspapers and journals year after year. Writing to solicitor E. S. P. Haynes, he says: 'I am not one of those who think literature ill-paid for I clearly perceive there is no economic reason why it should be paid at all, but I think the estimate put upon it by the public is lower now than it ever has been before in the course of our national life, and especially by the governing public. There is not enough pride taken in the national literature by those who are perpetually gassing about the greatness of the Nation. Dr Johnson well remarked that the greatness of the Nation necessarily lay in its men of letters. What is more, literature is the main symptom and the only surviving symptom of national dignity, or indignity, at any given moment. To judge our literature at the present moment, posterity will think us perverted in our instincts, cowardly or wholly inept. They would not think that, if what is best in our literature was sedulously fostered by what is best in society.'[1]

In 1906 he published Esto Perpetua, *his book about North Africa, where he had gone in the previous year to recuperate from an illness, as well as one of the first of his many collections of essays*—Hills and the Sea.

[1] Having read these views in 1906 the inquiring reader should refer to John Gross's *The Rise and Fall of the Man of Letters*, a remarkable assessment of the Man of Letters and his world during the nineteenth and present century.

Esto Perpetua *received a somewhat critical review in the* Times Literary Supplement: *'Belloc can express', they wrote, 'English with the purity and lucidity of the French, and French ideas with the restraint and force of an Englishman. But we never lay down a book of his without wondering whether he is ever going to make up his mind what he will be at.'*

But in retrospect one sees in this work some of his finest writing.

Timgad

When the morning came I looked out again from my window and I saw the last of the storm still hurrying overhead, and beneath and before me, of one even grey colour and quite silent, the city of Timgad. There was no one in it alive. There were no roofs and no criers. It was all ruins standing up everywhere: broken walls and broken columns absolutely still, except in one place where some pious care had led the water back to its old channels. There a little fountain ran from an urn that a Cupid held.

I passed at once through the gates and walked for perhaps an hour, noting curiously a hundred things: the shop-stalls and the lines of pedestals; the flag-stones of the Forum and the courses of brick—even, small, Roman and abandoned. I walked so, gazing sometimes beyond the distant limits of the city to the distant slopes of Atlas, till I came to a high place where the Theatre had once stood, dug out of a hillside and built in with rows of stone seats. Here I sat down to draw the stretch of silence before me, and then I recognized for the first time that I was very tired.

I said to myself: 'This comes of my long march through the night'; but when I had finished my drawing and had got up to walk again (for one might walk in Timgad for many days, or for a lifetime if one chose) I found a better reason for my fatigue, which was this: that, try as I would I could not walk firmly and strongly upon those deserted streets or across the flags of that Forum, but I was compelled by something in the town to tread uncertainly and gently. When I recollected myself I would force my feet to a natural and ready step; but in a moment, as my thoughts were taken by some new aspect of the place, I found myself walking again with strain and care, noiselessly, as one does in shrines, or in the room of a sleeper or of the dead. It was not I that did it, but the town.

I saw, some hundred yards away, a man going to his field along a street of Timgad: he showed plainly for the houses had sunk to rubble upon either side of his way. This was the first life I had seen under that stormy mountain morning, and in that lonely place which had been lonely for so very long. He also walked doubtfully and with careful feet; he looked downward and made no sound.

I went up and down Timgad all that morning. The sun was not high before I felt that by long wandering between the columns and peering round many corners and finding nothing, one at last became free of the city. An ease and a familiarity, a sort of friendship with abandoned but once human walls, took the traveller as he grew used to the silence; but whether in such companionship he did not suffer some evil influence, I cannot say.

I came to one place and to another and to another, each quite without men, and each casting such an increasing spell upon the mind as is cast by voices heard in the night, when one does not know whether they are of the world, or not of the world.

I came to a triumphal arch which had once guarded the main entry to the city from Lamboesis and the west. It was ornate, four-sided, built, one would think, in the centuries of the decline. Beyond it, the suburbs into which the city expanded just before it fell stretched far out into the plain. Not far from it a very careful inscription recalled a man who has thus survived as he wished to survive; the sacred tablet testified to the spirit which unites the religion of antiquity with our own—for it was chiselled in fulfilment of a vow. In another place was the statue of the gods' mother, crowned with a wall and towers. This also was of the decline, but still full of that serenity which faces wore before the Barbarian march and the sack of cities.

There is a crossing of the streets in Timgad where one may sit a long time and consider her desolation upon every side. The seclusion is absolute, and the presence of so many made things with none to use them gradually invades the mind. The sun gives life to you as you look down this Decumanian way, and see the runnels where the wheels ran once noisily to the market; it warms you but it nourishes for you no companions. The town stares at you and is blind.

Against the sky, upon a little mound, stand two tall columns, much taller than the rest. They shine under the low winter sun from every part of Timgad and are white over the plain of grey stones. They may have been raised for the Temple of Capitoline Jove.

These will detain the traveller for as long as he may choose to regard them, so violently do they impress him with the negation of time. It is said that in certain abnormal moods things infinitely great and infinitely little are present together in the mind: that vast spaces of the imagination and minute contacts of the finger-tips are each figured in the brain, the one not driving out the other. In such moods (it is said) proportion and reality grow faint, and the unity and poise of our limited human powers are in peril. Into such a mood is a man thrown by Timgad, and especially by these two pillars of white stone. They proceed so plainly from the high conceptions of man: so much were their sculptors what we are in every western character: so fully do they satisfy us: so recent and clean is the mark of the tool upon them that they fill a man with society and leave him ready to meet at once a living city full of his fellows. It only needs a spoken word or the clack of a sandal to be back into the moment when all these things were alive. And mean-while, with that impression overpowering one's sense, there, physic-ally present, is a desolation so complete that measure fails it. No oxen moving: no smoke: no roof among the rare trees of the horizon: no gleam of water and no sound. It is as though not certain centuries but an incalculable space of days coexisted with the present, and as though, for one eternal moment, a vision of the absolute in which time is not were permitted—for no good—to the yet embodied soul.

XII

The Mowing of a Field
(From *Hills and the Sea*)

1906

There is a valley in south England remote from ambition and from fear, where the passage of strangers is rare and unperceived, and where the scent of the grass in summer is breathed only by those who are native to that unvisited land. The roads to the Channel do not traverse it; they choose upon either side easier passes over the range. One track alone leads up through it to the hills, and this is changeable: now green where men have little occasion to go, now a good road where it nears the homesteads and the barns. The woods grow steep above the slopes; they reach sometimes the very summit of the heights, or, when they cannot attain them, fill in and clothe the coombes. And, in between, along the floor of the valley, deep pastures and their silence are bordered by lawns of chalky grass and the small yew trees of the Downs.

The clouds that visit its sky reveal themselves beyond the one great rise, and sail, white and enormous, to the other, and sink beyond that other. But the plains above which they have travelled and the Weald to which they go, the people of the valley cannot see and hardly recall. The wind, when it reaches such fields, is no longer a gale from the salt, but fruitful and soft, an inland breeze; and those whose blood was nourished here feel in that wind the fruitfulness of our orchards and all the life that all things draw from the air.

In this place, when I was a boy, I pushed through a fringe of beeches that made a complete screen between me and the world, and I came to a glade called No Man's Land. I climbed beyond it, and I was surprised and glad, because from the ridge of that glade I saw the sea. To this place very lately I returned.

The many things that I recovered as I came up the countryside were not less charming than when a distant memory had enshrined them, but much more. Whatever veil is thrown by a longing recollection had not intensified nor even made more mysterious the beauty of that happy ground; not in my very dreams of morning had I, in exile, seen it more beloved or more rare. Much also that I had forgotten now returned to me as I approached—a group of elms, a little turn of the parson's wall, a small paddock beyond the graveyard close, cherished by one man, with a low wall of very old stone guarding it all round. And all these things fulfilled and amplified my delight, till even the good vision of the place, which I had kept so many years, left me and was replaced by its better reality. 'Here', I said to myself, 'is a symbol of what some say is reserved for the soul: pleasure of a kind which cannot be imagined save in a moment when at last it is attained.'

When I came to my own gate and my own field, and had before me the house I knew, I looked around a little (though it was already evening), and I saw that the grass was standing as it should stand when it is ready for the scythe. For in this, as in everything that a man can do—of those things at least which are very old—there is an exact moment when they are done best. And it has been remarked of whatever rules us that it works blunderingly, seeing that the good things given to man are not given at the precise moment when they would have filled him with delight. But, whether this be true or false, we can choose the just turn of the seasons in everything we do of our own will, and especially in the making of hay. Many think that hay is best made when the grass is thickest; and so they delay until it is rank and in flower, and has already heavily pulled the ground. And there is another false reason for delay, which is wet weather. For very few will understand (though it comes year after year) that we have rain always in south England between the sickle and the scythe, or say just after the weeks of east wind are over. First we have a week of sudden warmth, as though the South had come to see us all; then we have the weeks of east and south-east wind; and then we have more or less of that rain of which I spoke, and which always astonishes the world. Now it is just before, or during, or at the very end of that rain—but not later—that grass should be cut for hay. True, upland grass, which is always thin, should be cut earlier than the grass in the bottoms and along the water meadows; but not even the latest, even in the wettest seasons, should be left (as it is) to flower and even to seed. For what we get when we store our grass is not a harvest of something ripe, but a thing just caught in its prime before maturity: as witness that our corn and straw are best yellow, but our hay is best green. So also Death should be represented with a scythe and Time with a sickle; for Time can only take what is ripe, but Death comes always too soon. In a word, then, it is always much easier to cut grass too late than too early; and I, under that evening and come back to these pleasant fields, looked at the grass and knew that it was time. June was in full advance: it was the beginning of that season when the night has already lost her foothold of the earth and hovers over it, never quite descending, but mixing sunset with the dawn.

Next morning, before it was yet broad day, I awoke, and thought of the mowing. The birds were already chattering in the trees beside my window, all except the nightingale, which had left and flown away to the Weald, where he sings all summer by day as well as by night in the oaks and the hazel spinneys, and especially along the little river Adur, one of the rivers of the Weald. The birds and the thought of the mowing had awakened me, and I went down the stairs and along the stone floors to where I could find a scythe; and when I took it from its nail, I remembered how, fourteen years ago, I had last gone out with my scythe, just so, into the fields at morning. In between that day and this were many things, cities and armies, and a confusion of books, mountains and the desert, and horrible great breadths of sea.

When I got out into the long grass the sun was not yet risen, but there were already many colours in the eastern sky, and I made haste to sharpen my scythe, so that I might get to the cutting before the dew should dry. Some say that it is best to wait till all the dew has risen, so as to get the grass quite dry from the very first. But, though it is an advantage to get the grass quite dry, yet it is not worth while to wait till the dew has risen. For, in the first place, you lose many hours of work (and those the coolest), and next— which is more important—you lose that great ease and thickness in cutting which comes of the dew. So I at once began to sharpen my scythe.

There is an art also in the sharpening of a scythe, and it is worth describing carefully. Your blade must be dry, and that is why you will see men rubbing the scythe-blade with grass before they whet it. Then also your rubber must be quite dry, and on this account it is a good thing to lay it on your coat and keep it there during all your day's mowing. The scythe you stand upright, with the blade pointing away from you, and you put your left hand firmly on the back of the blade, grasping it: then you pass the rubber first down one side of the blade-edge and then down the other, beginning near the handle and going on to the point and working quickly and hard. When you first do this you will, perhaps, cut your hand; but it is only at first that such an accident will happen to you.

To tell when the scythe is sharp enough this is the rule. First the stone clangs and grinds against the iron harshly; then it rings musically to one note; then, at last, it purrs as though the iron and stone were exactly suited. When you hear this, your scythe is sharp enough; and I, when I heard it that June dawn, with everything quite silent except the birds, let down the scythe and bent myself to mow.

When one does anything anew, after so many years, one fears very much for one's trick or habit. But all things once learnt are easily recoverable, and I very soon recovered the swing and power of the mower. Mowing well and mowing badly—or rather not mowing at all—are separated by very little; as is also true of writing verse, of playing the fiddle, and of dozens of other things, but of nothing more than of believing. For the bad or young or untaught mower without tradition, the mower Promethean, the mower original and contemptuous of the past, does all these things: He leaves great crescents of grass uncut. He digs the point of the scythe hard into the ground with a jerk. He loosens the handles and even the fastening of the blade. He twists the blade with his blunders, he blunts the blade, he chips it, he dulls it, or breaks it clean off at the tip. If anyone is standing by he cuts him in the ankle. He sweeps up into the air wildly, with nothing to resist his stroke. He drags up earth with the grass, which is like making the meadow bleed. But the good mower who does things just as they should be done and have been for a hundred thousand years, falls into none of these fooleries. He goes forward very steadily, his scythe-blade just barely missing the ground, every grass falling; the swish and rhythm of his mowing are always the same.

So great an art can only be learnt by continual practice; but this much is worth writing down, that, as in all good work, to know the thing with which you work is the core of the affair. Good verse is best written on good paper with an easy pen, not with a lump of coal on a whitewashed wall. The pen thinks for you; and so does the scythe mow for you if you treat it honourably and in a manner that makes it recognize its service. The manner is this. You must regard the scythe as a pendulum that swings, not as a knife that cuts. A good mower puts no more strength into his stroke than into his lifting. Again, stand up to your work. The bad mower, eager and full of pain, leans forward and tries to force the scythe through the grass. The good mower, serene and able, stands as nearly straight as the shape of the scythe will let him, and follows up every stroke closely, moving his left foot forward. Then also let every stroke get well away. Mowing is a thing of ample gestures, like drawing a cartoon. Then, again, get yourself into a mechanical and repetitive mood: be thinking of anything at all but your mowing, and be anxious only when there seems some interruption to the monotony of the sound. In this mowing should be like one's prayers—all of a sort and always the same, and so made that you can establish a monotony and work them, as it were, with half your mind: that happier half, the half that does not bother.

In this way, when I had recovered the art after so many years, I went forward over the field, cutting lane after lane through the grass, and bringing out its most secret essences with the sweep of the scythe until the air was full of odours. At the end of every lane I sharpened my scythe and looked back at the work done, and then carried my scythe down again upon my shoulder to begin another. So, long before the bell rang in the chapel above me—that is, long before six o'clock, which is the time for the *Angelus*—I had many swathes already lying in order parallel like soldiery; and the high grass yet standing, making a great contrast with the shaven part, looked dense and high. As it says in the *Ballad of Val-ès-Dunes*, where—

> The tall son of the Seven Winds
> Came riding out of Hither-hythe,

and his horse-hoofs (you will remember) trampled into the press
and made a gap in it, and his sword (as you know)

> . . . was like a scythe
> In Arcus when the grass is high
> And all the swathes in order lie,
> And there's the bailiff standing by
> A-gathering of the tithe.

So I mowed all that morning, till the houses awoke in the valley,
and from some of them rose a little fragrant smoke, and men began
to be seen.

I stood still and rested on my scythe to watch the awakening of
the village, when I saw coming up to my field a man whom I had
known in olden times, before I had left the Valley.

He was of that dark silent race upon which all the learned quarrel,
but which, by whatever meaningless name it may be called—
Iberian, or Celtic, or what you will—is the permanent root of all
England, and makes England wealthy and preserves it everywhere,
except perhaps in the Fens and in a part of Yorkshire. Everywhere
else you will find it active and strong. These people are intensive:
their thoughts and their labours turn inward. It is on account of
their presence in these islands that our gardens are the richest in the
world. They also love low rooms and ample fires and great warm
slopes of thatch. They have, as I believe, an older acquaintance with
the English air than any other of all the strains that make up
England. They hunted in the Weald with stones, and camped in
the pines of the green-sand. They lurked under the oaks of the
upper rivers, and saw the legionaries go up, up the straight paved
road from the sea. They helped the few pirates to destroy the towns,
and mixed with those pirates and shared the spoils of the Roman
villas, and were glad to see the captains and the priests destroyed.
They remain; and no admixture of the Frisian pirates, or the
Breton, or the Angevin and Norman conquerors, has very much
affected their cunning eyes.

To this race, I say, belonged the man who now approached me.
And he said to me, 'Mowing?' And I answered, 'Ar.' Then he also
said 'Ar', as in duty bound; for so we speak to each other in the
Stenes of the Downs.

Next he told me that, as he had nothing to do, he would lend me a hand; and I thanked him warmly, or, as we say, 'kindly'. For it is a good custom of ours always to treat bargaining as though it were a courteous pastime; and though what he was after was money, and what I wanted was his labour at the least pay, yet we both played the comedy that we were free men, the one granting a grace and the other accepting it. For the dry bones of commerce, avarice and method and need, are odious to the Valley; and we cover them up with a pretty body of fiction and observances. Thus, when it comes to buying pigs, the buyer does not begin to decry the pig and the vendor to praise it, as is the custom with lesser men; but tradition makes them do business in this fashion:

First the buyer will go up to the seller when he sees him in his own steading, and, looking at the pig with admiration, the buyer will say that rain may or may not fall, or that we shall have snow or thunder, according to the time of year. Then the seller, looking critically at the pig, will agree that the weather is as his friend maintains. There is no haste at all; great leisure marks the dignity of their exchange. And the next step is, that the buyer says: 'That's a fine pig you have there, Mr ——' (giving the seller's name). 'Ar, powerful fine pig.' Then the seller, saying also 'Mr' (for twin brothers rocked in one cradle give each other ceremonious observance here), the seller, I say, admits, as though with reluctance, the strength and beauty of the pig, and falls into deep thought. Then the buyer says, as though moved by a great desire, that he is ready to give so much for the pig, naming half the proper price, or a little less. Then the seller remains in silence for some moments; and at last begins to shake his head slowly, till he says: 'I don't be thinking of selling the pig, anyways.' He will also add that a party only Wednesday offered him so much for the pig—and he names about double the proper price. Thus all ritual is duly accomplished; and the solemn act is entered upon with reverence and in a spirit of truth. For when the buyer uses this phrase: 'I'll tell you what I *will* do', and offers within half a crown of the pig's value, the seller replies that he can refuse him nothing, and names half a crown above its value; the difference is split, the pig is sold, and in the quiet soul of each runs the peace of something accomplished.

Thus do we buy a pig or land or labour or malt or lime, always with elaboration and set forms; and many a London man has paid double and more for his violence and his greedy haste and very unchivalrous higgling. As happened with the land at Underwalt-ham, which the mortgagees had begged and implored the estate to take at twelve hundred, and had privately offered to all the world at a thousand, but which a sharp direct man, of the kind that makes great fortunes, a man in a motor-car, a man in a fur coat, a man of few words, bought for two thousand three hundred before my very eyes, protesting that they might take his offer or leave it; and all because he did not begin by praising the land.

Well then, this man I spoke of offered to help me, and he went to get his scythe. But I went into the house and brought out a gallon jar of small ale for him and for me; for the sun was now very warm, and small ale goes well with mowing. When we had drunk some of this ale in mugs called 'I see you', we took each a swathe, he a little behind me because he was the better mower; and so for many hours we swung, one before the other, mowing and mowing at the tall grass of the field. And the sun rose to noon and we were still at our mowing; and we ate food, but only for a little while, and we took again to our mowing. And at last there was nothing left but a small square of grass, standing like a square of linesmen who keep their formation, tall and unbroken, with all the dead lying around them when a battle is over and done.

Then for some little time I rested after all those hours; and the man and I talked together, and a long way off we heard in another field the musical sharpening of a scythe.

The sunlight slanted powdered and mellow over the breadth of the valley; for day was nearing its end. I went to fetch rakes from the steading; and when I had come back the last of the grass had fallen, and all the field lay flat and smooth, with the very green short grass in lanes between the dead and yellow swathes.

These swathes we raked into cocks to keep them from the dew against our return at daybreak; and we made the cocks as tall and steep as we could, for in that shape they best keep off the dew, and it is easier also to spread them after the sun has risen. Then we raked up every straggling blade, till the whole field was a clean floor for the tedding and the carrying of the hay next morning. The grass we had mown was but a little over two acres; for that is all the pasture on my little tiny farm.

When we had done all this, there fell upon us the beneficent and deliberate evening; so that as we sat a little while together near the rakes, we saw the valley more solemn and dim around us, and all the trees and hedgerows quite still, and held by a complete silence. Then I paid my companion his wage, and bade him a goodnight, till we should meet in the same place before sunrise.

He went off with a slow and steady progress, as all our peasants do, making their walking a part of the easy but continual labour of their lives. But I sat on, watching the light creep around towards the north and change, and the waning moon coming up as though by stealth behind the woods of No Man's Land.

XIII

'The Wing of Dalua'
(From *Hills and the Sea*)

1906

'*The Wing of Dalua*' *is among the finest of Belloc's essays. It is an account of a 'haunted' valley in the Pyrenees where he was accompanied by his close friend Phil Kershaw, whom he met at Baliol.*

*This was again a very active year. The last of his three great biographies of the French Revolution appeared—*Marie Antoinette (*the previous two being* Danton *and* Robespierre), *a further volume of essays—*On Everything, *as well as his social study* The Church and Socialism. *He also published the second of his political-satirical novels,* A Change in the Cabinet.

The Wing of Dalua

Time was, and that not so long ago, when the Two Men had revealed to them by their Genius a corner of Europe wherein they were promised more surprises and delights than in any other.

It was secretly made known to them that in this place there were no pictures, and that no one had praised its people, and further that no Saint had ever troubled it; and the rich and all their evils (so the two men assured) had never known the place at all.

It was under the influence of such a message that they at once began walking at great speed for the river which is called the River of Gold, and for the valleys of Andorra; and since it seemed that other men had dared to cross the Pyrenees and to see the Republic, and since it seemed also, according to books, records and what not, that may have been truth or may have been lies, that common men so doing went always by one way, called the Way of Hospitalet, the Two Men determined to go by no such common path, but to march, all clothed with power, in a straight line, and to take the main range of mountains just where they chose, and to come down upon the Andorrans unexpectedly and to deserve their admiration and perhaps their fear.

They chose, therefore, upon the map the valley of that torrent called the Aston, and before it was evening, but at an hour when the light of the sun was already very ripe and low they stood under a great rock called Guie, which was all of bare limestone with façades as bare as the Yosemite, and almost as clean. They looked up at this great rock of Guie and made it the terminal of their attempt. I was one and my companion was the other: these were the two men who started out before a sunset in August to conquer the high Pyrenees. Before me was a very deep valley full of woods, and reaching higher and higher perpetually so that it reminded me of Hyperion; but as for my companion, it reminded him of nothing, for he said loudly that he had never seen any such things before and had never believed that summits of so astonishing a height were to be found on earth. Not even at night had he imagined such appalling upward and upward into the sky, and this he said though he had seen the Alps, of which it is true that when you are close to them

98

they are very middling affairs; but not so the Pyrenees, which are not only great but also terrible, for they are haunted, as you shall hear. But before I begin to write of the spirits that inhabit the deserts of the Aston, I must first explain, for the sake of those who have not seen them, how the awful valleys of the Pyrenees are made.

All the high valleys of mountains go in steps, but those of the Pyrenees in a manner more regular even than those of the Sierra Nevada out in California, which the Pyrenees so greatly resemble. For the steps here are nearly always three in number between the plain and the main chain, and each is entered by a regular gate of rock. So it is in the valley of the Ariege, and so it is in that of the Aston, and so it is in every other valley until you get to the far end where live the cleanly but incomprehensible Basques. Each of these steps is perfectly level, somewhat oval in shape, a mile or two or sometimes five miles long, but not often a mile broad. Through each will run the river of the valley, and upon either side of it there will be rich pastures, and a high plain of this sort is called a *jasse*, the same as in California is called a 'flat': as 'Dutch Flat', 'Poverty Flat', and other famous flats.

First then will come a great gorge through which one marches up from the plain, and then at the head of it very often a waterfall of some kind, along the side of which one forces one's way up painfully through a narrow chasm of rock and finds above one the great green level of the first jasse with the mountains standing solemnly around it. And then when one has marched all along this level one will come to another gorge and another chasm, and when one has climbed over the barrier of rock and risen up another 2,000 feet or so, one comes to a second jasse, smaller as a rule than the lower one; but so high are the mountains that all this climbing into the heart of them does not seem to have reduced their height at all. And then one marches along this second jasse and one comes to yet another gorge and climbs up just as one did the two others, through a chasm where there will be a little waterfall or a large one, and one finds at the top the smallest and most lonely of the jasses. This often has a lake in it. The mountains round it will usually be cliffs, forming sometimes a perfect ring, and so called cirques, or, by the Spaniards, cooking-pots; and as one stands on the level floor of one such last highest jasse and looks up at the summit of the cliffs, one knows that one is looking at the ridge of the main chain.

Then it is one's business, if one desires to conquer the high Pyrenees, to find a sloping place up the cliffs to reach their summits and
to go down into the further Spanish valleys. This is the order of the
Pyrenean dale, and this was the order of that of the Aston.

Up the gorge then we went, my companion and I; the day fell
as we marched, and there was a great moon out, filling the still air,
when we came to the first chasm, and climbing through it saw
before us, spread with a light mist over its pastures, the first jasse
under the moonlight. And up we went, and up again, to the end of
the second jasse, having before us the vast wall of the main range,
and in our hearts a fear that there was something unblessed in the
sight of it. For though neither I told it to my companion nor he to
me, we had both begun to feel a fear which the shepherds of these
mountains know very well. It was perhaps midnight or a little more
when we made our camp, after looking in vain for a hut which may
once have stood there, but now stood no longer. We lit a fire, but
did not overcome the cold, which tormented us throughout the
night, for the wind blew off the summits; and at last we woke from
our half-sleep and spent the miserable hours in watching the Great
Bear creeping round the pole, and in trying to feed the dying
embers with damp fuel. And there it was that I discovered what I
now make known to the world, namely, that gorse and holly will
burn of themselves, even while they are yet rooted in the ground.
So we sat sleepless and exhausted, and not without misgiving, for
we had meant that night before camping to be right under the foot
of the last cliffs, and we were yet many miles away. We were glad to
see the river at last in the meadows show plainly under the growing
light, the rocks turning red upon the skyline, and the extinction of
the stars. As we so looked north and eastward the great rock of Guie
stood up all its thousands of feet enormous against the rising of the
sun.

We were very weary, and invigorated by nothing but the light,
but, having that at least to strengthen us, we made at once for the
main range, knowing very well that, once we were over it, it would
be downhill all the way, and seeing upon our maps that there were
houses and living men high in the further Andorran valley, which
was not deserted like this vale of the Aston, but inhabited: full, that
is, of Catalans, who would soon make us forget the inhuman loneliness of the heights, for by this time we were both convinced,

though still neither of us said it to the other, that there was an evil brooding over all this place.

It was noon when, after many hours of broken marching and stumbling, which betrayed our weakness, we stood at last beside the tarn in which the last cliffs of the ridge are reflected, and here was a steep slope up which a man could scramble. We drank at the foot of it the last of our wine and ate the last of our bread, promising ourselves refreshment, light, and peace immediately upon the further side, and thus lightened of our provisions, and with more heart in us, we assaulted the final hill; but just at the summit, where there should have greeted us a great view over Spain, there lowered upon us the angry folds of a black cloud, and the first of the accidents that were set in order by some enemy to ruin us fell upon my companion and me.

For a storm broke, and that with such violence that we thought it would have shattered the bare hills, for an infernal thunder crashed from one precipice to another, and there flashed, now close to us, now vividly but far off, in the thickness of the cloud, great useless and blinding glares of lightning, and hailstones of great size fell about us also, leaping from the bare rocks like marbles. And when the rain fell it was just as though it had been from a hose, forced at one by a pressure instead of falling, and we two on that height were the sole objects of so much fury, until at last my companion cried out from the rock beneath which he was cowering, 'This is intolerable!' And I answered him, from the rock which barely covered me, 'It is not to be borne!' So in the midst of the storm we groped our way down into the valley beneath, and got below the cloud; and when we were there we thought we had saved the day, for surely we were upon the southern side of the hills, and in a very little while we should see the first roofs of the Andorrans.

For two doubtful hours we trudged down that higher valley, but there were no men, nor any trace of men except this, that here and there the semblance of a path appeared, especially where the valley fell rapidly from one stage to another over smooth rocks, which, in their least dangerous descent, showed by smooth scratches the passage of some lost animal. For the rest, nothing human nor the memory of it was there to comfort us, though in one place we found a group of cattle browsing alone without a master. There we sat down in our exhaustion and confessed at last what every hour had inwardly convinced us of with greater strength, that we were not our own masters, that there was trouble and fate all round us, that we did not know what valley this might be, and that the storm had been but the beginning of an unholy adventure. We had been snared into Fairyland.

We did not speak much together, for fear of lowering our hearts yet more by the confession one to the other of the things we knew to be true. We did not tell each other what reserve of courage remained to us, or of strength. We sat and looked at the peaks immeasurably above us, and at the veils of rain between them, and at the black background of the sky. Nor was there anything in the landscape which did not seem to us unearthly and forlorn.

It was, in a manner, more lonely than had been the very silence of the further slope: there was less to comfort and support the soul of a man; but with every step downward we were penetrated more and more with the presence of things not mortal and of influences to which any desolation was preferable. At one moment voices called to us from the water, at another we heard our names, but pronounced in a whisper so slight and so exact that the more certain we were of hearing them the less did we dare to admit the reality of what we had heard. In a third place we saw twice in succession, though we were still going forward, the same tree standing by the same stone: for neither tree nor stone was natural to the good world, but each had been put there by whatever was mocking us and drawing us on.

Already had we stumbled twice and thrice the distance that should have separated us from the first Andorran village, but we had seen nothing, not a wall, nor smoke from a fire, let alone the tower of a Christian church, or the houses of men. Nor did any length of the way now make us wonder more than we had already wondered, nor did we hope, however far we might proceed, that we should be saved unless some other influence could be found to save us from the unseen masters of this place. For by this time we had need of mutual comfort, and openly said it to one another—but in low tones—that the valley was Faëry. The river went on calling to us all the while. In places it was full of distant cheering, in others crowded with the laughter of a present multitude of tiny things, and always mocking us with innumerable tenuous voices. It grew to be evening. It was nearly two days since we had seen a man.

There stood in the broader and lower part of the valley to which we had now come, numerous rocks and boulders; for our deception some one of them or another would seem to be a man. I heard my companion call suddenly, as though to a stranger, and as he called I thought that he had indeed perceived the face of a human being, and I felt a sort of sudden health in me when I heard the tone of his voice; and when I looked up I also saw a man. We came towards him and he did not move. Close up beside his form we put out our hands: but what we touched was a rough and silent stone.

After that we spoke no more. We went on through the gathering twilight, determined to march downwards to the end, but knowing pretty well what the end would be. Once only did we again fall into the traps that were laid about us, when we went and knocked at the hillside where we thought we had seen a cottage and its oaken door, and after the mockery of that disappointment we would not be deceived again, nor make ourselves again the victims of the laughter that perpetually proceeded from the torrent.

The path led us onwards in a manner that was all one with the plot now woven round our feet. We could but follow the path, though we knew with what an evil purpose it was made: that it was as phantom as the rest. At one place it invited us to cross, upon two shaking pine trunks, the abyss of a cataract; in another it invited us to climb, in spite of our final weariness, a great barrier of rock that lay between an upper and a lower jasse. We continued upon it determinedly, with heads bent, barely hoping that perhaps at last we should emerge from this haunted ground, but the illusions which had first mocked us we resolutely refused. So much so, that where at one place there stood plainly before us in the gathering darkness a farm-house with its trees and its close, its orchard and its garden gate, I said to my companion, 'All this place is cursed, and I will not go near.' And he applauded me for he knew as well as I that if we had gone a few steps towards that orchard and that garden close, they would have turned into the bracken of the hillside, bare granite and unfruitful scree.

The main range, where it appeared in revelations behind us through the clouds, was far higher than mountains ever seem to waking men, and it stood quite sheer as might a precipice in a dream. The forests upon either side ran up until they were lost miles and miles above us in the storm.

Night fell and we still went onward, the one never daring to fall far behind the other, and once or twice in an hour calling to each other to make sure that another man was near; but this we did not continue, because as we went on each of us became aware under the midnight of the presence of a Third.

There was a place where the path, now broad and plain, approached a sort of little sandy bay going down towards the stream, and there I saw, by a sudden glimpse of the moon through the clouds, a large cave standing wide. We went down to it in silence, we gathered brushwood, we lit a fire, and we lay down in the cave. But before we lay down I said to my companion: 'I have seen the moon—she is in the *north*. Into what place have we come ?' He said to me in answer: 'Nothing here is earthly', and after he had said this we both fell into a profound sleep in which we forgot not only cold, great hunger and fatigue, but our own names and our very souls, and passed, as it were, into a deep bath of forgetfulness.

When we woke at the same moment, it was dawn.

We stood up in the clear and happy light and found that everything was changed. We poured water upon our faces and our hands, strode out a hundred yards and saw again the features of a man. He had a kind face of some age, and eyes such as are the eyes of mountaineers, which seem to have constantly contemplated distant horizons and wide plains beneath their homes. We heard as he came up the sound of a bell in a Christian church below, and we exchanged with him the salutations of living men. Then I said to him: 'What day is this ?' He said 'Sunday', and a sort of memory of our fear came on us, for we had lost a day.

Then I said to him: 'What river are we upon, and what valley is this ?'

He answered: 'The river and the valley of the Aston.' And what he said was true, for as we rounded a corner we perceived right before us a barrier, that rock of Guie from which we had set out. We had come down again into France, and into the very dale by which we had begun our ascent.

But what that valley was which had led us from the summits round backward to our starting-place, forcing upon us the refusal of whatever powers protect this passage of the chain, I have never been able to tell. It is not upon the maps; by our description the peasants knew nothing of it. No book tells of it. No men except ourselves have seen it, and I am willing to believe that it is not of this world.

XIV

'Drouet's Ride'
(From *The Eye Witness*)

1908

In his preface to The Eye Witness *Belloc tells us that he 'has attempted, upon the model of one vivid experience, to reconstruct certain passages of the past'. He accordingly accumulated detail from personal visitations, later reconstructing the scene in his mind's eye.* The Eye Witness *contains imaginary as well as historic episodes, the episode chosen here being historic.*

This same year saw the publication of The Pyrenees *of which the last chapters were polished off in about four days! His activities were immense—as soon as he had finished this book he went off to the New Forest and rode hard for twenty-four hours.[1] He also published one of his famous collections of essays,* On Nothing, *the satirical novel,* Mr Clutterbuck's Election, *as well as* The Catholic Church and Historical Truth *and* An Examination of Socialism.

[1] R. Speaight: *Hilaire Belloc*, p. 269.

Drouet's Ride

JUNE 21, 1791

Louis XVI, and Marie Antoinette, King and Queen of France, attempting to fly from Paris in the midst of the Revolution, were intercepted just as they reached safety by one Drouet, who galloped near midnight by a short cut to the town of Varennes through the forest and roused the populace.

It was already dark. The longest day of the year had been cloudy, and though at sunset a lurid shaft of red shone from under the edges of the cloud, the sky soon covered again and one could see no stars. In the main room of the Town House of Ste Menehould a number of men were talking all at once, as is the French habit, and accomplishing things with an incredible rapidity. Outside the public square was filling, and though the mob as yet did not clamour, the noise from it was rising; in one place a man was struggling with a soldier, calling him a German, and the soldier was crying that it was false and that he was a Frenchman from Burgundy. In the ugly steeple which one could see squat against the night the bells rang continuously and furiously, and twice a pistol shot was heard in the darkness. All were now convinced that the carriage which had left them not an hour ago had contained the King. But with everyone volunteering at once to do this and to do that it was not until Drouet spoke with decision that the pursuit was determined.

Drouet was by nature a silent man; tall, and with a face like a hawk. He had long, clean legs, suitable for riding on a horse; he had the roll of the cavalry, for he had served in that arm. He went down to his stables and saddled the two horses by lantern-light, and so went riding out with his companion. The crowd gathered round him; as he came to the limit of the town he got free of them, and immediately broke into a gallop down the Clermont road. They listened to the distant beat of the hoofs, expecting the trot or the walk when he took the rise into Argonne, but they did not hear it. Even in its utmost faintness, and before the noise of the ride was lost in the distance, it was still a gallopade and a rhythmical pounding through the night.

Over the crest of the hill and down into the steep and muddy ravine where the mountain village of Islettes, dirty and clumped, squats by the brook-side, they galloped on, waking for one moment the villagers as they passed with the furious clatter of iron from the heavy hoofs of the posting horses; and again, after they had passed, there was heard that distant fading of the gallopade, for the long flat rise before them did not check their course. But just as they approached its summit in a place where the great trees of Argonne line the road upon the right, and upon the left are separated from it by nothing but a narrow strip of mead (where today the railway runs), there mixed with the noise of the hoof-beats beneath them the noise of a distant hail. They drew rein, and very soon tall riding figures loomed up in the night upon the skyline of the hill-top before them, and when they hailed again Drouet recognized his own grooms. The groups mingled, and to the panting of the two strained beasts, the occasional pawing of the tired post-horses of the others, the story of the coach was rapidly told. It was on two miles ahead, rolling rapidly to Neuville, and so to Varennes. It was bewildering news, for all Ste Menehould had thought that the King's flight was to Metz. And in a moment the active mind that lay behind the close-set eyes of Drouet seized the tactics of that night upon which depended the fate of the Capetian Monarchy, and of all Europe too. The coach had doubled. Its start upon him was too great to be caught up by following the road; they would be at Varennes and screened by a belt of soldiery before he could ride them down. He must—it was his one opportunity—plunge across the base of that triangle and head the fugitives; but this short cut lay not even over fields or common, it lay through the immense forest of Argonne and the high tangled ridge of the hill. He had, across such country, not an hour before him, and more than eleven miles to cover. He leapt the ditch, he crossed the meadow, he took the thick of the trees on his left, and urged his mount by a direct threading of the undergrowth, until he came to the summit whence proceeds the long line of the hills. For that short mile only was the sound of the hoof-beats hushed and time lost in necessity of walking his horse. At the summit an alley opened before him; he struck spurs and galloped furiously down again.

He was so native to Champagne that he knew what none of the countryfolk knew, and what indeed no historian has discovered, that an old track lay along the summit of the hill, open through the dense growth of the trees, dry from its situation on the ridge, with here and there a fallen trunk or a hummock of ground to imperil one, but still a road of a kind. It is of immense antiquity; the Gauls have used it, and the Romans, but the forest has grown up round its southern end; it comes up blindly against the undergrowth and leads nowhere. It had had no purpose in the history of the nation during all that thousand years in which the great edifice of the French Monarchy had risen to the benefit of mankind; and now this deserted and haunted lane in the wood was the instrument by which the Monarchy was destroyed.

Down it and down it, mile after mile, the horses thundered. The night wore on, and from the distant steeples of the villages in the plain beneath the half-hour struck; a couple of miles away down on the plain, and parallel to Drouet's riding, ran the straight high road, and on it, still rolling ahead, but gained on with every bound of the cavalryman's horses, went the berline and the destiny of the Bourbons.

The riders came to a place where years before murder had been done, and where a great white stone had been set by the peasantry, who dread the powers of evil that haunt such spots. This stone was Drouet's mark, for here there branches from the ridgeway a narrow and foul path which leads downwards on to the Varennes road, and strikes that road just as it issues from the forest and at the gate of the little town. By this way alone can a man on horseback get from the high ridgeway down to the plain, unless indeed he is to go all the way round and strike the main road through the pass which lies a mile or two ahead. This turning alone could accomplish Drouet's purpose, and even so the issue was very near. The hardest pace might fail to head the berline, and he might have ruined his mount and clattered into Varennes too late. They galloped and they galloped on, till the woods suddenly ceased upon either side. They heard beneath them the setts of the high road, and immediately saw before them such lights as still shone from the higher windows of Valmy. The clock was striking the hour. Drouet dismounted: wisely, for in the tortuous streets of the little place and with the business before him he was freer on the foot than in the saddle.

The whole place was silent. One would have said that no one watched. The sluggish river slipping between the piles of the bridge was the only sound. He ran breathlessly up the High Street. Between him and the archway that crossed clean over it up the hill there was not a human being nor light, save at one door, from which light streamed, and in which a group of men were talking—politics of course, for it was a tavern; but of the coach, of soldiers, even of the horses for the change, not a sign. He thought for a moment that he had failed. He dashed into the tavern and asked if a berline had rolled by. The stolid people of these hills looked at him rather stupidly, wondering what he meant. But he was known, and they answered him. Nothing had been heard, nothing had been seen. Then Drouet for the first time in that night of thundering hoofs and riding saw the conclusion of his plan. He told them that in the coach was the King. Such time as it took, not to convince them, but to get the mere fact into their heads, was wasted; but soon they had understood or believed; they rose, they scattered, one man to raise the militia, another to find the Mayor, a third to arm himself. As for Drouet, he went out into the air of the street, could see nothing at first for the glare of the light, waited a moment till his eyes should be accustomed to the darkness, then rapidly breasted the hill, keeping close upon the houses. And suddenly, before he quite knew it, there was the berline right on him, a huge mass of leather and of packages and of humanity within and without, girding on its brakes and sliding down the stone of the street. His work was done, and the doom of the Monarchy was accomplished.

XV

From *Verses*

1910

*This was a difficult period for Belloc. He had been for some time a
regular contributor to the* Morning Post, *and he now severed his connection with that paper and found it impossible to get another regular
commission. So he had to return to lecturing which was an ill-paid and
exhausting occupation. Nevertheless, the year 1910 saw the publication
of two volumes of essays, a satirical novel and a volume of verse.*

Stanzas Written on Battersea Bridge During a South-westerly Gale

The woods and downs have caught the mid-December,
　The noisy woods and high sea-downs of home;
The wind has found me and I do remember
　The strong scent of the foam.

Woods, darlings of my wandering feet, another
　Possesses you, another treads the Down;
The South West Wind that was my elder brother
　Has come to me in town.

The wind is shouting from the hills of morning,
　I do remember and I will not stay.
I'll take the Hampton road without a warning
　And get me clean away.

The channel is up, the little seas are leaping,
　The tide is making over Arun Bar;
And there's my boat, where all the rest are sleeping
　And my companions are.

I'll board her, and apparel her, and I'll mount her,
　My boat, that was the strongest friend to me—
That brought my boyhood to its first encounter
　And taught me the wide sea.

Now shall I drive her, roaring hard a' weather,
　Right for the salt and leave them all behind;
We'll quite forget the treacherous streets together
　And find—or shall we find?

There is no Pilotry my soul relies on
　Whereby to catch beneath my bended hand,
Faint and beloved along the extreme horizon
　That unforgotten land.

We shall not round the granite piers and paven
  To lie to wharves we know with canvas furled.
My little Boat, we shall not make the haven—
  It is not of the world.

Somewhere of English forelands grandly guarded
  It stands, but not for exiles, marked and clean;
Oh! not for us. A mist has risen and marred it:—
  My youth lies in between.

So in this snare that holds me and appals me,
  Where honour hardly lives nor loves remain,
The Sea compels me and my County calls me,
  But stronger things restrain.

England, to me that never have malingered,
  Nor spoken falsely, nor your flattery used,
Nor even in my rightful garden lingered:—
  What have you not refused?

The South Country

When I am living in the Midlands
  That are sodden and unkind,
I light my lamp in the evening:
  My work is left behind;
And the great hills of the South Country
  Come back into my mind.

The great hills of the South Country
  They stand along the sea;
And it's there walking in the high woods
  That I could wish to be,
And the men that were boys when I was a boy
  Walking along with me.

The men that live in North England
  I saw them for a day:

Their hearts are set upon the waste fells,
  Their skies are fast and grey;
From their castle-walls a man may see
  The mountains far away.

The men that live in West England
  They see the Severn strong,
A-rolling on rough water brown
  Light aspen leaves along.
They have the secret of the Rocks,
  And the oldest kind of song.

But the men that live in the South Country
  Are the kindest and most wise,
They get their laughter from the loud surf,
  And the faith in their happy eyes
Comes surely from our Sister the Spring
  When over the sea she flies;
The violets suddenly bloom at her feet,
  She blesses us with surprise.

I never get between the pines
  But I smell the Sussex air;
Nor I never come on a belt of sand
  But my home is there.
And along the sky the line of the Downs
  So noble and so bare.

A lost thing could I never find,
  Nor a broken thing mend:
And I fear I shall be all alone
  When I get towards the end.
Who will there be to comfort me
  Or who will be my friend?

I will gather and carefully make my friends
  Of the men of the Sussex Weald,
They watch the stars from silent folds,
  They stiffly plough the field.

VERSES

By them and the God of the South Country
    My poor soul shall be healed.

If I ever become a rich man,
    Or if ever I grow to be old,
I will build a house with deep thatch
    To shelter me from the cold,
And there shall the Sussex songs be sung
    And the story of Sussex told.

I will hold my house in the high wood
    Within a walk of the sea,
And the men that were boys when I was a boy
    Shall sit and drink with me.

XVI

From *The French Revolution*
1911

'*Belloc was generally regarded as a dogmatic person because he liked laying down the law, but he was a man who believed in dogmas before he believed in dogmatism. This was at the root of his religious faith and his literary practice. He believed that certain things were true and their converse was false; and these beliefs extended down to the smallest details of his daily life. We shall seize the character of his mind if we say that he was dogmatic where other men were opinionated. It was rarely, with him, a case of "I think"; it was nearly always a case of "this is so". He was in a very high degree a rational man, and even his prejudices and his exaggerations were rational rather than emotional. Whether reason and emotion can ever be kept as strictly separate as Belloc tried to keep them is a doubtful question. Is any reasoning quite unemotional? Nevertheless, it was Belloc's pride to proclaim the rights of reason to a world given over increasingly to violence and instinct. He was himself a man of large heart and healthy indignations, but both his anger and his affections were controlled.*

'*In the quest of the Republic which remained his central preoccupation right into middle age, he could not avoid the challenge of the French Revolution. There was no matter upon which the minds of educated Englishmen were more biased. Nourished on the rhetoric of Burke and the impressionism of Carlyle, they viewed it through a cloud of prejudice which Belloc made it his business to dispel. Those who regarded him as Defender of the Faith—as a man who would invariably take the Catholic side in any contemporary quarrel, or, more accurately, the side upon which a majority of Catholics were aligned— often expressed astonishment at his sympathy with his regicides of the*

Revolution. Because he was a Catholic, they expected him to defend the Ancien Régime.[1]

The French Revolution *was commissioned by H. A. L. Fisher for The Home University Library, and became one of his most successful works. It is now published by the Oxford University Press.*

[1] R. Speaight: *Hilaire Belloc,* p. 129.

The Characters of the Revolution

As might be expected, the character of King Louis XVI has suffered more distortion at the hands of historians than has any other of the revolutionary figures; and this because he combined with that personal character of his a certain office to which were traditionally attached certain points of view and methods of action which the historian takes for granted when he deals with the character of the man. As anyone thinking of a judge of some standing upon the English bench cannot but believe that he is possessed of some learning or some gravity, etc.; as anyone hearing of a famous soldier cannot but believe that he has certain qualities associated with the business of soldiering, so historians tend to confuse the personality and character of Louis XVI with that of his office; they either by contrast exaggerate his unkingly defects or by sympathy exaggerate his kingly opposition to reform.

The student will do well to avoid this error and its source, and to think of Louis as of a man who had been casually introduced, almost without preparation, into the office which he held. In other words, the student will do well, in his reading of the Revolution, to consider Louis XVI simply as a man, and his character as a private character. For this last of the long, unbroken line of Capetians possessed a character essentially individual. It was of a type which, no matter what accidents of fortune might have fallen upon its possessor, would have remained the same. Nor was ever a man possessed of high office whom high office had less moulded.

Men thus impervious to their environment are commonly so from two causes: either from an intense and vivid personal initiative which may border upon madness, or from something thick and heavy in their moral accoutrement which defends against external action the inner personal temperament. The latter was the case with Louis.

He was very slow of thought, and very slow of decision. His physical movements were slow. The movement of his eyes was notably slow. He had a way of falling asleep under the effort of fatigue at the most incongruous moments. The things that amused him were of the largest and most superficial kind. Horse-play, now and then a little touched with eccentricity, and very plain but un-expected jokes. One may express him from one aspect by saying that he was one of those men whom you could never by any chance have hoped to convince of anything. The few things which he accepted he accepted quite simply, and the process of reasoning in the mouth of any who approached him was always too rapid for him to follow. But it must not be imagined on this account that the moral integument so described was wrapped about a void. On the contrary, it enclosed a very definite character. Louis possessed a number of intimate convictions upon which he was not to be shaken. He was profoundly convinced of the existence and value of a certain corporate tradition in the organism which he ruled: the French nation. He was national. In this he differed from many a pedant, many a courtier, many an ecclesiastic, and many a woman about him, especially his wife.

He was, again, possessed of all the elements of the Catholic faith.

It was, indeed, a singular thing for a man of his position at such a time to hold intimately to religion, but Louis held to it. He con-fessed, he communicated, he attended mass, he performed his ordinary devotions—not by way of tradition or political duty, or State function, to which religious performance was now reduced in the vast majority of his wealthy contemporaries, but as an individual for whom these things had a personal value. Had he, with precisely the same interior spirit, woken in his bed some morning to find himself a country squire, and to discover that all his past kingship had been a dream of the night, he would have continued the practice of his religion as before.

Now this is a sufficiently remarkable point, for the country squire, the noble, the lawyer, the university professor of the genera-tion immediately preceding the Revolution had, as a rule, no con-ception of the Catholic Church. With them the faith was dead, save in the case of a very few who made it, if one may say so without disrespect, a mania, and in their exaggerations were themselves the proofs of the depth of decay into which the Church of Gaul had fallen.

Louis XVI was possessed, then, of religion: it appeared in many of his acts, in his hesitation to appoint not a few of the many atheist bishops of the time, in his real agony of responsibility upon the Civil Constitution of the clergy, and in nothing more than the peculiar sobriety and solid ritual whereby he prepared for a tragic, sudden, and ignominious death.

It is next to be observed that though he was a man not yet in middle age, and though he was quite devoid of ardour in any form, he had from the first matured a great basis of courage. It is well to admit that this quality in him was connected with those slow processes of thought and action which hampered him, but it is not to be explained by them. No man yet has become brave through mere stupidity.

It was not only the accidents of the Revolution that proved this quality in him: his physical habits proved it long before. He was a resolute and capable rider of the horse: an aptitude in that exercise is impossible to the coward. Again, in those by-products of courage which are apparent, even where no physical danger threatens, he was conspicuous; he had no hesitation in facing a number of men, and he had aptitude in a mechanical trade—a business by no means unconnected with virility.

Now in mentioning his virility, it is of prime importance for the student to remember, though the matter can be touched upon but lightly, that Louis, in this department of physical life, suffered from a mechanical impediment which gravely distorted the first years of his marriage, which undoubtedly wounded his self-respect, and which was perhaps the only thing that caused him permanent anxiety. He was cured by medical aid in the summer of the year 1777, but he was already three years a king and seven years a husband before that relief came to him. The tragedy affected his whole life, and, I repeat, must never be forgotten when one considers either him or Marie Antoinette in their intimate character, and in their effect as actors in the great drama.

For the rest, the character of Louis betrayed certain ineptitudes (the word ineptitude is far more accurate in this connection than the word weakness), which ineptitudes were peculiarly fatal for the military office which he held and for the belligerent crisis which he had to meet.

Few men are possessed of the eye, the subtle sympathy, the very rapid power of decision, and the comprehension of human contrasts and differences which build up the apt leader of an armed force great or small. Most men are mediocre in the combination of these qualities. But Louis was quite exceptionally hopeless where they were concerned. He could never have seen the simplest position nor have appreciated the military aspects, of any character or of any body of men. He could ride, but he could not ride at the head of a column. He was not merely bad at this trade, he was *nul*. Drafted as a private into a conscript army, he would never have been entrusted with the duties of a corporal. He would have been impossible as a sergeant; and, possessed of commissioned rank, ridicule would have compelled him to take his discharge.

This lack did not only, or chiefly, betray itself in his inability to meet personally the armed crisis of a revolution; it was not only, or chiefly, apparent in his complete breakdown during the assault upon the palace on the 10th of August: it was also, and much more, the disastrous cause of his inability to oversee, or even to choose, military advisers.

Those who propose in the early part of the Revolution to check the mob in Paris, are excellent commanders: but Louis does not know it. Those who succeed each other at the Ministry of War, or at the head of the armies during the active part of the revolution are various in the extreme: but they all seem one to him. Between a fop like Narbonne and a subtle, trained cavalry man like Dumouriez, Louis made no distinction. The military qualities of La Fayette (which were not to be despised) meant no more to him than does music, good or bad, to a deaf man. From the beginning to the end of the movement, the whole of the military problem escaped him.

Another hole in his character, which was of prime importance at such a time, was his inability to grasp in a clear vision any general social problem. Maps he could well comprehend, and he could well retain statistics; but the landscape, as it were, of the Revolution his protuberant and lethargic eyes completely missed. He was quite unable to see where lay danger and where support, in what large masses such and such forces were grouped, and the directions in which they were advancing, or upon which they must retreat. In this matter he was, as will be seen in a moment, the very opposite of Mirabeau, and it was on account of this weakness, or rather this form of nullity, that all Mirabeau's vision was wasted upon Louis.

Finally, he had no working comprehension of Europe. He did

not even exaggerate the powers of the allies in the later phases of the Revolution when they were marching upon France. He did not either underestimate or overestimate the policy and naval force of Great Britain, the military resources of his own subjects, the probable sympathies of the Netherlands (anti-Austrian but Catholic), the decay of Spain, the division and impotence of the Italian Peninsula. Louis saw nothing of all these things.

One may conclude the picture (for the purposes of such a short study as this) by saying that only one coincidence could have led him through the labyrinth of the time with success. That coincidence would have been the presence at his side of a friend fully trusted from childhood, loved, as religious as himself, and yet possessing precisely those qualities which he himself lacked. Had Louis found to hand such a lieutenant, the qualities I have mentioned would have been a sort of keel and ballast which would have secured the monarchy, for he was not weak, he was not impulsive, he was not even foolish: he was only wretchedly alone in his incapacities. Certainly such a nature could trust and rely upon no one who was not of this intimate kind, and he possessed no such intimate, let alone an intimate who could command the qualities I have suggested.

THE QUEEN

Marie Antoinette presents to history a character which it is of the highest interest to regard as a whole. It is the business of her biographers to consider that character as a whole; but in her connection with the Revolution there is but one aspect of it which is of importance, and that is the attitude which such a character was bound to take towards the French nation in the midst of which the Queen found herself.

It is the solution of the whole problem which the Queen's action sets before us to apprehend the gulf that separated her not only from the French temperament, but from a comprehension of all French society. Had she been a woman lacking in energy or in decision, this alien character in her would have been a small matter, and her ignorance of the French in every form of their activity, or rather her inability to comprehend them, would have been but a private failing productive only of certain local and immediate consequences, and not in any way determining the great lines of the revolutionary movement.

As it was, her energy was not only abundant but steadfast; it grew more secure in its action as it increased with her years, and the initiative which gave that energy its course never vacillated, but was always direct. She knew her own mind, and she attempted, often with a partial success, to realize her convictions. There was no character in touch with the Executive during the first years of the Revolution comparable to hers for fixity of purpose and definition of view.

It was due to this energy and singleness of aim that her misunderstanding of the material with which she had to deal was of such fatal importance.

It was she who chose, before the outbreak of the Revolution, the succession of those ministers both Liberal and Reactionary, whose unwise plans upon either side precipitated violence. It was she who called and then revoked, and later recalled to office the wealthy and overestimated Necker; she who substituted for him, and then so inopportunely threw over Calonne, the most national of the precursors of the Revolution, and ever after her most bitter enemy; it was she who advised the more particularly irritating details of resistance after the meeting of the first revolutionary Parliament; it was she who presided over (and helped to warp) the plans for the flight of the royal family; it was she who, after this flight had failed, framed a definite scheme for the coercion of the French people by the Governments of Europe; it was she who betrayed to foreign chanceries the French plan of campaign when war had become inevitable; finally, it was she who inspired the declaration of Brunswick which accompanied the invasion of French territory, and she was in particular the author of the famous threat therein contained to give over Paris to military execution, and to hold all the popular authorities responsible with their lives for the restoration of the pre-revolutionary state of affairs.

As research proceeds, the capital effect of this woman's continual and decided interference will be more and more apparent to historians.

Now Marie Antoinette's conception of mankind in general was the conception that you will find prevalent in such societies as that domestic and warm centre which had nourished her childhood.

The romantic affection of a few equals, the personal loyalty of a handful of personal servants, the vague histrionic content which permeates the poor at the sight of great equipages and rich accoutrements, the cheers of a crowd when such symbols accompanying monarchy are displayed in the streets—all these were for Marie Antoinette the fundamental political feelings of mankind. An absence of them she regarded with bewilderment, an active opposition to them she hated as something at once incomprehensible and positively evil.

There was in all this illusion, of course, a great element of what the English call middle class, and the French bourgeois. To be quite ignorant of what servitors will say of their masters behind their backs; not to appreciate that heroic devotion is the faculty of a few; never to have imagined the discontents of men in general, and the creative desire for self-expression which inspires men when they act politically; not to know that men as a whole (and particularly the French people) are not deceived by the accidents of wealth, nor attach any real inferiority to poverty; to despise the common will of numbers or to doubt its existence; to see society established in a hierarchy not of office but of leisure: all this may seem to the democrat a very unnatural and despicable mood. But it was not despicable, still less unnatural, in the case of Marie Antoinette: it was the only experience and the only conception of society which had ever been given her. She had always believed, when she gazed upon a mass of the populace, that the difference between the crowd and herself was a moral reality. The contrast in external habits between the wealthy, the middle class, and the poor—a contrast ultimately produced by differences in the opportunity and leisure which wealth affords—she thought to be fundamental. Just as children and certain domestic pet animals regard such economic accidents in society as something real which differentiates men, so did she—but she happened to nourish this illusion in the midst of a people, and within a day's walk of a capital, where the misconception had less hold than in any other district of Europe.

Of the traits peculiar to the French she knew nothing, or, to put it more strongly, she could not believe that they really existed.

The extremes of cruelty into which this people could fall were inconceivable to her, as were also the extremes of courage to which they can rise under the same excitements as arouse them to an excess of hatred. But that character in the French which she most utterly failed to foresee or to comprehend, was their power of *corporate organization.*

That a multitude could instruct and order themselves for a common purpose, rapidly acquire and nominate the officers who should bring that purpose to fruition, and in general pass in one moment from a mere multitude to an incipient army—that was a faculty which the French had and have to a peculiar degree, and which she (like so many of our own contemporaries, and especially those of German blood) could not believe to be real. This faculty in the French, when it took action and was apparent in the physical struggles of the Revolution, seemed to her, to the very end, a sort of nightmare; something which, by all the laws of reality, *ought not* to be happening, but somehow or other *was* happening in a manner evilly miraculous. It was her ignorance upon this main point of all that caused her to rely so continually upon the use of the regular forces, and of those forces in insufficient numbers. She could not but believe that a few trained soldiery were necessarily the masters of great civilian bodies; their uniforms were a powerful argument with her, and mere civilian bodies, however numerous, were always, in her conception, a dust of disparate and inchoate humanity. She believed there was nothing to attack or resist in popular numbers but the opinion, the fear, or the cupidity of the individual. In this error of judgement concerning the French people she was not peculiar: it is an error repeated over and over again by foreigners, and even by some native commentators when they seek to account for some national movement of the Gauls. The unlearning of it is the first lesson which those who would either administrate or resist the French should learn.

In the matter of religion (which the reader may see in these pages to be of such moment in the revolutionary story), the queen was originally far more indifferent than her husband, though she observed a certain measure of personal practice. It was not until her heavy misfortunes came upon her that any degree of personal devotion appeared in her daily life, though it must be admitted that, by a sort of premonition of disaster, she turned to religion in the months immediately preceding the outbreak of the reform.

It remains to describe the personal effect she had upon those who were in her immediate presence. Most of the French aristocracy she repelled. The same misfortune which made her unable to understand the French temperament as a whole divorced her from that particular corner of it which took the shape of French aristocratic tradition. She did not understand its stiffness, its exactitude, its brilliancy or its hardness: and she heartily disliked all four.

On this account she produced on the great families of her court, and especially upon the women of them, an effect of vulgarity. Had she survived, and had her misfortunes not been of so tragic an intensity, the legend she would have left in French society would certainly have been one of off-handed carelessness, self-indulgence, and lack of dignity which have for the French of that rank the savour that a loud voice, a bad accent, an insufficient usage in the rules of daily conduct, leave upon what is left of a corresponding rank in England today.

She was, on the other hand, easily deceived by the flattery of place seekers, and the great power which she wielded in politics just before the Revolution broke out made her, as it were, a sort of *butt* of the politicians.

They haunted her presence, they depended upon her patronage, and, at the same time, they secretly ridiculed her. Her carriage, which was designed to impress onlookers and did have that effect upon most foreigners, seemed to most of the French observers (of rank which permitted them to approach her familiarly) somewhat theatrical and sometimes actually absurd. The earnestness which she displayed in several lines of conduct, and notably in her determined animosity to certain characters (as that of La Fayette, for instance), was of an open and violent sort which seemed to them merely brutal and unintelligent; her luxury, moreover, was noticed by the refined world of Versailles to be hardly ever of her own choosing, but nearly always practised in imitation of others.

In connection with that trait of luxury, the reader must appreciate at the outset that it was grievously exaggerated by her contemporaries, and has been still more exaggerated by posterity. She was not a very frivolous, still less a dissipated, woman. She was woefully loose in tongue, but she was certainly virtuous.

She gambled, but as the times went, and the supposed unlimited fortune of the Crown, her gambling was not often excessive; her expenditure upon jewellery and dress would be thought most moderate today in the case of any lady of our wealthier families. On the other hand, her whims were continual and as continually chang-ing, especially in the earlier part of her life.

Since that surrounding world of the Court which she misunder-stood and which had no sympathy with her was ready to find some handle against her, that handle of dissipation was the easiest for them to seize; but the accusation was not a just one.

Had fortune made her the wife of a poor man in a lower class of society, Marie Antoinette would have been a capable housewife: her abundant energy would have found a proper channel, and she was in no way by nature extravagant.

She had a few very passionate and somewhat too sentimental friendships, some of which were returned, others of which their objects exploited to their own advantage. The two most famous were her friendship for the Princess de Lamballe and for Madame de Polignac. These moved her not infrequently to unwise acts of patronage which were immediately seized by the popular voice and turned against her. They were among the few weaknesses apparent in her general temper. They were certainly ill balanced and ill judged.

She indulged also in a number of small and unimportant flirta-tions which might almost be called the routine of her rank and world; she had but one great affection in her life for the other sex, and it was most ardently returned. Its object was a Swedish noble of her own age, the very opposite of the French in his temper, romantically chivalrous, unpractical in the extreme, gentle, intensely reserved; his name Count Axel de Fersen. The affair remained pure, but she loved him with her whole heart, and in the last months of her tragedy this emotion must be regarded as the chief concern of her soul. They saw each other but very rarely, often they were separated for years; it was this, perhaps, which lent both glamour and fidelity to the strange romance.

MIRABEAU

Mirabeau, the chief of the 'practical' men of the Revolution (as the English language would render the most salient point in their political attitude), needs a very particular examination. His influ-ence upon the early part of the Revolution was so considerable, the effect of his death was so determinant and final, the speculation as to what *might* have happened had he survived is so fruitful, so entertaining, and so common, and the positive effect of his attitude upon the development of the Revolution after his death was so wide, that to misunderstand Mirabeau is in a large measure to misunderstand the whole movement; and Mirabeau has unfortunately been ill or superficially understood by many among now three generations of historians; for a comprehension of this character is not a matter for research nor for accumulated historic detail, but rather a task for sympathy.

Mirabeau was essentially an artist, with the powers and the frailties which we properly associate with that term: that is, strong emotion appealed to him both internally and externally. He loved to enjoy it himself, he loved to create it in others. He studied, therefore, and was a master of, the material by which such emotion may be created; he himself yielded to strong emotion and sought it where it might be found. It is foolish alike to belittle and to exaggerate this type of temperament. Upon it or upon its admixture with other qualities is based the music, the plastic art, and in a large measure the permanent literature of the world. This aptitude for the enjoyment and for the creation in others of emotion clothes intellectual work in a manner which makes it permanent. This is what we mean when we say that *style* is necessary to a book; that a great civilization may partly be judged by its architecture; that, as Plato says, music may be moral or immoral, and so forth. The artist, though he is not at the root of human affairs, is a necessary and proper ally in their development.

When I say that Mirabeau was an artist I mean that wherever his energies might have found play he would there have desired to enjoy and to create enjoyment through some definite medium. This medium was in part literary, but much more largely oral expression. To be a *tribune*, that is the voice of great numbers, to persuade, nay, to please by his very accents and the very rhythm of his sentences, these things occupied the man; but he also brought into his art that without which no great art can exist: mere intellect.

He believed in the main principles at least which underlay the revolutionary movement, he understood them and he was prepared to propagate them; but his power over men was not due to this conviction: his power over men was wholly that of the artist, and had he by some accident been engaged in maintaining the attack against democracy, he would have been nearly as famous as he became under the title of its defender. We must then always consider Mirabeau as an orator, though an orator endowed with a fine and clear intelligence and with no small measure of reasoned faith.

Much else remains to be said of him.

He was a gentleman; that is, he both enjoyed and suffered the consequences which attach to hereditary wealth and to the atmosphere that surrounds its expenditure. On this account, he being personally insufficiently provided with wealth, he was for ever in debt, and regarded the sums necessary to his station in life and to his large opportunities as things due to him, so to speak, from society. We are right when we say that he took bribes, but wrong if we imagine that those bribes bound him as they would bind a man meaner in character or less lucky in his birth. He stooped as gentlemen will to all manner of low intrigues to, obtain 'the necessary and the wherewith'; that is, money for this *rôle*. But there was a driving power behind him, bound up with his whole character, which made it impossible for any such sums to control his diction or to make of such a man a mere advocate. He was never that dirtiest of political phenomena, the 'party man'. He would never have been, had he been born a hundred years later and thrust into the nastiness of modern parliamentary life, 'a parliamentary hand'.

Mirabeau had behind him a certain personal history which we must read in connection with his temperament.

He had travelled widely, he knew Englishmen and Germans of the wealthier classes well. The populace he knew ill even in his own country; abroad he knew it not at all. He had suffered from his father's dislike of him, from the consequence of his own unbridled passions, also not a little from mere accidental misfortune. Capable of prolonged and faithful attachment to some woman, the opportunity for that attachment had never been afforded him until the last few months before his death. Capable of paying loyal and industrious service to some political system, no political system had chosen him for its servant. It is a fruitful matter of speculation to consider what he might have done for the French monarchy had Fate put him early at Court and given him some voice in the affairs of the French Executive before the Revolution broke out. As it was, the Revolution provided him with his opportunity merely because it broke down old barriers and conventions and was destructive of the framework of the State in which he lived. He was compelled to enter the Revolution as something of a destroyer, for by no other avenue could he be given his chance; but by nature he detested destruction. I mean (since this phrase is somewhat vague) he detested that spirit which will disendow a nation of certain permanent institutions serving definite ends, without a clear scheme of how those institutions should be replaced by others to serve similar ends. It was on this account that he was most genuinely and sincerely a defender of the monarchy: a permanent institution serving the definite ends of national unity and the repression of tendencies to oligarchy in the State.

Mirabeau had none of the revolutionary Vision. In mind he was prematurely aged, for his mind had worked very rapidly over a very varied field of experience. The pure doctrine of democracy which was a religion to many of his contemporaries, with all the consequences of a religion, he had never thought of accepting. But certain consequences of the proposed reforms strongly appealed to him. He loved to be rid of meaningless and dead barriers, privileges which no longer corresponded to real social differences, old traditions in the management of trade which no longer corresponded to the economic circumstances of his time, and (this is the pivotal point) the fossils of an old religious creed which, like nearly all of his rank, he simply took for granted to be dead: for Mirabeau was utterly divorced from the Catholic Church.

Much has been said and will be said in these pages concerning the religious quarrel which, though men hardly knew it at the time, cut right across the revolutionary effort, and was destined to form the lasting line of cleavage in French life. There will be repeated again and again what has already been written, that a reconciliation between the Catholic Church and the reconstruction of democracy was, though men did not know it, the chief temporal business of the time, and the reader of these pages will be made well acquainted in them with the degradation to which religion had fallen among the cultivated of that generation. But in the case of Mirabeau this absence of religion must be particularly insisted upon. It would no more have occurred to Mirabeau that the Catholic Faith had a future than it could occur to (let us say) an English politician of thirty years ago that the Irish might become a wealthy community or that an English Government might within his own lifetime find itself embarrassed for money. I use this parallel for the sake of strengthening my contention, but it is indeed a weak parallel. No contemporary parallel in our strange and rapidly changing times corresponds to the fixed certitude which permeated the whole of the end of the eighteenth century that the Catholic Faith was dead. Mirabeau had perhaps never engaged in his life in intimate conversation a single man who took the Catholic sacraments seriously, or suffered a moment's anxiety upon the tenets of the creed.

He knew, indeed, that certain women and a much smaller number of insignificant men wrapped themselves up in old practices of an odd, superstitious kind; he knew that great, dull areas of ignorant peasantry, in proportion to their poverty and isolation, repeated by rote the old formulae of the Faith. But of the Faith as a living thing he could have no conception.

He saw on the one hand a clerical institution, economic in character, providing places and revenues for men of his own rank; he met those men and never discovered them to have any religion at all. He saw on the other hand a proposed society in which such a fossil, unjust and meaningless, must relinquish its grip upon those large revenues. But of the Faith as a social force, as a thing able to revive, he could have no conception. It would have seemed to him a mere folly to suggest that the future might contain the possibility of such a resurrection. The dissolution of the religious orders, which was largely his work, the civil constitution of the clergy which he presided over, were to him the most natural acts in the world. They were the mere sweeping away of a quantity of inorganic stuff which cumbered the modern State. He felt of them as we might feel of the purchase of waste spaces in our cities, or the confiscation of some bad landlords' property in them. The Church served no kind of purpose, no one who counted believed in it, it was defended only by people who enjoyed large revenues from the survival of what had once been, but was now no longer, a living, social function.

In everything of the Revolution which he understood Mirabeau was upon the side of caution. He was not oblivious to the conception of popular government, he was not even mistrustful of it, but he could not conceive of it save as acting through the established strength of the wealthier classes. Of military power he judged very largely through Prussian eyes. And in long and enthusiastic passages he described the Prussian army as invincible. Had he lived to see the military enthusiasm of the Republicans he would utterly have distrusted it. He favoured in his heart an aristocratic machinery of society—though not an aristocratic theory of the State; he was quite determined to preserve as a living but diminished national organ the traditional monarchy of France; he was curious upon a number of details which were present and close to his eyes: methods of voting, constitutional checks, commercial codes and the rest of it. The little equilibriums of diplomacy interested him also, and the watching of men immediately under his eye in the Parliament.

It was in the Parliament that his whole activity lay, it was there that he began to guide the Revolution, it was his absence from the Parliament after his death that the Revolution most feels in the summer of 1791.

This very brief sketch does not present Mirabeau to the reader. He can only be properly presented in his speeches and in the more rhetorical of his documents. It is probable as time proceeds that his reputation in this department will grow. His constitutional ideas, based as they were upon foreign institutions, and especially upon the English of that time, were not applicable to his own people and are now nearly forgotten: he was wrong upon English politics as he was wrong upon the German armies, but he had art over men and his personality endures and increases with time.

LA FAYETTE

The character of La Fayette has suffered chiefly from his own aloofness towards his contemporaries on the one hand, and from his rigid adherence to principle upon the other. Both these causes are clearly connected. The same quality in him which made him so tenacious of principle made him contemptuous of the run of men about him. Fundamentally, he was nearer the extreme Republicans than any other class, from the very fact of his possessing a clear political creed and a determination to follow it out to its logical consequence. But there was no chance of his comprehending the concrete side of the movement or the men engaged upon it, for his great wealth, inherited in very early life, had cut him off from experience. His moral fault was undoubtedly ambition. It was an ambition which worked in the void, as it were, and never measured itself with other men's capacities or opportunities. He made no plans for advancement, not because he would have despised the use of intrigue in reason, but because he was incapable of working it. He was exceedingly attached to popularity, when it came he thought it his due; unpopularity in its turn seemed to him a proof of the vileness of those who despised him. He made himself too much the measure of his world.

Undoubtedly a very great part in the moulding of his character proceeded from his experience in the United States of America. He was then at the most impressionable and formative period of human life, little more than a boy, or at least just entering early manhood. He had just married, he had just come into the administration of his vast fortune. At such a moment he took part in the victorious rebellion of the English colonies, and it may be imagined how powerful was the effect of this youthful vision upon the whole of the man's future life; because there was no proletariat in the colonies, he never saw or comprehended the dispossessed classes of Paris— for that matter he never saw or comprehended the French peasantry upon his own lands; because a chance and volunteer soldiery had, under the peculiar conditions of the half-populated Atlantic sea- board in conjunction with the French fleet and with the aid of French money and arms, got the better of the small and hetero- geneous forces of George III, he believed that a military nation like the French, in the midst of powerful enemies, could make some- thing of an amateur civic force; because a certain type of ease in social relations was the ideal of many, perhaps of most, of those with whom he had served in America, he confused so simple and mundane an ideal with the fierce crusading blast and the sacred passion for equality which was stirring his own nation when his opportunity for leadership came.

It may be said of La Fayette with justice that he never upon a single occasion did the right thing. It may also be said with justice that he never did politically any major thing for which his own conscience would later reproach him. It is noticeable that the Queen held him in particular odium. He had been a wealthy young noble about the Court, the friend of all her women friends, and his sympathy with the revolutionary movement at its inception there- fore seemed to her nothing better than treason. There was also undoubtedly something in his manner which grievously repelled her; that it was self-sufficient we cannot doubt, and that it was often futile and therefore exasperating to women, events are sufficient to show. But Marie Antoinette's violent personal antagonism towards La Fayette was not common, though several ardent spirits (Danton's, for instance) shared it. The mass of those who came across La Fayette felt in connection with him a certain irritation or a certain contempt or a certain rather small and distant respect; he inspired no enthusiasms, and when he timidly attempted a rebellion against the new Government after the fall of the monarchy, no one would sacrifice himself or follow him.

It may be affirmed of La Fayette that if he had not existed the Revolution would have pursued much the same course as it did, with this exception: that there would not have been formed a definitely middle class armed guard to provoke friction in Paris: the National Guard would have been more open to all ranks.

In religion the man was anodyne, Catholic of course by baptism, but distinctly Protestant in morals and in general tone, in dogma (until the end of his life) freethinking, of course, like all his contemporaries. He was personally courageous but foolishly despised the duel. One anecdote out of many will help to fix his nature in the mind of the reader. Mirabeau, casting about as usual for aid in his indebtedness, sent urgently to him as to a fellow noble, a fellow politician and a fellow supporter of the Crown, begging a loan of £2,000. La Fayette accorded him £1,000.

DUMOURIEZ

Dumouriez presents a character particularly difficult for the modern Englishman to comprehend, so remote is it in circumstance and fundamentals from those of our time.

Of good birth, but born in a generation when social differences had become a jest for intelligent and active men (and he was intelligent and active), courageous, with a good knowledge of his trade of soldiering, of rapid decision and excellent judgement where troops or *terrain* were concerned, he was all at sea in the comprehension of men, and he bore no loyalty to the State.

It is this last feature which will particularly surprise the English reader, for it is the singular and permanent advantage of oligarchic communities such as the British that they retain under any stress and show throughout the whole commonwealth the sense of the State. To betray the State, to act against its interests, to be imperfectly conscious of its existence, are crimes or weaknesses unknown to the citizens of an oligarchy, and a citizen of this country cannot easily conceive of them today. In democracies and despotisms, on the other hand, to forget one's duty to the State, to be almost oblivious of its corporate existence, is a common weakness. There is here a compensation, and by just so much as despotism and democracy permit rapid, effective and all-compelling action on the part of the State, by just so much as they permit sudden and sometimes miraculous enthusiasms which save or which confirm a State, by that also do they lack the quiet and persistent consciousness of the State which oligarchy fosters and determines.

Dumouriez' excellence as a general can only be appreciated by those who have looked closely into the constitution of the forces which he was to command and the adversaries with whom he had to deal. It is the prime quality of a great commander that his mind stands ready for any change in circumstances or in the material to his hand, and even when we have allowed for the element of luck which is so considerable in military affairs, we must not forget that Dumouriez saved without disaster the wretched and disorganized bands, inchoate and largely mutinous as to their old units, worthless and amateur as to their new, which had to meet, in and behind the Argonne, the model army of Prussia.

We must not forget that his plan for the invasion of the Low Countries was a just and sensible one, nor with what skill, after the inevitable defeat and retreat of the spring of 1793, he saved his command intact.

As a subordinate to an armed executive, to the Government of Napoleon, for instance, the man would have been priceless. Nay, had circumstances permitted him to retain supreme command of civil as of military power, he would have made no bad dictator. His mere technical skill was so considerable as to make the large sums paid him by the English Government seem a good bargain even at our distance of time, and his plans for the defence of England and for the attack on Napoleon are a proof of the value at which he was estimated.

But Dumouriez was quite unable to act under the special circumstances in which he happened to be placed at the moment of his treason. A mere ambition had carried him from intrigue to intrigue among the politicians. He despised them as an active and capable soldier was compelled to despise them; he was too old to share any of their enthusiasms, even had his temperament permitted him to entertain any vision, political or religious. He certainly never felt the least moral bond attaching him to what was in his eyes the chance anarchy of the last six months of French Government under which he served, and if he is to be branded with the title of traitor, then we must brand with the same title all that multitude of varied men who escaped from the country in the Emigration, who left it in disgust, or even who remained in France, but despaired of French fortunes, in the turmoil of 1793.

It is perhaps a worthy excuse for Dumouriez' failure to point out that he also was one of those whom the Court might have used had it known how to use men; but the Court had no such knowledge.

DANTON

The character of Danton has more widely impressed the world than that of any other revolutionary leader, because it contained elements permanently human, independent of the democratic theory of the time, and necessary neither to the support of that theory nor to the criticism of it.

The character of Danton appeals to that sense in man which is interested in action, and which in the field of letters takes the form of drama. His vigour, his personal strength of mind and body, the individuality of his outline, arrest equally the man who loves the Revolution, and the man who hates it, and the man who is quite indifferent to its success or failure.

It is on this very account that historians, especially foreign historians, have tended to misinterpret the man. Thus Carlyle, who has great intuition in the matter, yet makes him out farmer-like—which he certainly was not; Michelet, fascinated by his energy, presents him as something uncouth, and in general those who would describe Danton stand at a distance, as it were, where his loud voice and forcible gesture may best be appreciated; but a man to be seen truly must be seen in intimacy.

Danton was essentially a compound of two powerful characters in man. He was amative or constructive, and at the same time he not only possessed but liked to exercise lucidity of thought. The combination is among the strongest of all those that go to build up human personalities.

That which was amative and constructive in him, his virility if you will, brought him into close touch with reality; he knew and loved his own country, for instance, and infinitely preferred its happy survival to the full development of any political theory. He also knew and loved his fellow countrymen in detail and as persons; he knew what made a Frenchman weak and what made him strong. The vein of Huguenotry, though he did not know it for what it was, he disliked in his compatriots. On the other hand, the salt and freshness of the French was native to him and he delighted in it; the freedom of their expression, the noise of their rhetoric, and the military subsoil of them, were things to all of which he immediately responded. He understood their sort of laughter, nor was he shocked, as a man less national would have been, at their peculiarly national vices, and in especial their lapses into rage. It is this which must account for what all impartial judgement most blames in him, which is, his indifference to the cruelties, his absorbed interest in foreign and military affairs, at the moment of the Massacres of September.

This touch with reality made him understand in some fashion (though only from without) the nature of the Germans. The foolish mania of their rulers for mere territorial expansion unaccompanied by persuasion or the spread of their ideas, he comprehended. The vast superiority of their armies over the disorganized forces of the French in 1792 he clearly seized: hence on the one hand his grasp of their foreign policy, and on the other his able negotiation of the retreat after Valmy. He also understood, however, and more profoundly, the rapid self-organization of which his own countrymen were capable, and it was upon this knowledge that his determination to risk the continuance of the war reposed. It should be remarked that both in his military and in his quasi-military action he was himself endowed in a singular degree with that power of immediate decision which is characteristic of his nation.

His lucidity of thought permitted him to foresee the consequences of many a revolutionary decision, and at the same time inclined him to a strong sympathy with the democratic creed, with the doctrine of equality, and especially with the remoulding of the national institutions—particularly his own profession of the law—upon simple lines. He was undoubtedly a sincere and a convinced revolutionary, and one whose doctrine more permeated him than did that of many of his contemporaries their less solid minds. He was not on that account necessarily republican. Had some accident called his genius into play earlier in the development of the struggle, he might well, like Mirabeau, with whom he presents so curious a parallel, have thought it better for the country to save the Monarchy.

It must always be remembered that he was a man of wide culture and one who had achieved an early and satisfactory professional success; he was earning a sound income at the moment of his youthful marriage; he read English largely and could speak it. His dress was not inexpensive, and though somewhat disordered (as it often is with men of intense energy and constant gesture) it never gave an impression of carelessness or disarray. He had many and indifferent intellectual interests, and was capable, therefore, of intelligent application in several fields. He appreciated the rapid growth of physical science, and at the same time the complexity of the old social conditions—too widely different from contemporary truths.

To religion he was, of course, like all men of that time, utterly indifferent, but unlike many of them he seized the precise proportion of its remaining effect upon certain districts and certain sections of the countrysides. There has been a tendency latterly to exaggerate the part which Freemasonry played in the launching of him; he was indeed a member of a masonic lodge, as were, for that matter, all the men, conspicuous or obscure, democratic or utterly reactionary, who appeared upon the revolutionary stage: probably the king, certainly old aristocrats like the father of Madame de Lamballe, and the whole host of the middle class, from men like Bailly to men like Condorcet. But it is reading history backwards, and imagining the features of our own time to have been present a century ago, to make of Masonry the determining element in his career.

Danton failed and died from two combined causes: first his health gave way, secondly he obtruded his sanity and civilian sense into the heated fury and calculated martial law of the second year of the Republic. To both that fury and that calculation he was an obstacle; his opposition to the Terror lost him the support of the enthusiasts, but it was the interference which such a judgement made in the plans of the soldiers, and notably of Carnot, that determined his condemnation and death. He also, like Mirabeau, will undoubtedly increase as the years proceed, and, if only as a representative of the national temper, become more and more the typical figure of the Revolution in action.

CARNOT

Carnot, the predecessor of Napoleon, and the organizing soldier of the early revolutionary wars, owed his power to backbone.

He had not only a good solidity of brain, but an astonishing power of using it for hours and hours on end. This he owed perhaps to the excellent physical stock of which he came, the eldest of a very large family born to a notable lawyer in Burgundy.

It was Carnot's pride to hold a commission in the learned arms which were to transform at that moment the art of war: for as Bonaparte, his successor, was a gunner, so he was a sapper. His practice of exact knowledge in application, and the liberal education which his career demanded, further strengthened the strong character he had inherited. More important still, in his democratic views he was what none of the older officers had been, convinced and sincere. He had not come within the influence of the very wealthy or of the very powerful. He was young, and he knew his own mind not only in matters of political faith but in the general domain of philosophy, and in the particular one of military science.

It has been said of him that he invented the revolutionary method of strategical concentration and tactical massing in the field. There is some truth in this; but the method would not have been possible had he not also invented, in company with Danton, and supported after Danton left power, a universal system of conscription.

Carnot understood, as only trained soldiers can, the value of numbers, and *he depended with great sagacity upon the national temper*; thus at Wattignies, which was a victory directly due to his genius, though it was novel in him to have massed troops suddenly upon the right after a check on the extreme left of the field, yet the novelty would have been of no effect had he not comprehended that, with his young fellow countrymen as troopers, he could depend upon a charge delivered after thirty-six hours of vigil.

He used not only the national but also the revolutionary temper in war. One of the chief features, for instance, of the revolutionary armies when they began to be successful, was the development of lines of skirmishers who pushed out hardly before the main bodies and were the first in the history of modern warfare to learn the use of cover. This development was spontaneous: it was produced within and by each unit, not by any general command. But Carnot recognized it at Hoondschoote and used it ever after.

The stoical inflexibility of his temper is the noblest among the many noble characters of his soul. He never admitted the empire, and he suffered exile, seeming thereby in the eyes of the vilest and most intelligent of his contemporaries, Fouché, to be a mere fool. He was as hard with himself as with others, wholly military in the framework of his mind, and the chief controller of the Terror, which he used as it was intended to be used, for the military salvation of the republic.

MARAT

Marat is easily judged. The complete sincerity of the enthusiast is not difficult to appreciate when his enthusiasm is devoted to a simple human ideal which has been, as it were, fundamental and common to the human race.

Equality within the State and the government of the State by its general will: these primal dogmas, on the reversion to which the whole Revolution turned, were Marat's creed.

Those who would ridicule or condemn him because he held such a creed, are manifestly incapable of discussing the matter at all. The ridicule and condemnation under which Marat justly falls do not attach to the patent moral truths he held, but to the manner in which he held them. He did not only hold them isolated from other truths—it is the fault of the fanatic so to hold any truth—but he held them as though no other truths existed. And whenever he found his ideal to be in practice working at a friction or stopped dead, his unnourished and acute enthusiasms at once sought a scapegoat, discovered a responsible agent, and suggested a violent outlet, for the delay.

He was often right when he denounced a political intriguer: he often would have sacrificed a victim not unjustly condemned, he often discovered an agent partially responsible, and even the violent solutions that he suggested were not always impracticable. But it was the prime error of his tortured mind that beyond victims, and sudden violent clutches at the success of democracy, there was nothing else he could conceive. He was incapable of allowing imperfections, for stupidities, for the misapprehension of mind by mind, for the mere action of time, and for all that renders human life infinitely complex and infinitely adjustable.

Humour, the reflection of such wisdom, he lacked—'judgement' (as the English idiom has it) he lacked still more—if a comparative term may be attached to two such absolute vacuities.

It must not be forgotten that so complete an absence of certain necessary qualities in the building up of a mind are equivalent to madness. Marat was not sane. His insanity was often generous, the creed to which it was attached was obvious enough, and in the eyes of most of us it is a creed to be accepted. But he worked with it as a madman who is mad on collectivism, let us say, or the rights of property, might work in our society, thinking of his one thesis, shrieking it and foaming at the mouth upon it, losing all control when its acceptance was not even opposed but merely delayed. He was valueless for the accomplishment of the ends of the Revolution. His doctrine and his adherence to it were so conspicuously simple and sincere that it is no wonder the populace made him (for a few months) a sort of symbol of their demand.

For the rest, his face, like his character, was tortured; he carried with him a disease of the skin that irritated perpetually his wholly unbalanced temper.

Some say (but one must always beware of so-called 'Science' in the reading of history) that a mixture of racial types produced in him a perpetual physical disturbance: his face was certainly distorted and ill-balanced—but physical suggestions of that sort are very untrustworthy.

Those who met him in the management of affairs thought him worthless enough; a few who knew him intimately loved him dearly; more who came across him continually were fatigued and irritated by his empty violence. He was, among those young revolutionaries, almost an elderly man; he was (this should never be forgotten) a distinguished scholar in his own trade, that of medicine; and he effected less in the Revolution than any man to whom a reputation of equal prominence happened to attach. He must stand responsible for the massacres of September.[1]

ROBESPIERRE

No character in the Revolution needs for its comprehension a wider reading and a greater knowledge of the national character than Robespierre's.

Upon no character does the comprehension of the period more depend, and none (for reasons I will give in a moment) has been more misunderstood, not only in the popular legend but in the weighed decisions of competent historians.

So true is this that even time, which (in company with scholarship) usually redresses such errors, has not yet permitted modern authors to give a true picture of the man.

The reason of so conspicuous a failure in the domain of history is this: that side by side with the real Robespierre there existed in the minds of all his contemporaries *save those who actually came across him in the functions of government*, a legendary Robespierre— a Robespierre popularly imagined; and that this imaginary Robespierre, while it (or he) has proved odious to posterity, seemed, while he lived, a fascinating portrait ot the man himself, and therefore he accepted it. For Robespierre, though just, lacked humility.

The problem is an exceedingly subtle as well as an exceedingly difficult one. The historian, as he reads his authorities, has perpetually to distinguish between what is strong and what is weak evidence, and to recall himself, as he reads, to reality by a recollection of what Robespierre himself was. If he does not do so he falls at once into the legend; so powerful is that legend in the numbers that supported it, and so strongly did Robespierre himself support it by his own attitude. The legendary Robespierre may be described in a very few lines.

Conceive a man sincerely convinced of the purest democratic theory, a man who cared for nothing else but the realization of that theory, and who had never sacrificed his pursuit of its realization

[1] There is but one trustworthy monograph on Marat. It will interest the student as a proof of the enthusiasm which Marat can inspire. It is by Chèvremont.

in the State to any personal advantage whatsoever. This man, trusted by the people and at last idolized by them, becomes more and more powerful. He enters the governing body (the Committee of Public Safety), he is the master both within and without that body, and uses his mastery for establishing an ideal democracy which shall recognize the existence of God and repose upon civic virtue; and to establish this ideal he has recourse to terror. He finds that human defections from his ideal are increasingly numerous: he punishes them by death. The slaughter grows to be enormous; the best of Democrats are involved in it; at last it can be tolerated no longer, his immediate subordinates revolt against him in the Committee, he is outlawed, fails to raise a popular rebellion in his favour in Paris, is executed, and his system of terror falls to the ground.

This picture, though purely legendary in tone, contains not only much truth, but truth of precisely that sort which conspires to make credible what is false in the whole.

Robespierre was sincerely attached to the conception of an ideal democracy; he was incorruptible in the pursuit of it—and to be a politician and incorruptible amounts to something like what the Church calls heroic virtue in a man. He *did* enter the Committee of Public Safety; he *did* support the Terror, and when he was overthrown the Terror, *did* come to an end. Where then, does the legend differ from the truth?

In these capital points, which change it altogether; that Robespierre was not the chief influence in the Committee of Public Safety, i.e. the all powerful executive of the Republic; that he did not desire the Terror, that he did not use it, that he even grew disgusted with it, and that, in general, he was never the man who governed France.

It need hardly be pointed out how such a truth destroys such a legend. The whole nature of the twelve months between the summer of 1793 and the summer of 1794 must vary according as we regard them as Robespierrean or no: and they were not Robespierrean.

What were they then, and why has the error that Robespierre was then master, arisen?

Those months, which may be roughly called the months of the Terror, were, as we shall see later in this book, months of martial law; and the Terror was simply martial law in action—a method of enforcing the military defence of the country and of punishing all those who interfered with it or were supposed by the Committee to interfere with it.

No man in the Committee was the author of this system, but the one most determined to use it and the one who had most occasion to use it, was undoubtedly the military organizer, Carnot. Side by side with him one man, such as Barrère, supported it because it kept up the Committee of Public Safety which gave him all his political position. Another, such as Saint-Just, supported it because he believed that the winning of the war (in which he took an active part) would secure democracy everywhere and for ever. Another, such as Jean Bon, supported it from the old sectarian bitterness of the Huguenot. But of all men in the Committee, Robespierre supported the Terror least, and was most suspected by his colleagues —and increasingly suspected as time went on—of desiring to interfere with the martial system of the Terror and to modify it.

Why, then, was Robespierre popularly identified with the Terror, and why, when he was executed, did the Terror cease?

Robespierre was identified with the Terror because he was identified with the popular clamour of the time, with the extreme democratic feeling of the time, and its extreme fear of a reaction. Robespierre being the popular idol, had become also the symbol of a popular frenzy which was supposed to be ruling the country. But that frenzy was not ruling the country. What was ruling the country was the Committee of Public Safety, in which Carnot's was the chief brain. Robespierre was indeed the idol of the populace; he was in no way the agent of their power or of any power.

Why, when he fell, did the Terror cease if he were not its author? Because the Terror was acting under a strain; it was with the utmost difficulty that this absolute, intolerant and intolerable martial system could be continued when once the fear of invasion was removed. For some weeks before Robespierre fell the victories had begun to render it unnecessary. When the Committee saw to it that Robespierre should be outlawed by the Parliament, they knocked away, without knowing it, the keystone of their own policy; it was *his* popular position which made *their* policy possible. When he was destroyed they suddenly found that the Terror could no longer be maintained. Men had borne with it because of Robespierre, falsely imagining that Robespierre had desired it. Robespierre gone, men would not bear with it any more.

Now, finally, if Robespierre himself had always felt opposed to the system of the Terror, why did he not take the lead in the popular reaction against it?

He had his opportunity given him by Danton in December 1793 —seven months before his own catastrophe. The Committee determined to put Danton out of the way because Danton, in appealing for mercy, was weakening the martial power of their government. Robespierre might have saved Danton: he preferred to let him be sacrificed. The reason was that Robespierre wrongly believed popularity to lie upon the side of the Terror and against Danton; he was in no way a leader (save in rhetoric and in rhetoric directed towards what men already desired), and his own great weakness or vice was the love of popular acclaim.

Later on, in the summer of 1794, when he actually began to move against the Terror, he only did so privately. He so misread men that he still believed the Terror to be popular, and dared not lose his popular name. A man by nature as sincere as crystal, he was tempted to insincerity in this major thing, during the last months of his life, and he yielded completely to the temptation. For the sake of his memory it was deplorable, and deplorable also for history. His weakness has been the cause of an historical error as grave as any that can be discovered in modern letters, and at the same time has wholly maligned him to posterity.

A factor in Robespierre's great public position which is often forgotten is the great effect of his speeches. That men should still debate, after so vast a change in taste, whether those speeches were eloquent or no, is a sufficient proof of their effect. He spoke in an ordered and a reasoned manner, which bored the fine spirits of the earlier Parliaments, but well suited the violent convictions of the later Revolution. His phraseology, his point of view, just jumped with that of his audience. He could express what they felt, and express it in terms which they knew to be exact, and which they believed to be grand. For his manner was never excessive, and those excessive men who heard him in an excessive mood, were proud to know that their violence could be exposed with so much scholarship and moderated skill.

By birth he was of the smaller gentry, though poor. It is an indication of his character that he had thought of taking Orders, and that in early youth literary vanity had affected him. He has left no monument; but from the intensity of his faith and from his practice of it, his name, though it will hardly increase, will certainly endure.

XVII

The Party System

1911

This was another very active year and saw the publication of The
Party System, *a highly controversial work which he wrote with Cecil
Chesterton, G.K.'s brother.*

*Belloc had become disillusioned with Parliament and did not seek
re-election in 1910, The authors are outspoken and bitter for they had
decided that the party system was outmoded and that the private
member had become a cipher. Thus:*

'. . . it should be noted that the effect of the Party System on even
the cleverer politicians is to reduce the normal level of their intelligence. It is quite incredible that such men as Mr Asquith and
Mr Lloyd George, Mr Balfour and Mr F. E. Smith, could under
any other circumstances give expression to such imbecilities as
those which constantly adorn their public speeches. They would
not talk like that at dinner, or at their clubs. But the standard of
intellect in politics is so low that men of moderate mental capacity
have to stoop in order to reach it. Examples of this in men who are
after all highly educated and move in a well-instructed world, will
occur to everyone. They could hardly be explained in any other
way than by the proportion of energy which is wasted under the
Party System in bad rhetoric and worse intrigue, which are utterly
useless to the Commonwealth.'

*The authors continue their attack in maintaining that Front Bench
members from both sides of the House control legislation whether for
good or bad, and the volume concludes on a low note:*

'The degraded Parliament may ultimately be replaced by some

other organ; but no such other organ appears to be forming, and until we get our first glimpse of it we are in for one of those evil spaces, subject to foreign insults and domestic misfortune, which invariably attach to nations when, for a period, they lose grip over their destinies.'

As a result of the excitement that The Party System *had created, Belloc and Chesterton decided to publish a newspaper of their own. It began as* The Eye Witness *and was edited by Belloc from June 1911 to October 1912. When the paper went bankrupt it became* The New Witness, *which was edited by Cecil Chesterton, and when Cecil joined up in 1916, G. K. Chesterton himself edited it. It was certain articles in these journals which formed the basis of Belloc's* The Servile State.

XVIII

From *More Peers*

1911

*On December 31, 1910 Belloc wrote to his close friend George Wynd-
ham: 'Since you say (with justice) that I write too much against the
rich, the very rich, learn that in Basil Blackwood's book and mine
which (INTERVAL: Elodie has come in since I wrote that to tell me
it was ten minutes to twelve by her watch, five by Shipley time: I told
her it was sixteen by Big Ben. Anyhow we went out and ritualled:*
Haud Mora: *The servants are assembled and drink with us. We may
not drink after twelve: a bottle of wine for the heretic servants: then
all doors are opened to let the old year out: Then we all go out of
doors: then the bell stops and there is a signal gun fired Horsham way:
then the bells begin again and it is New Year: The House must first
be entered by a Male with his Right foot. This is done by my son. End
of Ritual. I found our tom cat, a eunuch, and hoped he had not sneaked
in after twelve: Now I am returned to finish this letter) is called* Old
Peers in New Bottles, *we introduce a defence of the Very Rich:*

> *No tenants groan beneath his heartless sway:*
> *The heartlessness was all the other way:*
> *They loved to contradict his mildest whim,*
> *And when they groaned at all, they groaned at him.*

There is a picture of him at a meeting being groaned at.'[1]

[1] R. Speaight: *Letters of Hilaire Belloc*, p. 33.

Lord Finchley

Lord Finchley tried to mend the Electric Light Himself.

It struck him dead: And serve him right!
It is the business of the wealthy man
To give employment to the artisan.

Lord Hippo

Lord Hippo suffered fearful loss
By putting money on a horse
Which he believed, if it were pressed,
Would run far faster than the rest:
For

    someone who was in the know

    Had confidently told him so.

But

on the morning of the race

It only took

the *seventh* place!

Picture the Viscount's great surprise!
He scarcely could believe his eyes!

He sought the Individual who
Had laid him odds at 9 to 2,
Suggesting as a useful tip
That they should enter Partnership
And put to joint account the debt
Arising from his foolish bet.

But when the Bookie—oh! my word,
I only wish you could have heard
The way he roared he did not think,
And hoped that they might strike him pink!
Lord Hippo simply turned and ran
From this infuriated man.

Despairing, maddened and distraught
He utterly collapsed and sought
His sire,

the Earl of Potamus,
And brokenly addressed him thus:
'Dread Sire—to-day—at Ascot—I . . .'
His genial parent made reply:
'Come! Come! Come! Come! Don't look so glum!
Trust your Papa and name the sum. . . .'

What?

    . . . *Fifteen hundred thousand?* . . . Hum!
However . . . stiffen up, you wreck;
Boys will be boys—so here's the cheque!'
Lord Hippo, feeling deeply—well,
More grateful than he cared to tell—
Punted the lot on Little Nell:—
And got a telegram at dinner

To say

that he had backed the Winner!

XIX

From *The Four Men*
1912

The Four Men *is an account of a walking tour through Belloc's beloved County of Sussex (the original title given the book). It was in 1906 that Belloc and his wife went to live in Sussex where they bought a house at Shipley, seven miles south of Horsham, called King's Land, and where the Bellocs lived for the rest of their lives.*

The Four Men who tramped through Sussex all might be reflections of Belloc himself (the 'Poet')—the 'Sailor', Grizzlebeard and the 'Author'. The book has memorable affinities with The Path To Rome *though* The Four Men *has an Autumnal philosophy.*

The Best Thing and the Worst Thing
in the World

We went through the dark trees by a long green ride, climbing the gate that a rich man had put up and locked, and passing deeper and deeper into the wild, and in the little that we said to each other, Grizzlebeard, the Sailor and I, we hoped for rest very soon; but the Sailor went on before, knowing his way like a hound, and turning down this path and that until we came suddenly to a blot in the darkness, and a square of black stretching across the trees from side to side. It was a little hut.

The Sailor first tried the door, then, finding it locked, he pulled a key from his pocket and entered, and when he had got inside out of the breeze, he struck a match and lit a candle that was there, standing on a copper stick, and we all came in and looked around.

It was one room, and a small one, of weather boarding on all the four sides. There were two small windows, which were black in the candle light, and on the side to the right of the door a great fireplace of brick, with ashes in it and small wood and logs laid, and near this fireplace was a benched ingle-nook, and there were two rugs there. But for these things there was nothing in the hut whatsoever, no book or furniture at all, except the candlestick, and the floor was of beaten earth.

'Sailor,' said I, 'how did you come to have the key of this place?'

It was wonderful enough that he should have known his way to it. But the Sailor said:

'Why not?' and after that would tell us no more. Only he said before we slept, late as it was, we would do well to light the fire, and put upon it two or three more of the great logs that stood by, since in the autumn cold, we none of us should sleep however much we wrapped our cloaks about our feet, unless we had our feet to a blaze. And in this he was quite right, for no matter what the weather, and even out in the open, men can always sleep if they have a fire. So we made an agreement between us that Grizzlebeard, being an old man, was to have the bench and the rugs, but that we three were to stretch ourselves before the fire, when it should be lit;

and, talking so and still wideawake, we struck matches and tried to coax the flame.

But, at first, on account of the wind without, it lit badly, and the small wood was damp and smoked, and the smoke blew into our faces and into the room; and the Sailor, shielding it with his coat and trying to get a draught in that great chimney-place, said that a smoking chimney was a cursed thing.

'It is the worst thing in the world,' said the Poet peevishly; to which the Sailor answered:

'Nonsense! Death is the worst thing in the world.'

But Grizzlebeard, from where he lay on the broad bench with rugs about him, and his head resting on his hand, denied this too, speaking in a deep voice with wisdom. 'You are neither of you right,' he said. 'The worst thing in the world is the passing of human affection. No man who has lost a friend need fear death,' he said.

The Sailor. 'All that is Greek to me. If any man has made friends and lost them, it is I. I lost a friend in Lima once, but he turned up again at Valparaiso, and I can assure you that the time in between was no tragedy.'

Grizzlebeard (solemnly). 'You talk lightly as though you were a younger man than you are. The thing of which I am speaking is the gradual weakening, and at last the severance, of human bonds. It has been said that no man can see God and live. Here is another saying for you, very near the same: No man can be alone and live. None, not even in old age.'

He stopped and looked for some little time into the rising fire. Outside the wind went round the house, and one could hear the boughs in the darkness.

Then Grizzlebeard went on:

'When friendship disappears then there is a space left open to that awful loneliness of the outside which is like the cold of space between the planets. It is an air in which men perish utterly. Absolute dereliction is the death of the soul; and the end of living is a great love abandoned.'

Myself. 'But the place heals, Grizzlebeard.'

Grizzlebeard (still more solemnly). 'All wounds heal in those who are condemned to live, but in the very process of healing they harden and forbid renewal. The thing is over and done.'

He went on monotonous and grave. He said that 'everything else that there is in the action of the mind save loving is of its nature a growth: it goes through its phases of seed, of miraculous sprouting, of maturity, of somnolescence, and of decline. But with loving it is not so; for the comprehension by one soul of another is something borrowed from whatever lies outside time: it is not under the conditions of time. Then if it passes, it is past—it never grows again; and we lose it as men lose a diamond, or as men lose their honour.'

Myself. 'Since you talk of honour, Grizzlebeard, I should have thought that the loss of honour was worse than the loss of friends.'

Grizzlebeard. 'Oh, no. For the one is a positive loss, the other imaginary. Moreover, men that lose their honour have their way out by any one of the avenues of death. Not so men who lose the affection of a creature's eyes. Therein for them, I mean in death, is no solution: to escape from life is no escape from that loss. Nor of the many who have sought in death relief from their affairs is there one (at least of those I can remember) who sought that relief on account of the loss of a human heart.'

The Poet. 'When I said "it" was the worst thing in the world just now so angrily, I was foolish. I should have remembered the toothache.'

The Sailor (*eagerly and contemptuously*). 'Then there you are utterly wrong, for the earache is much worse.'

The Poet. 'I never had the earache.'

The Sailor (*still contemptuously*). 'I thought not! If you had you would write better verse. It is your innocence of the great emotions that makes your verse so dreadful—in the minor sense of that word.'

Grizzlebeard. 'You are both of you talking like children. The passing of human affection is the worst thing in the world. When our friends die they go from us, but it is not of their own will; or if it is of their own will, it is not of their own will in any contradiction to ours; or even if it be of their own will in contradiction to ours and the end of a quarrel, yet it is a violent thing and still savours of affection. But the decay of what is living in the heart, and that numbness supervening, and that last indifference—oh! these are not to be compared for unhappiness with any other ill on this unhappy earth. And all day long and in every place, if you could survey the world from a height and look down into the hearts of men, you would see that frost stealing on.'

Myself. 'Is this a thing that happens, Grizzlebeard, more notably to the old?'

Grizzlebeard. 'No. The old are used to it. They know it, but it is not notable to them. It is notable on the approach of middle age. When the enthusiasms of youth have grown either stale or divergent, and when, in the infinite opportunities which time affords, there has been opportunity for difference between friend and friend, then does the evil appear. The early years of a man's life do not commonly breed this accident. So convinced are we then, and of such energy in the pursuit of our goal, that if we must separate we part briskly, each certain that the other is guilty of a great wrong. The one man will have it that some criminal is innocent, the other that an innocent man was falsely called a criminal. The one man loves a war, the other thinks it unjust and hates it (for all save the money-dealers think of war in terms of justice). Or the one man hits the other in the face. These are violent things. But it is when youth has ripened, and when the slow processes of life begin that the danger or the certitude of this dreadful thing appears: I mean of the passing of affection. For the mind has settled as the waters of a lake settle in the hills; it is full of its own convictions, it is secure in its philosophy; it will not mould or adapt itself to the changes of another. And, therefore, unless communion be closely maintained, affection decays. Now when it has decayed, and when at last it has altogether passed, then comes that awful vision of which I have spoken, which is the worst thing in the world.'

The Poet. 'The great poets, Grizzlebeard, never would admit this thing. They have never sung or deplored the passage of human affection; they have sung of love turned to hatred, and of passion and of rage, and of the calm that succeeds passion, and of the doubt of the soul and of doom, and continually they have sung of death, but never of the evil of which you speak.'

The Sailor. 'That was because the evil was too dull; as I confess I find it! Anything duller than the loss of a friend! Why, it is like writing a poem on boredom or like singing a song about Welbeck Street, to try and poetize such things! Turn rather to this fire, which is beginning to blaze, thank God! turn to it, and expect the morning.'

163

Myself. 'You Poet and you Sailor, you are both of you wrong there. The thing has been touched upon, though very charily, for it is not matter for art. It just skims the surface of the return of Odysseus, and the poet Shakespeare has a song about it which you have doubtless heard. It is sung by gentlemen painted with grease paint and dressed in green cloth, one of whom is a Duke, and therefore wears a feather in his cap. They sit under canvas trees, also painted, and drink out of cardboard goblets, quite empty of all wine; these goblets are evidently empty, for they hold them anyhow; if there were real wine in them it would drop out. And thus accoutred and under circumstances so ridiculous, they sing a song called "Blow, blow, thou winter wind". Moreover, a poet has written of the evil thing in this very County of Sussex, in these two lines:

> The things I loved have all grown wearisome,
> The things that loved me are estranged or dead.'

Grizzlebeard. ' "Estranged" is the word: I was looking for that word. Estrangement is the saddest thing in the world.'

The Sailor. 'I cannot make head or tail of all this!'

The Poet. 'Have you never lost a friend?'

The Sailor. 'Dozens—as I've already told you. And the one I most regret was a doctor man whom the owners shipped with us for a run to the Plate and back again. But I have never let it weigh upon my mind.'

Grizzlebeard. 'The reason that the great poets have touched so little upon this thing is precisely because it is the worst thing in the world. It is a spur to no good deed, nor to any strong thinking, nor does it in any way emend the mind. Now the true poets, whether they will or no, are bound to emend the mind; they are constrained to concern themselves with noble things. But in this there is nothing noble. It has not even horror nor doom to enhance it; it is an end, and it is an end without fruition. It is an end which leaves no questions and no quest. It is an end without adventure, an end complete, a nothingness; and there is no matter for art in the mortal hunger of the soul.'

And after this sad speech of his we were again silent, lying now at length before the fire, and the Sailor having lit a pipe and smoking it.

Then I remembered a thing I had read once, and I said:

Myself. 'I read once in a book of a man who was crossing a heath in a wild country not far from the noise of the sea. The wind and the rain beat upon him, and it was very cold, so he was glad to see a light upon the heath a long way off. He made towards it and, coming into that place, found it to be a chapel where some twenty or thirty were singing, and there was a priest at the altar saying Mass at midnight, and there was a monk serving his Mass. Now this traveller noticed how warm and brilliant was the place; the windows shone with their colours, and all the stone was carved; the altar was all alight, and the place was full of singing, for the twenty or thirty still sang, and he sang with them . . . But their faces he could not see, for the priest who said the Mass and the man who served the Mass both had their faces from him, and all in that congregation were hooded, and their faces were turned away from him also, but their singing was loud, and he joined in it. He thought he was in fairyland. And so he was. For as that Mass ended he fell asleep, suffused with warmth, and his ears still full of music; but when he woke he found that the place was a ruin, the windows empty, and the wind roaring through; no glass, or rather a few broken panes, and these quite plain and colourless; dead leaves of trees blown in upon the altar steps, and over the whole of it the thin and miserable light of a winter dawn.

'This story which I read went on to say that the man went on his journey under that new and unhappy light of a stormy winter dawn, on over the heath in the wild country. But though he had made just such a journey the day before, yet his mind was changed. In the interlude he had lost something great; therefore the world was worth much less to him than it had been the day before, though if he had heard no singing in between, nor had seen no lights at evening, the journey would have seemed the same. This advantage first, and then that loss succeeding, had utterly impoverished him, and his journey meant nothing to him any more. This is the story which I read, and I take it you mean something of the kind.'

'Yes, I meant something of the kind,' said Grizzlebeard in answer, sighing. 'I was thinking of the light that shines through the horn, and how when the light is extinguished the horn thickens cold and dull. I was thinking of irrevocable things.'

At this the Poet, whom we had thought dozing, started to his feet.

'Oh, let us leave so disheartening a matter,' said he, 'and consider rather what is the best thing in the world than what is the worst. For in the midst of this wood, where everything is happy except man, and where the night should teach us quiet, we ought to learn or discover what is the best thing in the world.'

'I know of no way of doing that,' said the Sailor, 'but by watching the actions of men and seeing to what it is they will chiefly attach themselves. For man knows his own nature, and that which he pursues must surely be his satisfaction? Judging by which measure I determine that the best thing in the world is flying at full speed from pursuit, and keeping up hammer and thud and gasp and bleeding till the knees fail and the head grows dizzy, and at last we all fall down and that thing (whatever it is) which pursues us catches us up and eats our carcases. This way of managing our lives, I think, must be the best thing in the world—for nearly all men choose to live thus.'

Myself. 'What you say there, Sailor, seems sound enough, but I am a little puzzled in this point: why, if most men follow their satisfaction, most men come to so wretched an end?'

The Sailor. 'Why that I cannot tell. That is their business. But certainly as I have watched men it seems to me that they regard being hunted as the best thing in the world. For one man having as much as would enable him (if he were so inclined) to seek the world of God, and to eat all kinds of fruit and flesh, and to drink the best of beer, will none the less start a race with a Money-Devil: a fleet, strong Money-Devil with a goad. And when this Money-Devil has given him some five years start, say until he is nearly thirty years of age, then will that man start racing and careering and bounding and flying with the Money-Devil after him, over hill and valley, field and fen, and wood and waste, and the high heaths and the wolds, until at last (somewhere about sixty as a rule or a little later) he gives a great cry and throws up his hands and falls down. Then does the Money-Devil come and eat him up. Many millions love such a course.

'And there is also that other sort of hunt, in which some appetite or lust sets out a-chasing the jolly human, and puts him at fence and hedge, and gate and dyke, and round the spinney and over the stubble and racing over the bridge, and then double again through copse and close, and thicket and thorn, until he has spent his breath upon the high Downs, and then, after a little respite, a second clear run all the way to the grave. Which, when the hunted human sees it very near at hand, he commonly stops of set purpose, and this thing that has chased him catches him up and eats him, even as did the other. Millions are seen to pursue this lust-hunted course, and some even try to combine it with that other sort of money-devil-huntedness. But the advice is given to all in youth that they must make up their minds which of the two sorts of exercises they would choose, and the first is commonly praised and thought worthy; the second blamed. Why, I do not know. Our elders say to us, 'Boy, choose the Money-Devil, give that Lord his run.' Both kinds of sport have seemed to me most miserable, but then I speak only for myself, and I am eccentric in the holidays I choose and the felicity I discover for myself in the conduct of my years.

'For, so far as I am concerned, my pleasure is found rather in having a game with that Great Three-toed Sloth, which is the most amiable of hell's emissaries, and all my life have I played the jolly game of tickling him forward and lolloping in front of him, now lying down until he has caught me up, and then slouching off until he came near again, and even at times making a spurt that I might have the longer sleep at the end, and give honest Sloth a good long waddle for his money.

'Yet after all, my method is the same as every one else's, and will have the same end.

'For when I see the grave a long way off, then do I mean to put on slippers and to mix myself a great bowl of mulled wine with nutmegs, and to fill a pipe, and to sit me down in a great armchair before a fire of oak or beech, burning in a great hearth, within sound of the Southern Sea.

'And as I sit there, drinking my hot wine and smoking my long pipe, and watching the fire, and remembering old storms and land-falls far away, I shall hear the plodding and the paddling and the shuffling and the muffling of that great Sloth, my life's pursuer, and he will butt at my door with his snout, but I shall have been too lazy to lock it, and so shall he come in. Then the Great Three-toed Sloth will eat me up, and thus shall *I* find the end of my being and have reached the best thing in the world.'

Myself. 'While you were speaking, Sailor, it seemed to me you had forgotten one great felicity, manly purpose, and final completion of the immortal spirit, which is surely the digging of holes and the filling of them up again?'

The Sailor. 'You are right! I had forgotten that! It is indeed an admirable pastime, and for some, perhaps for many, it is the best thing in the world!'

Myself. 'Yes, indeed, for consider how we drink to thirst again, and eat to hunger again, and love for disappointment, and journey in order to return. And consider with what elaborate care we cut, clip, shave, remove and prune our hair and beard, which none the less will steadfastly re-grow, and how we earn money to spend it, and black boots before walking in the mire, and do penance before sinning, and sleep to wake, and wake to sleep; and very elaborately do pin, button, tie, hook, hang, lace, draw, pull up, be-tighten, and in diverse ways fasten about ourselves our very complicated clothes of a morning, only to unbutton, unpin, untie, unhook, let down, be-loosen, and in a thousand operations put them off again when midnight comes. Then there is the soiling of things for their cleansing, and the building of houses to pull them down again, and the making of wars for defeat or for barren victories, and the painting of pictures for the rich blind, and the singing of songs for the wealthy deaf, and the living of all life to the profit of others, and the begetting of children who may perpetuate all that same round. The more I think of it the more I see that the digging of holes and the filling of them up again is the true end of man and his felicity.'

The Poet. 'I think you must be wrong.'

Myself. 'Well then, since you know, what is the best thing in the world?'

The Poet. 'It is a mixture wherein should be compounded and intimately mixed great wads of unexpected money, new landscapes, and the return of old loves.'

The Sailor. 'Oh, hear him with his return of old loves! All coming in procession, two by two, like the old maids of Midhurst trooping out of church of a Sunday morning! One would think he had slain a hundred with his eye!'

Grizzlebeard. 'All you young men talk folly. The best thing in the world is sleep.'

And having said so much, Grizzlebeard stretched himself upon the bench along one side of the fire, and, pulling his blanket over his head, he would talk to us no more. And we also after a little while, lying huddled in our coats before the blaze, slept hard. And so we passed the hours till morning; now waking in the cold to start a log, then sleeping again. And all night long the wind sounded in the trees.

XX

From *The Servile State*
1912

'Widely distributed property as a condition of freedom is necessary to the normal satisfaction of human nature,' Belloc.

The seeds of the Servile State based on the Papal encyclical De Rezum Novarum *began to ferment with the passing of Lloyd George's Compulsory Health Insurance Act, wherein every employed person (other than domestic servants and agricultural labourers) had by law to contribute to buying weekly insurance stamps, the employer paying rather more than the employed. It was a major act to help the labouring classes over medical assistance and one would have thought that Belloc would have seen in this act a major contribution to society, but he saw it in a very different light. Belloc (and Chesterton and his followers) saw such legislation as taking away the personal liberties of the working classes and regimenting them within a class, thus becoming slaves of the Servile State. Belloc himself labelled it as 'an arrangement of society in which so considerable a number of families and individuals are constrained by positive law to labour for the advantage of other families and individuals as to stamp the whole community with the mark of such labour'.[1] In short Belloc propounded that the masses should own co-operatively or individually the means of production, and of course to a very large extent this has come true. The nationalized industries, the Co-operative Societies, the opportunities of the workers to acquire shares in the businesses in which they work (in other contexts Belloc*

[1] Shaw wrote to G. K. Chesterton on October 27, 1911 about a public debate with Belloc they were trying to arrange in which he said 'The disadvantages for us are that we both want Belloc to let himself go (I simply thirst for the blood of his Servile State—I'll servile him)!'

expressed himself forcibly as to government by a strong Monarchy as against an aristocratic autocracy, for he disliked parliamentary government especially by the Front bench). As Robert Speaight has pointed out 'Belloc believed that the rich would acquire the poor with the poor's consent'.[1] We give here Belloc's opening outlines of his Servile State.

[1] Speaight, *Belloc*, p. 318.

Section the First: Definitions

Man, like every other organism, can only live by the transformation of his environment to his own use. He must transform his environment from a condition where it is less to a condition where it is more subservient to his needs.

That special, conscious, and intelligent transformation of his environment, which is peculiar to the peculiar intelligence and creative faculty of man we call the *Production of Wealth*.

Wealth is matter which has been consciously and intelligently transformed from a condition in which it is less to a condition in which it is more serviceable to a human need.

Without *Wealth* man cannot exist. The production of it is a necessity to him, and though it proceeds from the more to the less necessary, and even to those forms of production which we call luxuries, yet in any given human society there is a certain *kind* and a certain *amount* of wealth without which human life cannot be lived: as, for instance, in England today, certain forms of elaborately prepared food, clothing, fuel, and habitation.

Therefore, to control the production of wealth is to control human life itself. To refuse man the opportunity for the production of wealth is to refuse him the opportunity for life; and, in general, the way in which the production of wealth is by law permitted is the only way in which the citizens can legally exist.

Wealth can only be produced by the application of human energy, mental and physical, to the forces of nature around us, and to the material which those forces inform.

This human energy so applicable to the material world and its forces we will call *Labour*. As for that material and those natural forces, we will call them, for the sake of shortness, by the narrow, but conventionally accepted, term *Land*.

It would seem, therefore, that all problems connected with the production of wealth, and all discussion thereupon, involve but two principal original factors, to wit, *Labour* and *Land*. But it so happens that the conscious, artificial, and intelligent action of man upon nature, corresponding to his peculiar character compared with other created beings, introduces a third factor of the utmost importance.

Man proceeds to create wealth by ingenious methods of varying and often increasing complexity, and aids himself by the construction of *implements*. These soon become in each new department of the production as truly necessary to that production as *labour* and *land*. Further, any process of production takes a certain time; during that time the producer must be fed, and clothed, and housed, and the rest of it. There must therefore be an *accumulation of wealth* created in the past, and reserved with the object of maintaining labour during its effort to produce for the future.

Whether it be the making of an instrument or tool, or the setting aside of a store of provisions, *labour* applied to *land* for either purpose is not producing wealth for immediate consumption. It is setting aside and reserving somewhat, and that *somewhat* is always necessary in varying proportions according to the simplicity or complexity of the economic society to the production of wealth.

To such wealth reserved and set aside for the purposes of future production, and not for immediate consumption, whether it be in the form of instruments and tools, or in the form of stores for the maintenance of labour during the process of production, we give the name of *Capital*.

There are thus three factors in the production of all human wealth, which we may conventionally term *Land*, *Capital*, and *Labour*.

When we talk of the *Means of Production* we signify land and capital combined. Thus, when we say that a man is 'dispossessed of the means of production', or cannot produce wealth save by the leave of another who 'possesses the means of production', we mean that he is the master only of his labour and has no control, in any useful amount, over either capital, or land, or both combined.

A man politically free, that is, one who enjoys the right before the law to exercise his energies when he pleases (or not at all if he does not please), but not possessed by legal right of control over any useful amount of the means of production, we call *proletarian*, and any considerable class composed of such men we call a *proletariat*.

Property is a term used for that arrangement in society whereby the control of land and of wealth made from land, including therefore all the means of production, is vested in some person or corporation. Thus we may say of a building, including the land upon which it stands, that it is the 'property' of such and such a citizen, or family, or college, or of the State, meaning that those who 'own' such property are guaranteed by the laws in the right to use it or withhold it from use. *Private property* signifies such wealth (including the means of production) as may, by the arrangements of society, be in the control of persons or corporations *other* than the political bodies of which these persons or corporations are in another aspect members. What distinguishes private property is not that the possessor thereof is less than the State, or is only a part of the State (for were that so we should talk of municipal property as private property), but rather that the owner may exercise his control over it to his own advantage, and not as a trustee for society, nor in the hierarchy of political institutions. Thus Mr Jones is a citizen of Manchester, but he does not own his private property as a citizen of Manchester, he owns it as Mr Jones, whereas, if the house next to his own be owned by the Manchester municipality, they own it only because they are a political body standing for the whole community of the town. Mr Jones might move to Glasgow and still own his property in Manchester, but the municipality of Manchester can only own its property in connection with the corporate political life of the town.

An ideal society in which the means of production should be in the hands of the political officers of the community we call *Collectivist*, or more generally *Socialist*.[1]

A society in which private property in land and capital, that is, the ownership and therefore the control of the means of production, is confined to some number of free citizens not large enough to determine the social mass of the State, while the rest have not such property and are therefore proletarian, we call *Capitalist*; and the method by which wealth is produced in such a society can only be the application of labour, the determining mass of which must necessarily be proletarian, to land and capital, in such fashion that, of the total wealth produced, the Proletariat which labours shall only receive a portion.

The two marks, then, defining the Capitalist State are: (1) That the citizens thereof are politically free: i.e. can use or withhold at will their possessions or their labour, but are also (2) divided into

[1] Save in this special sense of 'Collectivist', the word 'Socialist' has either no clear meaning, or is used synonymously with other older and better-known words.

capitalist and proletarian in such proportions that the State as a whole is not characterized by the institution of ownership among free citizens, but by the restriction of ownership to a section markedly less than the whole, or even to a small minority. Such a *Capitalist State* is essentially divided into two classes of free citizens, the one capitalist or owning, the other propertyless or proletarian.

My last definition concerns the Servile State itself, and since the idea is both somewhat novel and also the subject of this book, I will not only establish but expand its definition.

The definition of the Servile State is as follows:

'*That arrangement of society in which so considerable a number of the families and individuals are constrained by positive law to labour for the advantage of other families and individuals as to stamp the whole community with the mark of such labour we call* THE SERVILE STATE.'

Note first certain negative limitations in the above which must be clearly seized if we are not to lose clear thinking in a fog of metaphor and rhetoric.

That society is not servile in which men are intelligently constrained to labour by enthusiasm, by a religious tenet, or indirectly from fear of destitution, or directly from love of gain, or from the common sense which teaches them that by their labour they may increase their well-being.

A clear boundary exists between the servile and the non-servile condition of labour, and the conditions upon either side of that boundary utterly differ one from another. Where there is *compulsion* applicable by *positive law* to men of a certain *status*, and such compulsion enforced in the last resort by the powers at the disposal of the State, there is the institution of *Slavery*; and if that institution be sufficiently expanded the whole State may be said to repose upon a servile basis, and is a Servile State.

Where such formal, legal status is absent the conditions are not servile; and the difference between servitude and freedom, appreciable in a thousand details of actual life, is most glaring in this: that the free man can refuse his labour and use that refusal as an instrument wherewith to *bargain*; while the slave has no such instrument or power to bargain at all, but is dependent for his well-being upon the custom of society, backed by the regulation of such of its laws as may protect and guarantee the slave.

XXI

The Outbreak of War
1914

Writing in The Cruise of the Nona *on the outbreak of the war Belloc said: 'I do not think that posterity will depart from the general conclusion of our own times (which is certainly mine) that an early declaration of the British attitude would have prevented war. It is a question easily confused with a totally different one, and the two must be kept carefully apart. The* right *of Great Britain to remain neutral should surely be admitted, not only in law but in common sense. In law there was no definite agreement with the French. There was no accepted obligation to support the French in the West or elsewhere.' Belloc was in London with Auberon Lucas when war was at last declared on August 4th, and his first care was to stress on all around him the importance of knowing the exact position of every sack of flour in the British Isles. He saw General Macdonaugh at the War Office and offered his services; but Macdonaugh replied that he did not know where to send him. Belloc persisted in his attempts and on September 12th he was writing to Lady Juliet Duff: 'Not a sign for me to go yet, not even a divisional one. It is an abominable shame, and when I chuck it in disgust and try through the French, it may be too late—they will wonder why I didn't ask before.'*

On September 9th, however, a rich Australian, Murray (Jim) Allison who had the control of Land *and* Water, *visited him at King's Land, and he asked Belloc if he would regularly contribute to his paper. Belloc agreed. 'Belloc's articles brought a wider fame than any earned by his previous writings.* Land *and* Water *reached a circulation of 100,000 and the articles were discussed by men in every street, club, railway train or mess. People read Belloc on the war who had never read him on anything else.'*[1]

[1] R. Speaight: *Hilaire Belloc*, p. 148.

XXII

A Letter to Mrs Reginald Balfour
1917

As the war went on so Belloc continued writing for Land and Water, *though the circulation began to decrease. With the lulls in the fighting with the stringent censorship, there were many dfficulties. Nevertheless Nelson's made arrangements to reissue the work in quarterly installments under the title of* General History of the War. *As a result Belloc met and discussed the war more and more with the leaders of the nation . . . the Asquiths, Reginald McKenna, Haldane, etc, who were all known to him. Belloc also went to France continually as this letter proves and where he met Foch and Pétain.*

(*The notes to this letter are Robert Speaight's who edited* Letters From Hilaire Belloc 1958.)

To Mrs Reginald Balfour

PARIS. LA REGENCE
June 26, 1917

On the 12th (July) I go North to take the girls from their Convent[1] and to pass a couple of nights with them at a friend's house in Manchester: the Goodwins, old friends of Elodie's and mine who used to subscribe vastly to my Parliamentary expenses and who very much want to know the girls—as I also want Eleanor and Elizabeth to know them . . . Then we settle down at home for the holidays, except the time we hope to be at Lynton. . . . I think the children particularly want the *bathing*. It is good for them, too.

I saw General Foch on Saturday. A *really* delightful man, full of genius and movement. He confirmed me in what I had said of the Marne and drew a little rough plan for me, which will be the most precious possession when I have it framed in my house. On Sunday I was at a crowded High Mass at Notre Dame. It is getting its own back in spite of being so far from the inhabited quarters. Then I saw the *Abbé Dimnet*. I don't know if you have met him. He is already, and can be much more, a link between the handful of English Catholics and the French. He is a wonderful English scholar.

Next time he is in London I will try and get him to a meal so that, if you will come too, you can make his acquaintance. I think you would like him. Eccles[2] knows him well and he is also, oddly enough, the French correspondent of the *Saturday Review*. I am to see him again before leaving.

Yesterday, Monday, I went to French Headquarters. I saw General Pétain at some length and then spent the day with the IInd Bureau, the Intelligence, to see all the latest statistics. It was a wonderful day's work! Difficult only for the slow journey in broiling heat. These journeys as a whole are terribly fatiguing but they

[1] The convent of Dominican Nuns at Stone, in Staffordshire, where Eleanor and Elizabeth Belloc were at school.
[2] Francis Yvon Eccles, Professor of French Literature in the University of London, 1920–34, and a close friend and Oxford contemporary of Belloc. See *The Life of Hilaire Belloc, passim*.

are worth it. The real strain is the journey to Paris—which this time I risked by night though I ought not to have done so. I happened to travel with Teano, the learned and very anti-Catholic Italian aristocrat whom they are always sending back and forth during the war between London and Rome.

Talking of which I cannot tell you what a relief it is to be with soldiers after, or in the intervals of, that political world which everywhere in this war is the opponent of the Faith. I get, too often, into the mood of finding this perpetual struggle in an isolated minority *useless*: like blows against the void. . . . But one has to go on: and getting into a fully Catholic atmosphere even for a few hours is like a bath, for refreshment.

I have the impression that after so tremendous a strain the partial government of Western and Southern Europe by anti-national cliques—mainly Masonic—will break down. But it may take longer. These recoveries of the Faith are slow things, and work in quite unexpected fashion by unexpected agents at unexpected times. At any rate both France and Italy had sickened of such minority Government long before the War and the War may bring a crisis, after victory. I pray God it may!

I am afraid I shall not be able to see Castelnau.[1] I very much wanted to, and Don Gregory[2] gave me a note for him, but it is an immense distance to go and very, very slow means of communication so I fear I shall not have the time. That probably means that I shall not see him in the course of the war unless he comes to London again.

I am afraid I shan't see Maurice Baring on the way back: I was at the Aviation Headquarters only a month ago and it is too early to ask myself again. But I shall try and stop at the PNTO office—the Naval Transport people—on the way back, and probably I shall get him on the telephone there . . .

Never did I think in the old days that there would come a time when I should find work too much for me and need rest—but I do now, and I envy those who obtain it beyond words . . .

By the way, did you read in the papers of the Poets' Gathering, where the rich made me read verses among others? It was extraordinarily funny.

[1] General de Castelnau (1851–1944).
[2] J. D. Gregory of the Foreign Office.

XXIII

A Letter to Lady Juliet Duff

1920

Belloc went to Morocco for the first time in September 1920, and as can be read in this letter, he met Lyautey, who was then Governor-General.

As to his travels in Spain, some of Belloc's best accounts of that country may be read in Many Cities *(1928).*

To Lady Juliet Duff

CORDOVA
October 11, 1920

I went through a desert to Taza where I supped with the soldiers who were going on to the mountain Atlas next day to try and frighten the Beni Warin, who had for many weeks been annoying them. They sent me on in the early morning by a motor car to Fez. All the way along under the bare mountains are stone block houses with barbed wire around them and these posts keep the road open by day, but by night no one can yet travel in that part which is called 'couloir de Taza' and still kept open with difficulty. But nearing Fez the country grows open and pacified though still all baked and treeless.

Fez is like what I have heard Damascus to be—a great island of green in the midst of hot bare sand and clay. It is on a slope through which pour the divided channels of a torrent, making a sound of water everywhere and feeding fountains in cool white courts. There are many fine houses of the Arabian sort in Fez with palm trees, shade and splashing jets and in one of these did I call on General Bertrand the Governor, a man grown sour through the excessive, the appalling, ugliness of his wife. I have always maintained that ugly women were the happiest and therefore good companions for men—but there are limits—and this women was quite beyond the line. At Fez they are building a large new French town.

From Fez I went to Meknes, where they are building a still larger French town, and from Meknes by a mountain tramway to Rabat. On the way to Rabat the little train went off the rails—a baby railway accident all on a tiny scale. At Rabat I dined with Lyautey—a remarkable man who talks all the time and says what he thinks—which is a relief nowadays. He had just had news of a remarkable thing. A certain negro chief of the south had sent him a deputation, a sort of nigger privy council to discuss matters with him. They were on a ship and on the same ship were 2 lions in a cage and 20 bullocks. At the port, as the ship was too deep to get in, the 20 cattle and the two lions and the nigger privy council were all put on to a lighter to be landed. A rope from the lighter tugged it toward the shore. But the rope broke, and as the wind was off-shore, the lighter, with the nigger right Honourables, the 2 lions and the 20 bullocks all drifted out into the Atlantic together and no one knows what become of them. Such news had I from Lyautey.

XXIV

A Letter to Mrs Raymond Asquith

1921

To Mrs Raymond Asquith

March 6, 1921

I have been all over the place. At Mons, where I had not been since 1912 and where I found a very active legend of the old Professional army of '14. It was touching to come across that memory. The English army, with its intense regimental traditions and its very high training, had remained something separate in Europe. It was vastly admired. It was very small, but this idea of *Une armée de Métier* appealed strongly to the body of officers in France, and by a repercussion to the half-soldier officers here. All the discipline and correctitude of that organism impressed civilians profoundly. Incidentally, they had much the best fire drill in Europe. All through the war the Guards, in spite of their flood of new recruitment, kept it up: they remained professional to the end: a singular proof of the value there is in a *cadre*. I am not sure that the astonishing effort which produced the two million fighting and organized men before the end and out of nothing was not a greater proof of the national vigour and spontaneity, but it was a different thing: and you will find, all over northern France (and over the border in Belgium), this tenacious recollection of the old army which England alone had preserved after the earthquake of the French Revolution.

They are rebuilding here, vigorously. They have not lost many of the young and active men: that gives them the power to work again. The French have lost about half of the men (by death or wounds or shock) of the ages which are now from 25 to 40, and which were in late '15 from 20 to 35. It is a startling gap, and it has—at least at first—paralysed them, though they are slowly recovering. Moreover in Belgium all the coal mines and most of the machinery remained intact—because the Germans meant to make a federal state of the place: whereas in France all was systematically destroyed in order to cripple rivalry after the war.

Next day I would have left by way of Casablanca and the sea. But the rains broke that very day in a violent storm and, as the port is unfinished, the boat that was due could not touch port and there was indefinite delay. I waited, but the storm still blew. So on the third day I hired a motor at vast expense to take me to Tangier whence I could get a boat any day to Spain. The new road is made for only ⅓ of the way. After that there is a track—often lost—over mere earth. The road stopped at the crossing of the large river Sebou (by a native ferry of huge size capable of taking many camels) beyond it was all dark earth. This the storm had somewhat thickened and the motor plowed through it slowly till dark at about 8 miles an hour. After dark we happily saw a light which was that of a lonely French farm and there we passed the night on hay. But that night a violent storm of rain drenched all the land and next day the motor hardly moved, so thick was the mud. By noon we had gone from 20 to 30 miles and were at the river Loukows, but trying to slide down the steep bank of this ditch (all mud and grease) the lowest gear of the motor broke so that its strongest power was gone: it could still crawl along flat earth fairly dry but could not move up any sharp rise or where any deep mud was. To reach Tangier (60 miles off still) over hills and deep mud was now impossible. So what I did was this. I hired 6 natives and a rope. Then, hearing that there was sand rather than mud on the track at Larache nearby on the coast I made for Larache. At every little rise the natives hauled the motor with the rope and when it could crawl they ran or walked by the side. At last—at dusk—I reached Larache (held by the Spaniards—a small delightful town with a neat little harbour) and there expected to remain bottled up indefinitely, but I had then my first piece of luck. I found a man in the darkness who told me of a little Spanish steamer that was going to try and start next day if the weather moderated. It was a wretched dirty little boat, laden with eggs, cocks and hens and stinking quite extraordinarily. It got out with some difficulty through very big waves and all next day rolled and pawed through the Atlantic. At sunset I saw the straits of Gibraltar far away eastward looking very fine. All that night I lay out on deck saying to myself that I was too old for that sort of thing. I had some bread with me and a little wine. We got into Cadiz harbour in the small hours before dawn. I was very tired. I gave the captain a pound—which was too much. But I was glad to get back to Europe. I went on to Seville, then here and tonight I go on to Madrid. The cathedral of Seville is the noblest work of man. The cathedral of Cordova which is an old mosque is absurdly overrated, but the more modern part of the sixteenth century is fine.

XXV

From *The Jews*

1922

One of Belloc's perpetual itches was 'the Jewish problem'; it was in truth far more a Belloc problem, for it gained him the tag of being an anti-semite. He therefore went to considerable lengths to prove that he had no quarrel with Jewry, and there appeared in 1922 his study The Jews. *He argued the age-long question as to whether Jewry was a race or was a religion, and on this vital point he maintained that the Jews were a race, and that therefore they could never be assimilated into a Western European society. His work received much critical comment, from both sides of the fence.*

This book, incidentally, was dedicated to Miss Ruby Goldsmith, who was Jewish, and was Belloc's secretary for over fourteen years, joining him in 1908.

The Thesis

It is the thesis of this book that the continued presence of the Jewish nation intermixed with other nations alien to it presents a permanent problem of the gravest character: that the wholly different culture, tradition, race and religion of Europe make Europe a permanent antagonist to Israel, and that the recent and rapid intensification of that antagonism gives to the discovery of a solution immediate and highly practical importance.

For if the quarrel is allowed to rise unchecked and to proceed unappeased, we shall come, unexpectedly and soon, upon one of these tragedies which have marked for centuries the relations between this peculiar nation and ourselves.

The Jewish problem is one to which no true parallel can be found, for the historical and social phenomenon which has produced it is unique. It is a problem which cannot be shirked, as the last generation of both Jews and of their hosts attempted to shirk it. It is a problem which cannot be avoided, nor even lessened (as can some social problems), by an healing effect of time: for it is increasing before our eyes. It must be met and dealt with openly and now. . . .

This book has been written to advocate a policy wherein the Jews on their side shall openly recognize their wholly separate nationality and we on ours shall equally recognize that separate nationality, treat it without reserve as an alien thing, and respect it as a province of society outside our own. . . .

Even today, in spite of a vast increase during our generation, both in the public appreciation of the problem and in its immediate gravity, there are very many men who still regard absorption as the natural end of the affair. These, though dwindling, are still numerous upon the non-Jewish side; upon the other, the Jewish side, they are, I think, a very small body. For I note that even those Jews who think absorption will come, admit it with regret, and certainly the vast majority would insist with pride upon the certain survival of Israel.

But here I maintain that we have the index of history against us. In point of fact absorption has not taken place. It has had a better chance than any corresponding case can show: ample time in which to work, wide dispersion, constant intermarriage, long periods of tolerant friendship for the Jew, and even at times his ascendancy. If ever there were conditions under which one might imagine that the larger body would absorb the smaller, they were those of Christendom acting intimately for centuries, in relation with Jewry . . . but the Jew has remained intact. . . . The continuous absorption of outlying fractions, a process continually going on wherever the Jewish nation is present, has not affected the mass of the problem at all. The body as a whole has remained separate, differentiated, with a strong identity of its own under all conditions and in all places, the *a priori* reasoning, by which men come to think this solution reasonable, is nullified by an experience apparent throughout history. That experience is wholly against any such solution. . . .

If the Jewish nation comes to express its own pride and patriotism openly, and *equally openly to admit the necessary limitations imposed by that expression*; if we on our side frankly accept the presence of this nation as a thing utterly different from ourselves, but with just as good a right to existence as we have; if we renounce our pretences in the matter; if we talk of and recognize the Jewish people freely and without fear as a separate body; if upon both sides the realities of the situation are admitted, with the consequent and necessary definitions with those realities imply, we shall have peace.

The advantage both parties—the small but intense Jewish minority, the great non-Jewish majority in the midst of which that minority acts—would discover in such an arrangement is manifest. If it could be maintained—as I think it could be maintained—the problem would be permanently solved. At any rate, if it cannot be solved in that way it certainly cannot be solved in any other, and if we do not get peace by this avenue, then we are doomed to the perpetual recurrence of those persecutions which have marred the history of Europe since the first consolidation of the Roman Empire. . . .

The opposition to it is diverse and formidable but can everywhere be reduced upon analysis to some form of falsehood. This falsehood takes the shape of denying the existence of the problem, of remaining silent upon it, or of pretending friendly emotions in public commerce which are belied by every phrase and gesture admitted in private. Or it takes the shape of defining the problem in false terms, in proclaiming it essentially religious whereas it is essentially national. Worst of all, it may be that very modern kind of falsehood, a statement of the truth accompanied by a statement of its contradiction, like the precious modern lie that one can be a patriot and at the same time international. In the case of the Jews, this particular modern lie takes the shape of admitting that they (the Jews) are wholly alien to us and different from us, of talking of them as such and even writing of them as such, and yet, in another connection, talking and writing of them as though no such violent contrast were present. That pretence of reconciling contradictions is the lie in the soul. Its punishment is immediate, for those who indulge in it are blinded.

All opposition that ever I have met to the solution here proposed is an opposition sprung from the spirit of untruth; and if there were no other argument in favour of an honest and moral settlement of the dispute, the one argument based on Truth would, I think, be sufficient. It is a social truth that there is a Jewish nation, alien to us and therefore irritant. It is a moral truth that expulsion and worse are remedies to be avoided. It is an historical truth that those solutions have always ultimately failed; the recognition of those three truths alone will set us right. . . .

If the solution I propose be the right solution, it yet remains to be determined whether it should first take the form of new laws from which a new spirit may be expected to grow, or first take the form of a new spirit and practice from which new laws shall spring. The order is of essential importance; for to mistake it, to reverse the true sequence of cause and effect, is the prime cause of failure in all social reform. . . .

If it be possible to create an atmosphere wherein the Jews are spoken of openly, and they in their turn admit, define, and accept the consequences of a separate nationality in our midst, *then*, such a spirit once established, laws and regulations consonant to it will naturally follow. But I am convinced that the reversing of this process would only lead first to confusion and next to disaster, both for Israel and for ourselves.

The Special Causes of Friction

There are two special forces upon the Jewish side which nourish and exasperate the inevitable friction between the Jewish race and its hosts. It will be well to deal with these before passing to the corresponding forces upon our side. For to find a remedy it is necessary to diagnose the disease.

The two main Jewish forces which exasperate and maintain the sense of friction between the Jews and their hosts are first of all the Jewish reliance upon secrecy, and, secondly, the Jewish expression of superiority.

THE JEWISH RELIANCE UPON SECRECY

It has unfortunately now become a habit for so many generations, that it has almost passed into an instinct throughout the Jewish body, to rely upon the weapon of secrecy. Secret societies, a language kept as far as possible secret, the use of false names in order to hide secret movements, secret relations between various parts of the Jewish body: all these and other forms of secrecy have become the national method. It is a method to be deplored, not because of its indignity and falsehood degrade the Jew—that is not our affair—but rather on account of the ill effects this policy produces on our mutual relations. It feeds and intensifies the antagonism already excited by racial contrast.

But before we go further it is essential to be just: for no one understand anything if he attacks it unjustly.

The Jewish habit of secrecy—the assumption of false names and the pretence of non-Jewish origin in individuals, the concealment of relationships and the rest of it—have presumably sprung from the experience of the race. Let a man put himself in the place of the Jew and he will see how sound the presumption is. A race scattered, persecuted, often despised, always suspected and nearly always hated by those among whom it moves, is constrained by something like physical force to the use of secret methods.

Take the particular trick of false names. It seems to us particularly odious. We think when we show our contempt for those who use this subterfuge that we are giving them no more than they deserve. It is a meanness which we associate with criminals and vagabonds; a piece of crawling and sneaking. We suspect its practisers of desiring to hide something which would bring them into disgrace if it were known, or of desiring to overreach their fellows in commerce by a form of falshood.

But the Jew has other and better motives. As one of their community said to me with great force, when I discussed the matter with him many years ago at a City dinner, 'When we work under our own names, you abuse us as Jews. When we work under *your* names you abuse us as forgers.' The Jew has often felt himself so handicapped if he declared himself, that he was half forced, or at any rate grievously tempted, to a piece of baseness which was never a temptation to us. Surely all this carefully arranged code of assumed patronymics (Stanley for Solomon, Curzon for Cohen, Sinclair for Slezinger, Montague for Moses, Benson for Benjamin, etc. etc.) had its root in that.

The Jew can plead something further in extenuation of this practice. Family names did not grow up naturally with them, as with us, in the course of the Middle Ages. The Jew retained, as we long retained in the middle and lower ranks of European society, the simple habit of possessing one personal name and differentiating a man from his fellows by introducing the name of his father. Thus a Jew in the sixteenth century was Moses ben Solomon, just as the Cromwell's ancestor of the same generation was William ap Williams. He had not what we call a surname or family name. In the same way until varying dates, early in France and England and other western countries, much later in Wales, Brittany, Poland and the Slav countries of the East, a man was known only by his personal name, distinguished, if that were necessary, by mentioning also the name of his father, or, in some cases, of his tribe.

Properly speaking the Jews have no surnames, and they may say with justice, 'Since we were compelled to take surnames arbitrarily' (which was the case in the Germanies and sometimes elsewhere as well), you cannot blame us if we attach no particular sanctity to the custom.' If a Jew of plain Jewish name was compelled by alien force to take the fancy name of Flowerfield, he is surely free to change that fancy name, for which he is not responsible, to any other he chooses. There was a good reason for the Government to force the name upon him. Only thus could he be registered and his actions traced. But forced it was, and therefore, on him, not morally binding.

All this is true, but there remains an element not to be accounted for on any such pleas. There are in the experience of all of us, an experience repeated indefinitely, men who have no excuse whatsoever for a false name save that advantage of deceit. Men whose race is universally known will unblushingly adopt a false name as a mask, and after a year or two pretend to treat it as an insult if their original and true name be used in its place. This is particularly the case with the great financial families. Some, indeed, have the pride to maintain the original patronymic and refuse to change it in any of their descendants. But the great mass of them concealed their relations one with another by adopting all manner of fantastic titles, and there can be no object in such a proceeding save the object of deception. I admit it is a form of protection, and especially do I admit that in its origin it may have mainly derived from a necessity for self-protection. But I maintain that today the practice does nothing but harm to the Jew. There are other races which have suffered persecution, many of them, up and down the world, and we do not find in them a universal habit of this kind.

Again, who can say that the bearing of a Jewish name today, or at any rate in the immediate past, is or was a handicap in commerce where occidental nations were concerned? And as for the Eastern nations, the Jews there are so sharply differentiated that a false name can be of no service merely to hide the racial character of its bearer. There must be another motive present.

The same arguments apply for and against other forms of secrecy. A man may plead that if secrecy in relationship were not maintained the dislike of the Jews would lead to false accusations. The Jew is highly individual, especially in intellectual affairs. He takes his own line. He expresses his opinions with singular courage. And such individual opinions will often differ violently from those of men with whom he is most closely connected. 'Why', I can understand some distinguished Jewish publicist saying, 'should I be compromised by people knowing that such-and-such a Bolshevist in Moscow or in New York is my cousin or nephew? I am conservative in temperament; I have always served faithfully the state in which I live; I heartily disapprove of these people's views and actions. If their relationship with me were known I should fall under the common ban. That would be unjust. Therefore I keep the relationship secret.'

The plea is sound, but it does not cover the ground. It is not sufficient to explain, for instance, the habit of hiding relationship between men equally distinguished and equally approved in the different societies in which they move. It does not explain why we must be left in ignorance of the fact that a man whom we are treating as the best of fellow-citizens should hide his connection with another man who is treated with equal honour in another country. There are occasions where national conflicts make the thing explicable. A Jew in England with a brother in Germany and a father at Constantinople might well be excused in 1915 for calling himself Montmorency. Yet we note that often where there is most need to hide the connection, the connection is not hidden at all. . . . The Rothschilds, present in the various capitals of Europe, have never pretended to hide their mutual relationships, and no one has thought any the worse of them, nor has this open practice in any way diminished their financial power.

There must be more than necessity at work; I suggest there is something like instinct, or, at any rate, an inherited tradition so strong that recourse to it seems natural.

Now it cannot be too forcibly emphasized that secrecy in any of these forms—working through secret societies, using false names, hiding of relationships, denying Jewish origin—specially exasperates this, our own race, among which the Jews are thrown in their dispersion. It is invariably discovered, sooner or later, and whenever it is discovered men have an angry feeling that they have been duped, even in cases where the practice is most innocent and no more than the following of something like a ritual.

I doubt whether the Jews have any idea how strongly this force works against them. . . . Everybody knows the international position of the Jew. Everybody knows that he cannot avoid that position. Everybody makes allowances for it. And I conceive that the abandonment of this habit of secrecy is not only possible but would be very greatly to the advantage of the whole race.

Perhaps its most absurd form (not its most dangerous form) is the secrecy maintained by distinguished men with regard to their Jewish ancestors. They and their Jewish relations often suppress it altogether or, at best, touch on it rarely and obscurely. Why should they act thus? Take the case of two men at random out of hundreds whose names are universally known and by most people respected, the name of Charles Kingsley, the writer, and the name of Moss-Booth, the founder of the Salvation Army. Here are two men who in very different fields played a great part in English life and who both owed their genius and nearly all their physical appearance to Jewish mothers. I should have thought it to the advantage of the Jewish race and of the individuals concerned that this fact should be widely known. The literary abilities of Charles Kingsley, the organizing and other abilities of Booth are not lessened in people's eyes, but, if anything, enhanced, by a knowledge of their true lineage. Yet the mention of that lineage is treated as though it were a sort of insult. . . . The Jews cannot have their cake and eat it too. If it is—surely it must be—in their eyes a matter for pride to belong to blood which they hold to be superior and to a tradition of such immense antiquity, then it cannot be at the same time a matter of insult. Yet the convention is desperately maintained by the Jews themselves. If a man tells me that he hates the English, and in reply I say, 'That's because you're an Irishman,' he does not fly at my throat. He takes it as a matter of course that the history of the English government in Ireland excuses his expression. So far from being insulted at being called an Irishman he would be insulted if you said he was not an Irishman. And so it is with many another nationality which has suffered oppression and persecution. I can find no rational basis for a contrary policy in the case of the Jews. Moreover the habit does this further harm: it makes men ascribe a Jewish character to anything they dislike, and thus extends undeservedly the odium against the race. . . .

It is not always recognized in this connection that the Jewish 'booms' which are so fruitful a cause of exasperation, depend on this same policy of concealment and on that account add to the volume of anger as each new trick is discovered.

Not that the objects of these world-wide campaigns are unworthy of attention. The Jewish actor, or film-star, or writer or scientist selected is usually talented; the victim of injustice whose case is advertised on the big drum has often a genuine grievance. But that the notice demanded is out of all proportion and that its dependence on Jewish organization is always kept hidden.

THE JEWS

So much for the element of secret action. A great deal more might be written upon it, but there are two reasons against enlarging thereon. First, a full discussion would take up far too much of my space; secondly, it would tend to add what I particularly wish to avoid in these pages, I mean emphasis upon the errors of the Jew. It would continue a quarrel, our whole object in which is to find peace.

THE EXPRESSION OF SUPERIORITY BY THE JEW

This is a very different matter. The mere *sense* of superiority is not something in which any special policy can be recommended, because it is there and cannot be remedied. It is part of the whole position. But it is possible to restrain its expression. For that purpose it is of value to define it, to put it upon record and to estimate its effect upon our issue.

The Jew individually feels himself superior to his non-Jewish contemporary and neighbour of whatever race, and particularly of our race; the Jew feels his nation immeasurably superior to any other human community, and particularly to our modern national communities in Europe.

The frank statement of so simple and fundamental a truth is rarely made. It will sound, I fear, shocking in many ears. To many others it will sound not so much shocking as comic, and to many more stupefying.

The idea that the Jew should think of himself our superior is something so incomprehensible to us that we forget the existence of the feeling. If it be constantly reiterated for the purpose of dealing with this great political difficulty, it is perhaps reluctantly admitted, but still held as a sort of abnormal, bewildering truth. I contend that the forgetfulness of that truth, the attempt to solve the problem without that truth remaining constant and fixed in the mind of the statesman, is in a very large measure the cause of our failure in the past; and that the way the Jew openly acts upon it in gesture, tone, manner, social assertion, is a very important factor in the quarrel between his race and ours. . . .

There is one last thing to be said, which it is almost impossible to say without the danger of giving pain and therefore of confusing the problem and making the solution more difficult. But it must be said, because, if we shirk it, the problem is confused the more. It is this: While it is undoubtedly true, that a Jew feels himself the superior of his hosts, it is also true that his hosts feel themselves immeasurably superior to the Jew. We can only arrive at a just and peaceable solution of our difficulties by remembering that the Jew to whom we have given special and alien status in the Commonwealth, is all the while thinking of himself as our superior. But on his side the Jew must recognize, however unpalatable to him the recognition may be, that those among whom he is living and whose inferiority he takes for granted, on *their* side regard him as something much less than themselves. . . .

In general, there is no success over others, nor even (which is much more necessary), any permanent arrangement possible with others, unless we know, allow for, and act upon the self-judgement of others, however wrong we may believe that self-judgement may be.

In the way of frankly recognizing, examining, taking an open interest in the Jewish minority in our midst there lie three very powerful obstacles. First, the inherited convention of polite society, secondly, and much the most powerful, fear; and thirdly, the very reputable desire to avoid offence. . . . You can meet an Irishman and discuss with him the conditions of his nation. You can ask an Italian when he was last in Italy; or congratulate a Frenchman upon his acquisition of your tongue or tell him that it is difficult for him to understand your own customs: but a convention arose under the Liberal fiction. . . that to do any of these very natural things in the case of Jew is monstrous. Your audience is shocked if you ask some learned Jew at a public table a question upon his national history of literature. It is a solecism to refer to his nationality at all, save perhaps now and then in terms of foolish praise—in nine times out of ten praise not to the point and not desired by its recipient. . . . I do not take offence if some chance acquaintance, noting my French name, talks to me about France, or is interested in my experience as a conscript long ago in that country. . . . But in the matter of the Jew there is this convention cutting you off from any such straightforward and simple way of dealing with a fellow-being. That convention, I say, must be broken down if we are to get any results at all and to establish a permanent peace.

The thing was not, of course, entirely irrational in origin. No custom is. It was to be excused upon several grounds.

First, there was the fact that many people were known to cherish so strong an hostility to Jews that to emphasize the Jewish character of anyone present might awaken that hostility. . . . But much the strongest excuse for the convention was the well-founded idea that its exercise pleased the Jews themselves. Men avoided the direct mention of Jewish nationality because it was felt that such direct mention was almost an insult. It was a thing which the Jew in whose presence you found yourself desired to have kept in the background; and though we might not understand why he desired it, yet we respected his desire as we do that of anyone with whom we wish to preserve harmonious relations. . . . Whether the Jews were wise or not to cherish that convention, as they undoubtedly did, does not concern this part of my argument. I am talking of our duty and not of theirs. But I say that unless the convention is softened and at last dissolved, nothing can be done. Both parties should know that it only does harm. It renders stilted and absurd all our relations; it fosters that suspicion of secrecy which I have insisted upon as the chief irritant in those relations, and it creates a feeling of exception, of oddity, which is the very worst service that could be rendered to the Jews themselves.

For whatever reason open discussion is burked, even for the reason of charity, we only put off the evil day, and charity so used may be compared to the charity which refuses to take action in any other critical problem of increasing gravity. The charity which hesitates to control the supplies of a spendthrift, or to wage a defensive war in a just cause, or to defend an oppressed man at the risk of quarrelling with his oppressor, is a charity mis-directed.

There remains the chief obstacle—that of fear.

There is no doubt that the strongest force still restraining an expression of hostility to the Jew is fear.

In a sense, of course, there is a 'fear' of breaking convention—but that is fear only in metaphor. I mean not this, but the very real dread of consequences; the feeling that an expression of hostility to Jewish power may bring definite evils on the individual guilty of it, and a panic lest those evils should fall upon him. How strong this feeling is, anyone can testify who has explored, as I have this most insistent of modern political ills; and doubtless the greater part of my non-Jewish readers will recall example to the point.

It is a fear of two consequences, social and economic, and even of both combined. Men dread lest hostile to the Jewish Domination should bring them into the grip of some unknown but suspected world-wide power—some would call it a conspiracy—which can destroy the individual who shall be so rash as to challenge it. Some perhaps have gone to the length—the insane length—of reading the word 'destroy' in its literal sense and of fearing for their lives. Such an illusion is laughable. But very many more are affected by the reasonable conception that they will have against them, if they provoke it, an intelligent, combined action which they cannot meet because there is no organization upon their side: because it is international; because there is behind it a great intensity of feeling; because through finance it controls the political machines of all the nations, because it is all-powerful in the Press—and so forth.

They dread, I say, the social consequences. They also (and that with more definition and more sense) dread the economic consequences. They recognize (they also exaggerate) the grip of the Jew over finance. They conceive that if they speak they will be dragged down, their enterprises ruined, their credit dissolved. And that is the most powerful instrument which can be brought to bear. When supernatural motives disappear the strongest motive remaining after appetite is avarice; and avarice is more universal than appetite and more continuous. Nor is it only avarice which is at work here, but also the respectable desire for security. There are today innumerable men who would express publicly on Jews what they continually express in private, but who conceal their feelings for fear that their salaries may be lost or their modest enterprises wrecked, their investments lowered, and their position ruined. Above them are a lesser number, equally convinced that their large fortunes would be in peril were they so to act.

The characteristic of all this feeling is two-fold. In the first place, as would seem to be the case with convention, though in a much greater degree, it dams up and enormously increases the latent force of anger against Jewish power both real and imaginary. It is like the piling up of a head of water when a river valley is obstructed, or like the introducing of resistance into an electric current. The suppression of resentment, though that suppression is the act of the men who themselves feel the resentment and not directly of their opponents, is a fierce irritant and accounts for the high pressure at which attack escapes when once it is loosened. . . .

Herein lies the peril to Israel of such a state of affairs. But with that I am not here concerned. I am only concerned with its effect upon ourselves. So long as we degrade ourselves, so long as we humiliate ourselves by our own cowardice, so long as we shirk all reasonable discussion, let alone all expression of hostility because we dread the consequences at the hands of our opponents, so long there are present in rising intensity two evil things: first, the postponement of the right solution; secondly, the turning of a reasoned policy into mere hatred with all the consequences which flow from such evil emotion.

The longer we maintain whatever remains of that barrier to free speech (happily it is already crumbling) the longer do we produce the two fatal results of postponing justice and of creating enmity. The destruction of that barrier, the ridding of ourselves of fear in the matter, is, as is always the case in the exercising of this un-manly thing, a matter for individual effort. As the proverb goes, 'Someone must bell the cat', which is another way of saying that if each man waits upon his neighbour, things will only grow worse and worse.

It is for each in his place, before it is too late, to approach the Jewish problem and to discuss it openly; to preface that discussion by a frank interest and a general expression upon all those things in the minority which directly concern its relations with the majority; to deal with the Jewish nation exactly as one would wish any other. . . .

XXVI

From *The Mercy of Allah*

1922

The English novel has produced some admirable examples of the school of The Thousand Nights and One. *Morier's* Haji-Baba, *Beckford's* Vathek, *Pickthall's* Saïd the Fisherman *are all classics of this genre. Belloc's variation on the theme was however ironic and peppered with Swiftian satire.*

A Levantine merchant regales his nephews day by day of how he had acquired position and wealth by his devious crafty nature and how he outwitted his inferiors and betters! Belloc's publishers thought the merchant was Jewish and when he originally published the book they announced this fact on the wrapper. Belloc was enraged and made them retract.

Al-Jamal Wa'l-Nakhl, or Camels and Dates

When the hour of public execution had arrived the boys came timorously into their rich uncle's presence, and seating themselves upon the expensive carpet at the feet of his divan, prepared to hear the continuation of his adventures.

That excellent old man began as follows:

'I warn you, my children, that the path to wealth, which (by the Mercy of Allah) I have been allowed to tread, is varied and difficult. Profit by my misadventures! Remain determined to enrich yourselves, even after the worst mishaps! Yea! After wealth and poverty (like mine) renewed wealth and (alas!) renewed poverty never despair. Still hold to gold and still determine your fate. Still thirst for money. But all the while most reverently worship Him the Supreme, the All-compelling, the Giver of Great bags of coin. No talent in the deception of individuals or the gulling of the crowd can of itself bring the great reward. The acquirement of those immense sums which are the chief glory of man, is, like all else, in the Hand of God.

'My brother, your worthy though impecunious father, has sufficiently grounded you in the essentials of our holy religion. You will not repine if you turn out to be one of the ninety-nine who end their lives in the gutter, rather than the blessed hundredth who attains, as I have attained, to the possession of a palace and of innumerable slaves. . . .'

Having so spoken the aged merchant bent for a moment in silent prayer and then proceeded:

'You will remember that at the conclusion of my last adventure I had reached a position, not of affluence, but at least of tolerable fortune. I was possessed of a train of camels, each heavily laden with two large panniers of dates, and drivers to conduct the whole.

'You will further remember how, on my arrival in Laknes, as I was anxious to make the best of my time I spoke freely to all of my merchandise, extolled its character, described how I intended to put it up for sale next day in the public markets, and spread abroad the name of Ismaïl-of-Taftah which happened for the moment to be mine.

'The rumour spread (as I had intended it should). I strolled through the narrow streets of the town after sunset, and was glad to hear my arrival discussed, and my wares. I had promise for the morrow. I returned to my men.

'I had already spread out my bed upon the corner of the yard, when there came up a slave magnificently dressed, who bowed to the ground, and approaching my presence asked whether he had the honour and felicity to address the renowned merchant Ismaïl. He bore an invitation from the greatest merchant in the city, whose name I had already heard half a dozen times in Taftah, and whom all the merchants there revered from afar for his enormous riches: a certain Yusouff ben Ahmed, also called "El-Zafari", or the Triumphant.

'Late as was the hour I purchased finery; with my last gold I hired a donkey of strange magnificence, and arrived at the palace of Yusouff, dressed in a fashion which I could ill afford, but which I regarded as an investment.

'I had expected to find within this palace that admirable simplicity of manner which is inseparable from really great wealth: Nor was I disappointed. The inner room to which I was led, encrusted everywhere with black marble, boasted no ornament save three white alabaster jars as tall as a man and of immense antiquity. They had formerly been the property of a young noble whom Yusouff had ruined, and *he* had them of the Sultan. In the midst shone the single pure flame of a massive silver lamp, rifled from the tomb of a saint. It now hung dependent from a chain of the same metal, the height of which was lost in the gloom of the lofty cupola.

'A fountain of scented water—I could not name its odour precisely, but I guessed it to be Fior de Goyim—plashed gently into a basin of porphyry at the end of the apartment.

'Yusouff and two other guests (who alone had been asked to meet me), rose from the exceedingly costly rugs of Persia whereon they had reclined, and gravely saluted me. The master of the house, after the first salutations and an invocation upon my head of the Mercy of Allah, told me that the feast was ready prepared, but that before summoning it he would ask me to honour the house and survey what poor ornaments he might be able to show me.

'I was expressly delighted at his tone. It was that which I had always heard to be native to princes of commerce. He had already acquired, in the few years that had elapsed since he had cleaned the streets for a living, a well-bred restraint of gesture, and when he spoke it was in the tone of one who thought negligible the whole world, including his guest. I prayed fervently, as I accompanied the leisurely steps of my great entertainer, that when I should have achieved a similar fortune I should myself as quickly acquire this distinctive manner of the great. I watched him narrowly in order to imitate (when I should have left his presence) those peculiar little details which mark affluence and are of such service in negotiation. He would often interpose words of his own into the midst of another's sentence. It pleased him not to answer some repeated question. He would change the conversation at his pleasure without too much regard for what I might have been saying immediately before. He also turned to another guest while I was addressing him and in every way showed his superiority.

'When we had sat down to meat I was further edified by the varied information, the extensive culture of my host. He would lead the talk on to some subject which he had recently acquired from his numerous secretaries, and dally upon it at a length which would have been tedious in one of lesser station. But all this was done with such an air of *money* that it was impossible to feel the slightest tedium, though his minute description of things which we all knew by heart extended more than once to a full quarter of an hour.

'During the progress of this divine repast I noted with pleasure that the distinguished master of the house never once introduced the subject of my affairs.

'I would have you remember, my dear nephews,' said Mahmoud at this point, 'that nothing is less pleasing in a merchant, especially in one of approved success than the introduction of profit and loss at a meal, for profit and loss are of such profound importance that their mere mention must distract from the legitimate pleasures of the table.

'It was not until a late hour, when the two other guests (whose insignificant names I have not attempted to retain) had arisen to depart, that affairs began.

'With the subtle tact of commercial genius my host retained me, gripping my arm. I ventured in the absence of any witness to say a few words upon what was nearest my heart: I asked him '*How were dates?*'

'To my delight he proved affable. He unbent in a degree unworthy of so small an occasion and listened with the greatest attention to my simple tale. I told him frankly that I had with me at the moment but few camels (I was under no necessity to confess that I had not another asset in the world). I suggested by my negligent tone that such a number could hardly be called a caravan and was little more than a distraction with which I amused myself on my travels. I then dropped the fact that I had loaded them—more as a pastime than anything else—with a few *dates*.

'At this second mention of the word "*dates*" the face of Yusouff-the-Blessed suddenly changed. He at first cast his eyes down in an expression of real concern. Then, looking up at me anxiously and steadily, he said:

' "This is no affair of mine. . . . You may resent my interference."

'I assured him that I desired nothing more than a hint from one so favoured of Heaven. How I had better dispose of my trifling merchandise? I was more anxious to hear his reply than it is possible to say!

'He sighed heavily, shook his head, and answered with a certain familiarity that I could not resent:

' "My poor friend . . .!"

'He then sighed again and added:

' "I really do not see how I can advise you. . . . The truth is that dates will from henceforth be almost unsaleable here. There has lately taken place—indeed it was but last week—an extraordinary thing. The mother of our Emir—the dowager—has left by will the whole of her immense date groves in trust to the nation with orders that regular weekly distribution shall be made *free* to all the citizens. We are bidden praise her generosity and the masses are of course delighted. But it is ruin for the poor merchants whose stocks of dates are now so much dross. They cannot sell to our neighbours in the country over the border, for these hold dates to be evil from their effect in giving the toothache. Their new law, called the Date Prohibition Act, is of the most rigorous kind. I have myself (from a sense of public duty) bought up the greater portion at a ruinous loss to prevent the failure of smaller men and to avoid a panic. I have sacrificed myself to the public good." He sighed heavily once more and was silent.

'You may imagine, my dear nephews, the effect of this news upon your unfortunate uncle! The panniers of dates (two for each camel) were, save the animals themselves, all that I had in the world. I had traversed the waste at the cost of much labour, infinite privation, and mortal perils, precisely because this district had the reputation of being by far the best market for dates, and here was I, with an enemy left behind me, alone in the world, and my sole venture ruined. . . . I remembered my dreadful poverty, only so recently past, and I shuddered as I considered those unsaleable dates and my black future! Before me was a country where dates were rigorously forbidden by law; behind me a hue and cry. Despair was in my heart!

'Though I trust I have a sufficient degree of the arts essential to our profession, Yusouff must have guessed my thoughts. Ignoring my former statement that the goods I had with me were but a toy, and that I was indifferent to their fate, he expressed the deepest sympathy with my plight and begged me to bear with him while he reflected within himself how he might be of service.

'Having said this he covered his face with his right hand, bowed his head, leant his elbow upon his knee, and for some moments was plunged in what merchants use as thought. When he raised his face I was shocked to see how haggard it had become, and I marvelled that one so circumstanced should care so much for the chance misfortunes of a stranger. But I had read that these Princes of Commerce were often of tenderest heart and that one should never be surprised at any freak of generosity on their part.

'Judge therefore of my delight on hearing Yusouff say in a determined voice that he had concluded upon the only issue and that he would purchase my dates himself!

' "I cannot" (he frankly added) "give you as good a price even as I could have given a day or two ago; the old Queen's idea of free dates has swamped everything. But I will pay a good quarter of the customary price—which is far more than you now could obtain elsewhere. I am very wealthy. You are a stranger and, as it were, our guest in this town. A good deed is never thrown away. Perhaps some day I shall be glad of your aid also. I have seen you a few hours only, but I think we know each other's hearts already. Moreover, I do not conceal it from you, I *may* save much of the loss. I have special correspondents in distant towns, and opportunities of sale which others do not possess. . . . Come! I'll do it! I will offer you this price of one-third. It is but a poor price," said he, sighing yet again most heavily, "but it is far, far better than no price at all."

'My relief was beyond words. I had seen myself leaving my merchandise unsold or sacrificing it at a ruinous nothing. That which Yusouff offered me was the difference between despair and a shred of hope, and though the loss was severe it left me at least with some capital for a further venture.

'Great men have a sort of simplicity in their dealings. Hardly had Yusouff discovered my gratitude and my immediate acceptance of his gift (for I could call it by no other name), than the princely fellow clapped his hands, sent for his treasurer, and had counted to me upon the spot a hundred pieces of gold. I gave him my writing of delivery, which he handed to another slave with a few words in a low voice. Then he continued to talk to me, for he was determined to detain me far into the night. Indeed it was near dawn before he whom I will now call my friend, and to whom I felt bound for life by the greatest ties of grateful affection, allowed me to pass his gates and to return to my hostelry.

'There I found that my panniers had already been removed and their contents conveyed to the purchaser's warehouse. I admired the promptitude in business which so often accompanies a generous heart.

'With the early hours of the next day, before the sun had yet acquired too great power, I strolled through the bazaar, not so much cast down at the thought of my loss as cheered by the recollection that I possessed, after all, one hundred good pieces of solid gold.

'With a malicious pleasure I approached the stall of a fruit-seller. Putting down a small copper coin I begged him for a handful of dates.

' "I need not full measure," said I; "only a handful to munch as I go along." For I knew that in the state of the market my penny might have purchased a gallon. I desired to show a neglect for small sums.

To my surprise the fruit-seller stared at me and said:

' "Dates ? From what country do you come that you ask for *dates* in our town ?"

' "Why!" said I, "is there not a glut of these ? I am told the place is overflowing with them."

' "There is One-who-judges," said the fruit-seller resignedly. "But as for dates—you will not find one in the whole town; our last month's arrival was pillaged by robbers in the hills. If you will but procure me a single gallon I will readily give in return two pieces of gold, so great is the demand. Of supply there is none whatever, nor, alas! any prospect of such."

'I was so bewildered that I hardly know what next I said, but at any rate, in reply to it, my new acquaintance told me that there were, indeed, *suspected* to be certain dates in the possession of Yusouff-the-Triumphant, "who" (he remarked aside) "has all the luck." He next said it was also rumoured that Yusouff's slaves had been seen in the last hours of the night going in procession with a great number of panniers laden on mules towards Yusouff's ware-house, and those who brought the news swore that they could smell the smell of dates.

' "But beyond that smell", he ended, "we have had nothing of dates in the place for three weeks. And if you understood our habit in the matter of food you would feel for us!"

'I have already described to you, my dear nephews, my admira-tion for Yusouff-the-Triumphant. Long before I had seen him his distant reputation had inflamed me. My brief acquaintance with him had exalted that feeling to what I had thought the highest pitch. But now it passed all bounds. A man so subtle in negotiation! So ready in affairs! So rapid and conclusive in a bargain! With so marvellous a command of feature and of tone! A man (in a word) so infinitely my superior in that profession of commerce to which Allah calls all great souls and in which I also was engaged! Such a man I had never thought to meet! Nay—I had never thought such a one to exist upon this poor earth. I could have kissed the ground upon which he walked or have borne upon me for ever, as a relic, some thread of his purse.

' "Here," I exclaimed, "is the true merchant! Here is the model of all that a man of affairs should be!" Oh! Mahmoud, you thought yourself something in your trade, but you have met your master, and more than your master! You have met one who is to you as the most holy of saintly men is to the basest of the Kafir. There is *none* on earth like him. Allah has raised him beyond all others.

'But it is not enough, my dear nephews,' continued the old man, whose eyes were now filled with a sort of sacred light, 'it is not enough to admire those who set us great examples. We should also imitate them. I determined after so rare an experience to follow as best I might in the footsteps of one who had shown himself raised high above the level of mortality.

' "Him," said I to myself, "him will I copy! *He* shall be my guide! *His* manner and his tone, on that unforgettable evening, shall be my exact model! Then perhaps in time I shall do as he has done and accumulate so great a store of money as shall put me among the greatest of mankind."

'I hastened to summon my slaves. I paid my score for the stabling, and as I looked at my small capital and surveyed my beasts I hesitated what I should do. Yusouff-the-Triumphant had, by God's special grace overshadowing him, got hold of my substance. Nothing was left me but the camels. In such a strait I abandoned the thought of men and turned at once to heaven. I lifted up my heart to my Maker and prayed for guidance. He that has never for very long abandoned. His servant answered my prayer with singular alacrity, for even as I prayed I heard two men who passed me muttering one to the other.

'The first, as they hurried along, was saying in fearful undertones: "They have not yet a camel among them! Yet camels they must have or the terrible sentence will be pronounced!"

' "Yes!" returned his companion in a horrified whisper, "I fear greatly for my relatives in that town, and I am proceeding there to make certain that they shall have at least *one* camel in so terrible a time! For if a sufficiency of camels is not there by tomorrow noon I hear they are all to be impaled!"

'So speaking in subdued accents of terror, little knowing they were overheard, they walked on while I followed and noted every word.

'My mind was immediately made up. I continued, with stealthy feet, to follow these two anxious beings who were so engrossed in the coming misfortunes of their native place. At last, when we had come to an empty space where three streets met, I caught them up and faced them. Accosting them I said:

' "Sirs, are you bound for such and such a place?" (naming a town of which they could never have heard—for indeed it did not exist).

'They stopped and looked at me in surprise.

' "No, sir," they answered me together, "we are bound in all haste for our native place which is threatened with a great calamity. Its name is Mawur, but, alas, it is far distant from us—a matter of some twenty leagues—the desert lies between, and we shall hardly reach it within the day that remains. For we are poor men, and only with fast *camels*" (at this word they glanced at each other and shuddered) "could the journey be accomplished in the time."

'I thanked them politely, regretted that I had disturbed them for so little, proceeded with the utmost haste to my caravan, inquired the road for Mawur (the track for which lay plain through the scrub and across the sand), and hastened with the utmost dispatch all that burning day and all the succeeding night without repose, until at dawn I passed with my exhausted train through the gates of the city. I had covered in twenty hours twice as many leagues.

'Five of my beasts I left upon the road; and some few of my slaves—how many I had not yet counted—had fallen out and would presumably die in the desert. But there was a good remainder.

'Unfortunately I was not alone in my venture, for I discovered that early as was the hour another man had arrived already with two camels and was standing with them under the dawn in the market-place. Poor beasts they were, and bearing every mark of fatigue. But I was determined upon a monopoly I had hoped from the conversation I had overheard that not a single camel would be present in the place. I would secure myself against even the slightest competition. I approached the leader of the two sorry camels and asked him there and then what he would take for his cattle. He stared at me for a moment, but to my astonishment when I offered him for a beginning the derisory price of ten pieces of gold, he accepted at once, put the coins into his pouch, smiled evilly, and moved off at a great pace.

'To my chagrin there approached within a very few moments yet another peasant, leading this time but one camel, a rather finer beast than the others. I hoped, I believed, he would be the last. I made haste to follow the same tactics with him as with the first. Like the first he took the five gold pieces without so much as bargaining, but he looked me up and down strangely before shrugging his shoulders and taking himself off hastily down a side lane.

'And then (the people beginning to drift into the street as the day rose) appeared a man leading not less than ten camels in a file. I was seriously alarmed, but I bethought me of my reading: how all great fortunes had been acquired by speculation, how caution and other petty virtues were the bane of true trade. I boldly approached him and offered him my remaining gold for the whole bunch. Instead of meeting my offer with a higher claim, he asked to look narrowly at the pieces, and then looked as narrowly into my face. He took one of the gold pieces and bit it. He stooped and rang it upon the cobble-stones. He determined apparently that it was good, and without another word took my gold, appealed to those around as witnesses to the transaction, handed me the leading cord, and with a burst of laughter ran off at top speed.

'Here, then, was I with my thirteen new camels and what was left of my original caravan. I will not deny that I was somewhat disturbed in mind; but I could only trust in Allah. I did so with the utmost fervour, and implored Him to consider His servant, and to see to it that not another camel should reach the town before I began to sell.

'But what is man? What is he that he should order the movements of the Most High?

'I lifted up my eyes and saw approaching down the narrowness of the street a file of certainly not less than one hundred camels led by a great company of ragged men and walking with that insolent and foolish air which this beast affects and which at such a moment provoked me to rage.

'Then a slave, trembling lest he should give me offence, bade me come apart with him where steps led up the city wall. These I climbed, and from the summit I saw a sight that broke my heart.

'For there, across the plain that surrounded the city, came such a mass of camels as I hardly thought the universe contained. They came in batches of twenty, fifty, two hundred, herds and flocks of camels, driven, led, ridden, conducted in every shape from one direction and another, through the desert and cultivated land, from track and path, a very foison and cataract of camels. It was as though all the camels of Arabia, India, Bactria, and Syria had been summoned to this one place.

'And, alas, so they had! or at least as many as the King of that region could command. . . .

'For this was the explanation. . . .'

Here the old man's eyes grew dim with tears, his voice faltered, and in spite of his present riches he broke down at the recollection of his past ill-fortune.

'Oh, my dear nephews,' he said in broken accents, 'hardly will you believe the magnitude of my misfortune! For it turned out, as I eagerly questioned the people of the place, that a war having broken out against their King on account of the Date Prohibition of which I have told you, that ruthless monarch had ordered them to collect as best they might so many thousands of camels to be present within the walls by noon of that day, or suffer massacre. If the full tale were not present every man, woman, and child would be killed. For he had been suddenly alarmed by this declaration of war and caught with an insufficient provision of sumpter beasts. His Emirs had advised him that his salvation lay in seizing without payment every beast for leagues around.

'In proportion as my soul sank so did the hearts of the townsmen rise, to see the number gradually fulfilled. By noon all was well for them—but very ill for me! The officers of the king arrived, the beasts were counted and set apart, with not an ounce of copper to pay for any one of them! All seized! And my poor herd, alone and in that vast multitude, suffered the fate of all the rest, and, what was worse, every one of my slaves—all were taken off to serve as drivers.

'There in a far land, alone, I stood, with not a gold piece left in my pouch and not a head of cattle to my name; once more quite destitute.

'I spent the remainder of that day debating whether to hang myself on a beam or throw myself from a minaret. The arguments in favour of either course were so evenly balanced that the sun set before I could decide between them, and even at sunset there appeared, through the Mercy of Allah, a new relief.'

'There did?' said the second of the nephews eagerly, but before his uncle could reply the intolerable noise of the Muezzin was heard and the boys, rising at the signal, bowed low to their uncle and were gone.

XXVII

From *Sonnets and Verse*

1923

In 1923 Belloc returned to America. He had not visited that country since 1898, and like most English authors he went there to lecture. As a result of the visit he wrote The Contrast *which recorded his impressions of that country. When he returned to Britain to his famous house King's Land, his family life was to be broken up, for his son Peter went to Spain, whilst his elder brother Hilary went to America. Many of his closest friends had died.*

Apart from his volume of essays On, Sonnets and Verse *appeared. This book was subsequently revised and was republished in 1938, with additional material.*

Sonnets

I

Lift up your hearts in Gumber, laugh the Weald
And you my mother the Valley of Arun sing.
Here am I homeward from my wandering,
Here am I homeward and my heart is healed.
You my companions whom the World has tired
Come out to greet me. I have found a face
More beautiful than Gardens; more desired
Than boys in exile love their native place.

Lift up your hearts in Gumber, laugh the Weald
And you most ancient Valley of Arun sing.
Here am I homeward from my wandering,
Here am I homeward and my heart is healed.
If I was thirsty, I have heard a spring.
If I was dusty, I have found a field.

XXIV

Hoar Time about the House betakes him slow
Seeking an entry for his weariness.
And in that dreadful company distress
And the sad night with silent footsteps go.
On my poor fire the brands are scarce aglow
And in the woods without what memories press
Where, waning in the trees from less to less
Mysterious hangs the hornéd moon and low.

For now December, full of agéd care
Comes in upon the year and weakly grieves;
Mumbling his lost desires and his despair
And with mad trembling hand still interweaves
The dank sear flower-stalks tangled in his hair,
While round about him whirl the rotten leaves.

XXV

It freezes: all across a soundless sky
The birds go home. The governing dark's begun.
The steadfast dark that waits not for a sun;
The ultimate dark wherein the race shall die.
Death with his evil finger to his lip
Leers in at human windows, turning spy
To learn the country where his rule shall lie
When he assumes perpetual generalship.

The undefeated enemy, the chill
That shall benumb the voiceful earth at last,
Is master of our moment, and has bound
The viewless wind itself. There is no sound.
It freezes. Every friendly stream is fast.
It freezes, and the graven twigs are still.

XXVI

O my companion, O my sister Sleep,
The valley is all before us, bear me on.
High through the heaven of evening, hardly gone,
Beyond the harbour lights, beyond the steep,
Beyond the land and its lost benison
To where, majestic on the darkening deep,
The night comes forward from Mount Aurion.
O my companion, O my sister Sleep.

Above the surf-line, into the night-breeze;
Eastward above the ever-whispering seas;
Through the warm airs with no more watch to keep.
My day's run out and all its dooms are graven.
O dear forerunner of Death and promise of Haven.
O my companion, O my sister Sleep.

XXVIII

But oh! not Lovely Helen, nor the pride
Of that most ancient Ilium matched with doom.
Men murdered Priam in his royal room
And Troy was burned with fire and Hector died.

For even Hector's dreadful day was more
Than all his breathing courage dared defend
The armouréd light and bulwark of the war
Trailed his great story to the accustomed end.

He was the city's buttress, Priam's Son,
The Soldier born in bivouac praises great
And horns in double front of battle won.
Yet down he went: when unremembering fate
Felled him at last with all his armour on.
Hector: the horseman: in the Scaean Gate.

XXIX

The world's a stage. The light is in one's eyes.
The Auditorium is extremely dark.
The more dishonest get the larger rise;
The more offensive make the greater mark.
The women on it prosper by their shape,
Some few by their vivacity. The men,
By tailoring in breeches and in cape.
The world's a stage—I say it once again.

The scenery is very much the best
Of what the wretched drama has to show,
Also the prompter happens to be dumb.
We drink behind the scenes and pass a jest
On all our folly; then, before we go
Loud cries for 'Author' . . . but he doesn't come.

The Winged Horse

I

It's ten years ago to-day you turned me out o' doors
To cut my feet on flinty lands and stumble down the shores,
And I thought about the all-in-all, oh more than I can tell!
But I caught a horse to ride upon and I rode him very well,
He had flame behind the eyes of him and wings upon his side.
      And I ride, and I ride!

II

I rode him out of Wantage and I rode him up the hill,
And there I saw the Beacon in the morning standing still,
Inkpen and Hackpen and southward and away
High through the middle airs in the strengthening of the day,
And there I saw the channel-glint and England in her pride.
                    And I ride, and I ride!

III

And once a-top of Lambourne down toward the hill of Clere
I saw the Host of Heaven in rank and Michael with his spear,
And Turpin out of Gascony and Charlemagne the Lord,
And Roland of the marches with his hand upon his sword
For the time he should have need of it, and forty more beside.
                    And I ride, and I ride!

IV

For you that took the all-in-all the things you left were three.
A loud voice for singing and keen eyes to see,
And a spouting well of joy within that never yet was dried!
                    And I ride.

Tarantella

Do you remember an Inn,
Miranda?
Do you remember an Inn?
And the tedding and the spreading
Of the straw for a bedding,
And the fleas that tease in the High Pyrenees,
And the wine that tasted of the jar?
And the cheers and the jeers of the young muleteers
(Under the vine of the dark verandah)?
Do you remember an Inn, Miranda,
Do you remember an Inn?
And the cheers and the jeers of the young muleteers

Who hadn't got a penny,
And who weren't paying any,
And the hammer at the doors and the Din?
And the Hip! Hop! Hap!
Of the clap
Of the hands to the twirl and the swirl
Of the girl gone chancing,
Glancing,
Dancing,
Backing and advancing,
Snapping of a clapper to the spin
Out and in——
And the Ting, Tong, Tang of the Guitar!
Do you remember an Inn,
Miranda?
Do you remember an Inn?

Never more;
Miranda,
Never more.
Only the high peaks hoar:
And Aragon a torrent at the door.
No sound
In the walls of the Halls where falls
The tread
Of the feet of the dead to the ground
No sound:
But the boom
Of the far Waterfall like Doom.

Ballade of Unsuccessful Men

I

The cause of all the poor in '93:
    The cause of all the world at Waterloo:
The shouts of what was terrible and free
    Behind the guns of *Vengeance* and her crew:

The Maid that rode so straightly and so true
  And broke the line to pieces in her pride—
They had to chuck it up; it wouldn't do;
  The Devil didn't like them, and they died.

II

Caesar and Alexander shall agree
  That right athwart the world their bugles blew:
And all the lads that marched in Lombardy
  Behind the young Napoleon charging through:
All that were easy swordsmen, all that slew
  The Monsters, and that served our God and tried
The temper of this world—they lost the clue.
  The Devil didn't like them, and they died.

III

You, the strong sons of anger and the sea,
  What darkness on the wings of battle flew?
Then the great dead made answer: 'Also we
  With Nelson found oblivion: Nelson, who
When cheering out of Portsmouth harbour grew
  To make one purpose with the wind and tide—
Our nameless hulks are sunk and rotted through:
  The Devil didn't like us and we died.'

Envoi

Prince, may I venture (since it's only you)
  To speak discreetly of The Crucified?
He was extremely unsuccessful too:
  The Devil didn't like Him, and He died.

Ha'nacker Mill

Sally is gone that was so kindly
Sally is gone from Ha'nacker Hill.
And the Briar grows ever since then so blindly
  And ever since then the clapper is still,
  And the sweeps have fallen from Ha'nacker Mill.

Ha'nacker Hill is in Desolation:
   Ruin a-top and a field unploughed.
And Spirits that call on a fallen nation
   Spirits that loved her calling aloud:
   Spirits abroad in a windy cloud.

Spirits that call and no one answers;
   Ha'nacker's down and England's done.
Wind and Thistle for pipe and dancers
   And never a ploughman under the Sun.
   Never a ploughman. Never a one.

XXVIII

A Reply to Compton Mackenzie
on Music

1923

In 1923 Compton Mackenzie wrote to a number of distinguished persons asking them what was their favourite song, their favourite composer, and their favourite tune.

Here is Belloc's reply:

'For a song, the love-song in "Don Juan", Mozart's. For a composer, Mozart. For a tune, why that of the song. For a singer, I can't judge; but the one I liked best was a man who sang tenor in the puppet show in Rome '21, the show called "The Little Ones"; or else Mignon Nevada.

XXIX

From *The Cruise of The Nona*

1925

Belloc was something of a latter-day Carlyle. The nearest he got to an autobiography was The Cruise of the Nona. *Anyone desiring to savour the writings of Belloc in one volume would be best served by reading this book. There they will find something of all his varying and discursive moods, and especially of his love of the sea. His beloved little boat was the* Nona—*an old-fashioned cutter of ten tons, some thirty feet long, slow but reliable. Built in 1874 she had belonged to Lord Stanley of Alderley's father, who gave her to Belloc.[1] The basic fabric of the book tells of a cruise southward from Holyhead, finally docking at Folkestone. It was not an easy voyage, but Belloc never was afraid of the elements. Interspersed between descriptions of his voyaging from port to port are the outpourings of his ever active mind—many of his opinions are biased and cantankerous, for Belloc was hardly an accommodating person. Yet however wrong he is, and wrong he was as well as right, his opinions are stimulating.*

We have endeavoured here to give extracts showing his many facets of argument and thought as well as the trials and tribulations of the cruise of the Nona.

[1] See the Introduction to *The Cruise of the Nona* in the 1955 edition by Lord Stanley of Alderley, p. xxii.

'Death by Drowning'

I looked at the Carnarvonshire coast there close at hand, the sinking lines of the mountains as they fell into the sea, and I discovered myself to be for the first time in my life entirely indifferent to my fate. It was a very odd sensation indeed, like the sensation I fancy a man must have to find he is paralysed. Once, under the influence of a drug during an illness some such indifference had pervaded me, but here it was in the broad daylight and the sun well up above the mountains, with a clear sky, in the grip of a tremendous gale and of an angry countering sea, ravening like a pack of hounds. Yet I could only look with indifference on the sea and at the land. The sensation was about as much like courage as lying in a hammock is like a hundreds yards race. It had no relation to courage, nor, oddly enough, had it any relation to religion, or to a right depreciation of this detestable little world which can be so beautiful when it likes.

Such as it was, there it was. I had always particularly disliked the idea of death by drowning, and I had never believed a word of the stories which say that at the end it is a pleasant death. Indeed, as a boy I was once caught under the steps of a swimming bath and held there a little too long before I could get myself out, and pleasant it was not at all. But here in Bardsey Sound, I was indifferent, even to death by drowning. All I was really interested in was to watch what way we lost and what chance we had of getting through.

Indeed, the whole question of fear is beyond analysis, and there is only one rule, which is, that a man must try to be so much the master of himself that he shall be able to compel himself to do whatever is needful, fear or no fear. Whether there be merit or not in the absence of fear, which sentiment we commonly call courage when it is allied to action, may be, and has been, discussed without conclusion since men were men. The absence of fear makes an admirable show, and excites our respect in any man; but it is not dependent upon the will. Here was I in very great peril indeed off Bardsey, and utterly careless whether the boat should sink or swim; yet was I the same man who, in a little freshness of breeze that arose off the Owers a year or two ago, was as frightened as could well be—and with no cause. And if this be true of change of mood in one man, it must be true of the differences of mood in different men.

I had occasion during the war, when I had been sent to write upon the Italian front, to be swung to the high isolated rock of a mountain peak in the Dolomites by one of those dizzy wires which the Italian engineers slung over the gulfs of the Alps for the manning and provisioning of small high posts. It was an experience I shall ever remember, a vivid, hardly tolerable nightmare; but the man I was with, an Italian officer of great and deserved fame, earned during that campaign, not only felt nothing, but could not understand what my terror was. We sat, or rather lay, in one of those shallow trays which travel slowly along these wires over infinite deeps of air; and during the endless crawling through nothingness he told me, by way of recreation, the story of a private soldier who had been coming down from the isolated post some weeks before. The machinery had gone wrong, and the tray remained suspended over the gulf, half-way across, for some twenty minutes. When it worked again and they hauled it in they found that the man had gone mad.

When the time came for the return journey, I very well remember asking myself whether I had the control to face that second ordeal or no. It was an obscure crisis, unknown to others, but as real and as great within as any of those which stand out in fiction or history. I would rather have gone down by the path which clung to the steep, the precipitous mountain side. This was forbidden because it was under direct Austrian fire; I knew that I should not be allowed. So I faced the return—and it was worse than the going.

Also in my life I have known two men who have hunted lions, and each of them has told me that fear in the presence of peril from the beast was wholly capricious, and that sometimes when an exceedingly unpleasant death seemed certain, the man who had just missed his shot felt indifferent. I can believe it.

Anyhow, here I was in Bardsey Sound, with many deaths moving over the howling fury of the sea, and not one of them affecting me so much as a shadow passing over a field.

The end of that adventure was odd and unreasonable—as things will be at sea. It was perhaps because we had been buffeted and pushed into some edge of the conflict between wind and water where the tide runs slacker; or it was perhaps because the wind had risen still higher. But, at any rate, after three separate raids forward (in the second of which we were very nearly out of our peril and into smooth water), and as many set-backs (one of which got us into the worst violence we had yet suffered) the *Nona*, in a fourth attempt (it was her own, not ours—we could do nothing but keep her, as best we might, to her course), slipped out and reached an eddy beyond the tide. For a moment it was very difficult to keep her to it, she slewed round; but then again she got her head southerly, and we found ourselves running past the great Black Rock which stands there—the Carrig Dhu—and marks the smooth water beyond the edge of the tide.

We breathed again; and as I took her on through an easy sea, close under the land with not too much strain upon the helm (for the high shore now broke the gale), I was free to look over my right shoulder and watch, passing away behind us, further and further, the hell of white water and noise, through which we had barely come to safety.

Danger keeps men awake and makes them forget necessity, but with this relief, our fatigue came upon us. My friend and I had now been awake for some twenty-five or twenty-six hours, and it was time for sleep.

We got the poor *Nona* which had behaved so well, up into a lonely little bay where was an old abandoned mine working, but no other sign of man. The Welshman with us told us it was good holding ground; we let go the anchor and stowed sail. I remember how I fell half asleep as I stretched the cover over the mainsail boom and yard and tied it down at the after end. The gale still blew, yet, as it seemed, more steadily and less fiercely. There was no danger of dragging. We were well under the lee of the land. I gave one look, under the violent but clear morning sky, to seaward before I went below; and there I saw how, at a certain distance from the land, in a long line, the white water began. It was like being in a lagoon, like being protected by a bank from the sea outside; but really it was only the effect of the lee of the land making a belt of smooth water along shore. Then we all lay down to sleep and slept till evening.

An Experience in the House of Commons

A man can only talk of the things he himself has known, and I myself have only seen one example of this inspiration in its perfection. It was (I regret to say) an experience of the House of Commons, a nasty place in which to find anything remarkable. There I saw the Speaker of my time (Mr Lowther, as he then was) exercising the art through two Parliaments with a perfection which I had thought impossible, and which moved me, at the watching of it, as much as I am moved by great lines of Milton or Racine, or the harmonies of certain musics.

Consider what the business was! He had before him in an ill-lit, dull, hideous, oblong room six hundred men, dully ranged in ten or a dozen dull rows; half to his left, half to his right. In that dull air of futile vulgar and unreal verbiage there could arise, in a moment, absurdly acrid emotions. These had to be tamed and resolved whenever they should bubble up like gas from a marsh. It was a necessity to the dull life of the place, if it were to crawl along at all, that such accidents should not wholly destroy its dull function.

This great body of men would dwindle in a moment to a dozen or less—a dozen who only remained for the chance of speaking, and of whom each individual would jump up like a jack-in-the-box the very instant the last mouther had sat down. It would swell again to a full complement, a crowded House, with equal rapidity.

The man managing that assembly had to remember each man by name. Those faces, which would, for any of *us*, have become mere blobs of white within half an hour of fatigued observation, had to be recognized as individuals. The relations of each with all had to be remembered; the nature of the matter under debate, the right of one man, through experience of office or of personal work, to be remembered; the claim of another man (suffering some unjust failure) to be recognized; the danger of a third who was repetitive; of a fourth who was mad. At the same time, the very subtle distinctions between the lesser and the greater claim to speak, the length of the debate, even the excessive tedium of each speaker had to be weighed. On the top of all that, it had to be remembered of what importance was each discussion (in so far as you can call any of them important—but they seem absurdly important to the participants). On the top of all that, again, was the general arrangement of the debate suggested by the Whips and in possession of the Chair.

Now in all this incredibly complicated task, involving, I suppose, some hundreds of interior decisions during the day, Mr Lowther never once failed. The House of his time was an instrument over which he had complete mastery through a complete comprehension and a rapidity of just decision which I have never seen equalled in any field of command.

We have a tendency today to use words too strong for the occasion, and the word genius is a very strong word; but I have no more doubt that Mr Lowther, as I watched him day after day, displayed genius than I have a doubt that Mozart in music, or Houdon in sculpture, had genius. It was amazing, it was satisfactory, it was continuous.

There was an old squire with whom I often dined in those years, and who had great knowledge of men and things in that club, still aristocratic, which England then still was. Not long after my first election to the august Assembly, I told him with enthusiasm at his own table what my judgement was of this achievement. He answered me, wearily, 'Oh! I have heard that said of every Speaker since I can remember!' To which I re-answered, 'Yes; but this time they were right.'

Which reminds me of how a modern poet, spared to middle age in spite of the wrath of God, famous for that he could neither scan nor rhyme—let alone think or feel—once made a speech in which he carefully set out those things which had been said against Swinburne when first that meteor flamed across the heaven of English verse. The modern poet next read to this assembly the things that had been written against himself when he first blurred into the murk of our evening. He triumphantly concluded: 'What was said against Swinburne they have said against me!' Then there arose an aged writer of reviews, a man whose hair, whose voice, and whose Aura were all three of delicate silver. He said: 'Yes! But in what they said of him they were wrong; in what they said of you, they were right.'

This was not an epigram, it was a paving-stone; and it reminded me of that line in the Epic of Roncesvalles, 'Christians are right and Pagans are wrong'.

So in the matter of Speakers. I have seen the action of four; but of none would I say even that they had talent, saving in this case alone, where I have used another word. . . .

On Dr Jowett

The truth Dr Jowett gave me came thus. He asked me the political question which was always uppermost in his mind, and which he believed all young men should consider. It was, 'Under what form of government is the state of man at its best?' I answered as all young men should answer, 'A Republic', to which he answered gently in his turn, 'You cannot have a Republic without Republicans.' Now that, for terseness and truth and a certain quality of *revelation*, was worthy of Aristotle. It is the full answer, historical and moral, to every honest man who desires, as most honest men do, democracy, and who wonders why it is so hard to attain. But I had never considered that answer; and I think if I had not heard these half dozen words I might never have considered it.

Democracy, that is, the government of the community by the community: a State wherein a man stands equal with his fellows, and has to suffer neither subservience nor the corruption of flattery and power: a State in which office alone commands and not the being clothed with office—that is the ideal at the back of every man's mind who cares for right in public affairs, and who has within himself anything left of private honour. It is simplest put by saying that democracy is the noblest form of government. But the moment you begin to deal with men, you find in varying degree, according to the human material handled, a difficulty in the direction of such an affair. You have experience of the wickedness and folly of men, and if you add to such growing experience the vast experience of history, you find that, save in some few, and those small, communities, the ideal of democracy must break down in practice; and that so far from enjoying the noblest of social conditions, men attempting democracy in great States are soon suffering the basest forms of control by the rich. That is because most men, though intimately desiring a republic, are not republicans: when you have great numbers, those worthy of democracy are few. In the same way most men, though individually desiring peace within, have not the control of themselves which makes such peace possible.

So much for the Master's excellent platitude.

It is strange that things worth saying and hearing, guiding things, should always have that quality of turning into platitudes, once they are familiar; for they were sudden revelations when first they came. To me now the impracticability of democracy among men indifferent to honour and justice is so clear that I never pause to consider it, well knowing that you cannot have the thing in any modern plutocratic State; that even in small States it needs a peculiarly admirable and rare temper in the human material of them. But this conviction came slowly, and all started from those few words.

And what has all this to do with the sailing of the sea? Nothing, save that it is during the sailing of the lonely sea that men most consider the nature of things.

'Wild Goose Race'

The *Nona* came therefore grandly out of Ramsey Sound with a sweep and dignified nod into the calm of St Bride's Bay, but I knew very well that there was before me another trial, more difficult still, called Jack Sound, between Skomer and the mainland, seven miles to the south.

Lord, what a tangle of dangers are here for the wretched mariner! Rocks and eddies and overfalls and shooting tides; currents and (as you shall shortly hear) horrible great mists, fogs, vapours, malignant humours of the deep, mirages, false ground, where the anchor will not hold, and foul ground, where the anchor holds for ever, spills of wind off the irregular coast and monstrous gales coming out of the main west sea; and, most terrible of all, Wild Goose Race.

I will maintain with the Ancients that there are some parts of the sea upon which a God has determined that there shall be peril: that these parts are of their inward nature perilous and that their various particular perils are but portions of one general evil character imposed by The Powers. For you will notice that wherever there is one danger of the seas there are many. If it is an overfall or a race then in that neighbourhood you will also have reefs, unaccountable thick weather, shifting soundings, bad holding and all the rest of it. Witness the western approach to the Isle of Portland, or the Bight of St Malo, with the Channel Islands and their innumerable teeth; the entry to the Straits of Messina and other places recorded in histories and in pilot books. Our moderns will have it that such things are chance and an accumulation of them a blind accident, but I hold with those greater men, our Fathers. Some one here in these places, some early captain, first sailing offended the Gods of the Sea. Hence all the tangle of the southern corner of Wales, Jack Sound and Ramsey Sound and the Bishop and his clerks and, worst of all, Wild Goose Race.

I write without knowledge of the Wild Goose Race. I have never been through it; neither have you been through death, you who read this. Yet, as we all know that death is a perilous passage and in accordance dread it, so I with the Wild Goose Race, well so named. My book told me that little ships like mine getting into that water were often dismasted and 'even foundered'. I like that word 'even'.

It seems that in Wild Goose Race a boat is taken up and pitched to heaven and let drop again, twirled round like a teetotum, thrown over on her side, banged off sideways with great stunning blows upon the cheek-bone and blinded all the time with cataracts of spray, the while the air is filled with a huge mocking laughter. Many races do I know, Portland Race and Alderney Race and Little St Alban's Race, of which you shall later hear, and the Race round the Skerries of Anglesey, if you may call that a race, and the Race in Bardsey Sound. But there are many races, which, thank heaven, I do not know and which I do not propose to know, such as the Race of Ushant, and the very damnable races of the northern headlands, including that Great Maelstrom of which we hear so much and see so little, and which puts on great airs: but none of these, I am told, is comparable to Wild Goose Race, therefore did I let it alone upon this passage. Do not believe it when you read it in books that a race is made by anything so simple as a tide against a wind or a sudden precipice in the depths of the sea. It is made by the anger of those that rule the sea. And yet of races there is one that has always treated me kindly, and that is the race off the Start. I have been through it I know not how many times and always was the sea there either quite smooth, gentle, purring and domestic; or an honest running sea, parallel and ordered. But perhaps, whatever governs the Start Race had received from me without my knowing it, some courtesy. I take this opportunity to thank whatever Powers govern that little corner of the watery world for their kindness.

I have often seen pictures of these Powers, horses and men and women with fishes' tails and scales, and Gods without scales that ride in chariots over the sea. I suppose in that world, or in those circles, the scales are a badge of service, making the link between the immortals and the dumb fishes of the sea; just as our highbrows make a link between the rich masters who rob the modern world and the millions who work. Only there is this difference, that our highbrows have no scales; they have nothing in common with the dumb millions who work. But I will not pursue this metaphor lest I should offend Mr and Mrs Able, who themselves indeed live in western suburbs but, upon the other hand, are perpetually in the houses of the great.

Where then was I ? Why, coming into the quiet and amplitude of St Bride's Bay, but having before me the terrors of Jack Sound. For it is true of the sea here as everywhere, that it is the symbol of life, and of our ceaseless duties, and of death. We must never expect long quiet in the business of our living, nor any long security in any passage of the sea. But I must say that this run across St Bride's Bay was very genial upon that summer noon, only there came with the early afternoon those ominous patches of an oily look to windward, the falling of the breeze; the sea still running, and yet the canvas not always over well filled: briefly, the renewed menace of a deadly calm. That calm fell upon us suddenly enough, just at the moment when we might, with the last of the ebb, have run through Jack Sound. It came upon us at the mouth of that forbidden passage, and left us idle and foolish, pointing anyhow and seeing, to our despair, the marks upon the distant shore slowly moving backward as (alas!) we drifted north.

Truly, indeed, did the immortal trio—Swift, Arbuthnot and Pope—exclaim in chorus: 'What is mortal man but a broomstick!' Never are we in half a gale of wind but we pray crapulously for calm. Never are we in a calm but we whine peevishly for wind. What, Dog, would you have the weather cut out for you like a suit of clothes? Is all the universe to arrange itself simply to your convenience, as it does for the very rich—so long as they keep off the sea? Will you not be content with sailing unless just that wind plays which is exactly trimmed for your miserable barque, neither too strong nor too light nor too far forward, so that you have to beat, nor so far aft that you fear a gybe, or pooping from a running sea? Will you never repose in the will of your Maker and take things as they come? Why then drift round Skomer like a fool!

Which, indeed, was what the *Nona* did, for as it fell dead calm, the set of the sea took her in the most amusing unaccountable way on a jolly little voyage of exploration. The sea took charge. The tiller was not worth holding, the helm swung idle, and the canvas hung like the flabby muscles on the face of an Opposition leader towards the end of the third hour of a speech from the Front Bench to which he has had to listen, sorely against his will. It hung loose and inept, like the hands of a poor man, waiting orders in the presence of a rich man, or, like the mind of a sceptic, when he considers the ultimate nature of good and evil—let alone beauty. The sea took charge and trolled the little boat along, keeping her just so far from the shore, as who should say, 'See, my child, how remarkable is the Island of Skomer! Come with me, I will show you every cranny of its outer shore.' So were we taken off round Skomer by the tide in that calm, further and further from Jack Sound.

When they had played this farce with us long enough, the Powers halted the sea, as is their fashion every six hours, and we found ourselves close aboard a large ketch which lay at anchor off that Skomer shore. There was one man upon the deck, smoking a pipe and keeping his mind empty, as is the duty of all mortals in such few intervals of leisure as heaven affords us. He bade us not knock into him, and we called out to him (but not very loud, for we were at a familiar cast of but few yards) that if we came too close aboard we would shove off and do him no harm. We asked him who he was and where he was going. He did not tell us who he was, but he told us where he was going, which was to Cork, and what he had on board, which was a cargo of coal.

The lazy sun, half-way down the sky, looked indifferently upon us; the quite smooth sea turned again in its perpetual come and go, and took us slowly back in so many hours, till we found ourselves again by evening where we had started, at the mouth of Jack Sound. What this current or tide movement was which had thus taken us nearly round Skomer and back again, I know not, but it was a journey that cost nothing, and, tedious as it was, we had at least learned another few miles of shore. It seemed, however, all of a set purpose, for the wind now blew again lightly but steadily from the north-east. The ebb was well on its way, and we could point through Jack Sound, and hope to be in Milford Haven, round St Anne's Head before the late darkness of this day in early June.

So did we enter that passage.

Jack Sound in that evening light was a repetition of Ramsey, only more violent, for we were more in the full roar of the ebb. There was the same rush as of a millrace, the same cataracts of falling water over the landward rocks. We came out of it with the setting sun glorious upon our starboard quarter, and ran quickly for the end of Skokholm—another Scandinavian name—sure (in that steady breeze) of rounding St Anne's Head easily before darkness, and dropping anchor in some cove of Milford Haven.

But nothing is certain at sea. We were, perhaps, a mile from the Head when there rolled up with astonishing rapidity from out the main ocean a solid bank of cloud, sweeping the level of the sea. I say cloud rather than fog, because it was so solid and so dark. It caught us like a cloak thrown over a man's head; and, before we knew where we were, we found ourselves steering hopelessly by the card, not daring to keep too much out, lest we should lose the mouth of the haven; not daring to keep too much in, lest we should strike: and nothing to prevent that but listening anxiously to the great fog-blast, which was now hooting regularly in its panic from the height of the headland.

What followed for nearly two hours was such an adventure as only wretched amateurs would indulge in, and amateurs in a craft which did not draw more than six feet of water. The wind, such as it was, had dropped, of course, with the fog. It gave us only enough way to creep eastward before it; and what we proposed to do was so to feel our way in the fading light through that dense mist until we should hear the slight surge of water upon the rocks of the haven mouth to port, that is, on the north side of the haven entry. I had a large plan aboard, and I knew that there was water close up to the shore, and that it was plain enough going, with nothing hidden beneath the surface. So we gingerly put her head slightly round, when we made out the mournful menace of the fog-horn to have come just aft of the beam; my companion took the helm, and I went forward with the lead, and also to call out to him to put the helm up whenever that might be made necessary by our getting too close. We faintly heard already the slight wash of the gently heaving water, and I saw, some few yards off the bow, little gleams of white through the mist, which were the foam sliding from the rock surfaces, as we slipped by. The *Nona*'s movement was so very slight that even if she had struck a glancing blow, nothing that was not jagged would have harmed her greatly; but we were preserved and did not touch.

We had this further good fortune, that, just as it grew quite dark, the sound of the slight surge to leeward receded and disappeared so that we knew we had turned the headland and opened the first bay of that long inland arm of the sea. Our chart showed us good depth and good holding ground, and a good berth for the night granted that there should be no other craft about. We heard none such through the fog; no voices, no swinging spars, no movement at all. So when we had got well into the bight, we dropped anchor; trusting to luck that, as she swung to her chain, she would not strike shoal ground nor anything near. Had we still had the dinghy I would have gone out and explored, and made certain and risked my chance of getting back aboard through the mist, but having no dinghy, we had to take things as they were, and these seemed secure enough, for we were well out of the fairway. The first of the night was interrupted by that perpetual call of the great horn upon the headland, but before midnight the fog lifted, the sound ceased, and a profound silence fell upon the sea and the land. We had also the comfort of seeing that we had plenty of room to swing, with the shore perhaps a quarter of a mile away.

That night as I fell asleep I designed the second and third verses of the 'Chaunty of the "Nona"'.

Tides

There are many parts of the sea where the tide goes round like a clock, and no one can tell you why. Instead of the stream setting first east, let us say, with the flood and then west with the ebb, it goes all round the compass. It sets north-west with the beginning of the flood, then north, then north-east, then east, and so on. Looking all round about itself like a performing dog, and slowly and ceaselessly revolving. It behaves not like an eddy, but like spokes. It is perfectly incomprehensible.

There is also this about the tides, which we all know to be true, and which we can see at work any day, but which I defy any man to rationalize: when the tide runs up a narrow river—or, indeed, any river—it will be still running up, say, ten miles from the mouth, when it is running *down* again, say, five miles from the mouth. What happens in between? Slack water, of course. But *how* is there slack water? How can the running *down* be going on at one point and, immediately beyond, the running *up*, without a division? How can the water go on running up from a reservoir below which it is running down? It does so, and it is all in God's providence, and I accept it as I do teeth, or any other oddity. But I will not pretend to explain it.

The sea teaches one the vastness and the number of things, and, therefore, the necessary presence of incalculable elements, perpetually defeating all our calculations. The sea, which teaches all wisdom certainly does not teach any man to despise human reason. I suppose there was never yet any Kantian fool or worser pragmatist who would not have been cured of his folly by half a week of moderate weather off the Onion. No one can at sea forego the human reason or doubt that things are things, or that true ideas are true. But the sea does teach one that the human reason, working from a number of known premises, must always be on its guard, lest the conclusion be upset in practice by the irruption of other premises, unknown or not considered. In plain words, the sea makes a man practical; and the practical man is, I suppose, as much the contrary of the pragmatist as the sociable man is the contrary of the socialist, or the peaceable man the contrary of the pacifist.

A Man & His Song

On the bar there was no end of a lump, and, as we were blanketed by that high cliff, the *Nona* took it uneasily, chucking up and down with flapping sails and rolling damnably, but in a few moments the strength of the ebb had swept us far enough out to catch the wind again, and we set a course full-and-by; right out for the open, for the large. For we designed to beat in again after a few miles, and so make our way down Channel toward the Cornishmen.

There was certainly quite enough wind: 'All the wind there is.' as an old Irish sailor said to me once during an Atlantic gale so abominable that he and I could not walk against its icy, sleeting December fury, but had to crawl forward tugging along the rail by main force, all up the windward side. . . . That was a passage worthy of remembrance, for we took three weeks between Europe and the Delaware, the engines and the old frame quite unfit for their task; and in that cheap passage also. I learnt from a stoker two songs: one called 'The Corn Beef Can', and the other called 'The Tom Cat'. They are of the great songs of this world.

A man should learn all the songs he can. Songs are a possession, and all men who write good songs are benefactors. No people have so many songs as the English, yet no people sing less in these last sad days of ours. One cannot sing in a book. Could a man sing in a book, willingly would I sing to you here and now in a loud voice 'The Corn Beef Can' and 'The Tom Cat', those admirable songs which I learnt in early manhood upon the Atlantic seas.

'The Dutch Invasion of England'

I should like to have seen that big Dutch fleet, with its few English renegades on board, come sweeping into Torbay. I should like to have seen the crowded boats passing to and fro, landing the Dutchmen and other foreign troops, and the great lords who were conspiring against their king, and the saturnine William himself. I should like to have seen that mercenary army of adventurers, hired to give the last blow to so great a victim as the wounded kingship of the English, formed in column, and the march up to Exeter: with the villagers timidly peeping from behind closely-shut windows at the strange faces, hearing alien speech, and wondering what the issue of the invasion would be.

There was a fine pageantry about all that miserable business which ended the age-long, but dying, tradition of monarchy in Britain, and put the rich in the saddle for good, without a master. From the moment when the huge armament bowled through the Straits of Dover under a south-east wind (forming such a crescent that the horns of it neared either shore) to that afternoon, two days later, when the high gilded poops of the Dutchmen stood out in line across Torbay, the whole evil thing was full of grandeur and of colour.

Whenever I recollect that business of the fall of the Stuarts, two things stand out in my mind: so much pageantry and so much comic stuff. For, to my thinking, there is something comic in the financing of the expedition with Dutch money, secured upon taxes promised *beforehand* as sure to be levied from the English (specifically on their tobacco), should it succeed. This way of making the victim pay for his own execution without his knowing it, and without consulting him, is full of the spirit of comedy. There are a hundred other comic details. Churchill leaning his handsome, villainous face over the dinner table of the inn and trying to persuade the unfortunate James to come out for a ride on that fine moonlight night; Churchill well knowing how, on that fine moonlight night, the scouts of the enemy were waiting to carry off the King. And, again, the picture of the subsequent dinner at Andover; James dining with his daughter's husband, the Prince of Denmark, and that great bagful of stupidity, repeating to everything that was said, '*Est-il possible!*'; then he and his suite excusing themselves for a moment to attend to some business; James, the King, wondering when they would return to the room. They never returned. That business on which they had excused themselves was treason, and the woman in town and her husband at Andover had betrayed.

What a Cavalry James had to climb! It is a pity that Anne should have done such a thing, for she seems to have been the best of all that gang—which is not saying much. I have always trusted Swift's judgement, who wrote of her: 'The only good woman I ever met in my life.' But there he exaggerated; for he certainly profoundly admired at least two others, and he would not have admired them if he had not thought them good in a very evil world.

Lyme Regis

There is also in this coast an entry called Charmouth, where the Danish pirates of the Dark Ages fought hard against the King of Winchester, but I know it only as a slight mark caught far off from the sea.

What I have made over and over again in this way, in one boat or another, and often in the *Nona*, is Lyme Regis.

What produced Lyme Regis? How came there to be a harbour there?

Men need harbours almost as much as they need the gods.

Men so much need harbours that in any long stretch of harbourless coast they will catch at any small advantage of reef, or projecting headland, and make shift with that. Thus, all down the line of eastern Italy, where for hundreds of miles the Adriatic meets nothing but one low even line of coast, they have caught at the sorry opportunity of Ancona. But this coast has plenty of harbours, small and large. A British or Roman road came down to Lyme Regis, but that could not have produced the harbour. It must have been the other way about. The road can only have come down here

because there was a harbour here. Perhaps there was here something like what was for centuries at Hastings (but is now washed
away), a crumbling piece of harder rock curling out to sea in an arm
and giving shelter within, and perhaps it was upon this that the Cob
was afterwards built.

The modern great havens, which we can artificially make, spoil
us for the harbours of antiquity, and make them small in our eyes,
but Lyme Regis was a port of entry all through history, and did not
lose its position until almost within the memory of men now alive.
How characteristic it is of the growth of our towns inland, and of
the change in English life through that growth, that, when men and
women hear of Lyme Regis today, they think not of the English
seas, nor of armed men landing here, but of works of fiction by
Miss Austen. Tennyson wrote admirably of the *Revenge*, and
believed himself a seer in the matter of the English waters and their
command, but his interest in Lyme Regis was from Miss Austen.
For my part, I am not ashamed to say that in my nineteenth year,
when I capsized all by myself in a little open boat under Golden
Cap, and with difficulty saved myself, though I was quite close to
shore (it was in the month of December, dear friends, and poor
weather for such gambols), I had not so much as heard of Jane
Austen: nevertheless from that moment Lyme Regis was vivid
enough to me without her aid, and so it was when, three years ago,
touching Lyme Regis again for the tenth of twentieth time, the
Nona herself capsized.

'Twas a dark and stormy night, *camaradoes*, and the wind blew
from the south-west, which is the stance it likes to take up when
it proposes to drive at doing a devilry. I knew well that the tide
running out during the darkness would leave us high and dry, and
by lantern light I made every kind of contraption and fastening
from the mast to the quay, so that she should lie even when she
took the ground. But at four in the morning, with a noise like
thunder, she fell over enormously to starboard upon the then dry
bottom of the harbour and threw us all one on top of the other—we
were three. That night we slept no more.

The English do well to build their boats deep, for only such
boats can hold the sea, or rather I should say, they 'did' well to
build their boats deep in the days when they did so build them,
before lines were ruined by racing. But there is this disadvantage

about your deep boat: that it will not sit, but lies over. So did the *Nona* on that stormy night; and damnably. You will tell me that when the tide rose she floated. Yes; but not until very much water had trickled in through the dry seams, so that the pale and stormy dawn from over Dorset, and the distant grey of Chesil and the Bill saw us still bailing—and so much for Lyme Regis.

Thence eastward, coasting back home, any man who belongs to my county and to its harbours must face the passage of Portland Race and the difficult rounding of the Bill. So had I always done, whether coming or going, whether easting or westing, leaving aside all that long coast of Dorset hither of the Isle of Portland, and watching afar off the endless unbroken patch called the Chesil Beach quite empty of men.

What a gift of compensation it is that the horror of our great towns and the ease of our new communications has produced deserts in between!

No one knows those deserts as well as the man who sails along the sea, following the coasts of England. The foulness of the great towns is discharged by the trainload upon beaches of sand; but all in between, or nearly all, is left more lonely than ever it was before in our history. Those cliffs of Dorset coming down on to the sea are less known to travelling Englishmen than much of foreign land.

Great Trials

The tendency of men to believe what it makes them happier to believe is so strong that one should lean with all one's weight against it in public as in personal affairs. But that does not mean that the verdict was not just: it only means that the accepted legend has no authority in itself. During my boyhood the opinion of men amply qualified to judge, men eminent in the legal profession, men of the Tichbornes' social standing and religion, was as violently divided as were later men of the same capacity for judgement in the matter of the Dreyfus affair.

Though I was too young to remember the heat of the quarrel, yet I always listened with interest to the violent disputes I heard between my elders, especially those which regularly took place in one of the Sussex houses, the Squire, of which had no doubt at all of the claimant's right; and my reason for such interest in a matter to me remote is this: that the Tichborne verdict is the first thing I remember. We were living in a house in Westminster, and my nurse who was excited in the matter, as all folk then were, rich and poor, took me into the press of people at Westminster Hall to hear the result. Of course, very early memories like this (I was but three years old) are falsified by the continual repetition of the subject by one's elders, but I am as certain as any one can be of such a memory, and I believe it is the earliest thing of which I have any clear memory left.

Upon a similar very early memory depends one of the longest links with history with which I am acquainted. Mademoiselle de Montgolfier, the daughter of the man who made the first balloons, lived as a life-long companion of my Irish grandmother in France, and died well after her ninetieth year, when I was a boy of ten or eleven. That woman as a child of four was present in Paris when the mob poured up the Faubourg of St Antoine to the capture of the Bastille in 1789, and I, as a child of seven, eight and onwards, was brought to her time and again to hear her tell the story. I am now in my fifty-fifth year, and the stretch of time is already remarkable. Were I in extreme old age, and told a child of this incident, that child himself, living to a similar old age, would be able to say that he had spoken to one who had heard of the fall of the Bastille from an eyewitness; and that would be as though some very old person today were to tell one that he had spoken to one who had known a page at Charles II's court, and had seen as a child the funeral of General Monk; or again, it is as though some very old person today were to remember having met in childhood a person who had talked to one who had seen John Milton.

The Dreyfus case, after all these years, still rouses such passions that I tremble even to mention it. I have myself (so many years after!) been subject to mournful rebuke in public from the excellent pen of Dean Inge, who has reproached me in well-knit prose for being the only man in England who did not take the side of the accused. He is wrong there; for I could cite the names of half a dozen prominent Englishmen who had the right to judge through a knowledge of European affairs, and who remained in doubt of Dreyfus' innocence, notably Lord Russell of Killowen, the Lord Chief Justice, and Mr Labouchere—and there were many others.

Here also the difficulty lay in weighing opposing sets of un-disputable facts. The nearer men were to a position where they could fully judge all the technical details of that highly technical evidence, and the probable motives of the clashing witnesses, the more were they divided; they remained divided today upon the issue after more than thirty years. On the one hand was present an overwhelming motive to secure the conviction of a man against whom there was strong *primâ facie* evidence. That motive was the desire to preserve the Intelligence Department of the French Army intact, though rival powers were bent on its destruction. On the other side was another motive: the overwhelming motive of freeing a man who was believed innocent, and the lesser, but still very strong, motive of defending the immunity of that small immensely wealthy, very powerful clique of international financiers, one member of which—the first and the last in our time—had been challenged by the authority of a modern State. Such men regard themselves, and are, in practice, usually treated, as though they were above the law.

I, for my part, pretend to no certain conclusion in the matter, for I doubt whether any man could do that who was not on the Bench in court, and physically confronted with the witnesses, and acquainted with all the documents, and able to weigh them all—even the use of the most technical terms in gunnery. But it is to be remembered that there was division upon that Bench itself, and that a minority of the five judges—two out of three—were (I am told) for acquittal.

Of my own intimate acquaintance who were on the spot and competent to judge, most were for the innocence of Dreyfus: but the rest, fully competent also, were and are, convinced of his guilt.

There are in England today two Englishmen whose wide know-ledge of Europe and especially of Paris, and the French tongue and society, enable them to judge. They are both close friends of mine. One is for, the other against.

I believe that, when the passions have died down, the Dreyfus case will remain for history very much what the Diamond Necklace has remained, or the Tichborne case; that is, there will be a popular legend, intellectually worth nothing; and, for the historian, the task of criticizing that legend, but hardly of solving the problem.

The historian will have one point to make in connection with it,

and that a point of capital importance. It is to the Dreyfus case that
we owe the four years of war, 1914–18: for it destroyed the French
Intelligence Bureau and so permitted the German surprise on Mons
and Charleroi.

Perhaps problems depending upon human psychology can never
be finally determined. But there are others equally absorbing which
involve no such heats, and no such moral doubts: only physical and
mathematical oppositions.

It would be a worthy task to draw up a list of such essentially
historical problems not involving guess-work upon human motives,
but dealing with plain, physical facts; problems which have remained unsolved, and which do not seem to be in the way of being
solved either. Your academic writer shirks them nearly always; he
writes as though they had been solved, and as though he knew the
solution; so that his readers go on imagining they have been given
an explanation which as a fact has been carefully avoided.

'Reminiscences of Youth'

It was a time when men who have since been caught into the net
of professional politics, and have lost their souls, went down to
speak fiercely at street corners, and to light in the hearts of broken
men the flame of human dignity.

I have seen in those days a young man, the heir to a great fortune
(later a minister of sorts) standing under the flaring naphtha lamps
of a muddy London evening, calling out the new gospel and the
promised land. I remember the eager, stupid, upturned faces of the
men and women, who had come there from bestial depths of the
slums to hear him; to go back into those depths, and there to remain. They lie in those depths today. It is not such a creed that
will save them. I remember the great mobs that followed John
Burns, and how I myself would go miles through the East End to
hear him; and I remember that great whirlpool of men in Trafalgar
Square on the most critical day when he and others accepted
imprisonment. There is nothing now for which men would act so;
no one now has a creed; therefore, I call that time of my youth a
better time.

Of all that enthusiasm and conviction nothing came; the mill
turned noisily enough, but it ground no corn. Those fevered exalta-

tions were transformed within a few years to a contemptible shrieking and raving called 'imperialism', and that also went its way, and
worked itself out to its ignoble end. . . . We survive today to hear
a perpetual flattering of America, a perpetual grumbling against the
workers, their sullenness, and, overseas, the increasing peril of
control over the alien races once so easily governed. The vulgarians
who invented this music-hall cry of empire now suffer the vacillation and the increasing peril into which their own base bullyings
have led them. They must live a little time longer and dree their
weird, and learn what happens to those forms of pride which have
not even the merit of dignity.

Of these years, one thing remains: the dock strike made
Southampton.

I see the monstrous ships of the Atlantic passage pass up and
down the dredged channel to Southampton Water, and, as I look
at them earning their millions for the few masters of such machines,
I say to myself: 'This was the fruit—here is the only fruit—of
those nightly enthusiasms by the London Docks, and of the cry for
freedom, and of the passionate belief that within a few years after 1899
the poverty of London would have passed into an evil memory.'

I carried on between the forts at Spithead under the new day,
with the wind steady from just west of south until I was relieved
at the helm, and hour by hour we made for the Looe.

Now with the Looe stream, which is the gateway to the Sussex
seas, I knew not whether I should take the coast in its order between
the Owers and the Forelands, or carry on day and night to the
straits. For I have cruised up and down that garden wall of my own
land so much that it stands in my mind as a perpetual come and go,
sometimes far out into the salt beyond sight of England, sometimes
a run in before too much wind, sometimes a beating up for Beachy,
sometimes just missing, and at others just making, any one of the
impossible entries of my harbours.

For the county of Sussex—and Kent, too, for that matter—up
to Folkestone, and beyond has had tricks played with it by the
Creator of the sea and land. There has been done to it what is often
done to a human life—that is, the granting of an insufficient
opportunity; opportunity enough to compel the use of a function,
not enough opportunity for the fulness of that use. All the harbours

are such that they can be made, but only on sufferance; Chichester Harbour, which is also Bosham, Littlehampton, Shoreham, New-haven, Folkestone in its day, are not to be approached at low tide save for the work of man, and Pevensey is dead, and what was once the shelter of Hastings has been worn down by the seas, the chalk reef which came out like an arm to keep off the south-west weather; nor is the breakwater they have made there sufficient. Newhaven is dredged, indeed, and they have pushed out a great pier of stone into the sea to stop the eastward making of the bank at its mouth, and Folkestone has a roadstead made for it though it is incomplete and open, but in their nature all these harbours are to be used by the favour of the tide, and that is why it is so awkward to be caught in a gale outside while Arundel River, or the Bramber River, is still ebbing out over Littlehampton or Shoreham Bar; for both those bars show out at a low spring tide. Sussex in this is less favoured than the Caux Country of Normandy, which is her opposite num-ber. For Trouville and Dieppe, of course, and Fécamp, and even St Valery, a boat like mine can get into at any time. This is for two reasons, first, because the Norman streams do not come from the country beyond the chalk hills as do our Sussex rivers, but are mere brooks, so that there is no weight of water to bring the clay silt down through the harbour mouths; next, because they are not open to the south-west wind and to the eastward drift.

The Sussex rivers left to themselves get a bar piled up in front of their mouths by the south-west wind and the in-shore tide, so that a bank of gravel grows up eastwardly continually in front of them. Thus the mouth of Shoreham river, the Adur, travelled eastward for three miles and more between the Conquest and the civil wars; until at last it came out into the sea right up near Hove. But later a great storm burst through the bank and made the present entry, half-way down.

Exactly the same thing happened with the Ouse. Its bank of shingle crept out eastward until, in the Middle Ages, the entry was at Seaford, and that is why Seaford was called 'Sea' Ford, and that is why the French would attack Sea Ford, and that is why when they so attacked 'This Pelham did repel 'em back aboard', as you may read in Lewes Church. After that a storm broke through the shingle bank, making a new entry right down to the westward, and so brought into being what is still called the 'New Haven'.

'To London River'

I could wish that this book, already so long as to have become intolerable to the reader, the writer, the printer, and all others concerned in its production, already so heavy as to have become a business to the publisher, the carman, and the railway people (if, indeed, they transport it, but I have known of books transported in bulk on shipboard, and sinking to the glory of God, before they reached their destination, and that to the great advantage of our miserable world, which is abominably overcrowded with books); I could wish that this book, already so prolix, so otiose, so weary of its way that no poor gabbler in an inn ever more offended his audience than I will mine; I could wish that this book, which may be called the Great Sea Serpent of books, or again, The Cromwell Road of Books, or once again, The Pambiblicon, or endless Compendium, or again, The Long Arctic Night—what you will—I could wish that this book were longer still, I say, in order that I might drag you to perdition with the tedium of a million memories north of the Forelands, north of the Goodwins, north of Long Nose: memories of the Muddy Rivers of the Trinobantes, whose descendants inhabit rather than cultivate the Essex clay: memories of sandbanks rising out of the misty seas like whales, and of the platters of Harwich, and of the King's ship called *The Serpent*, and of Orford River, and of the Onion, and of Lowestoft, Yarmouth, and the exceedingly difficult labyrinth of the Wash, and of the awful great tide at King's Lynn.

But I renounce—not so much for your sakes as for my own, nor do I even speak of that Thames River which sailors called London River, and of the getting across it slantwise in spite of the great ships and the way in which time has silted up that harbour.

There are many curious things to be noted about the opening of London River. There is the double tide, so that a man making Long Nose from the Channel finds a new tide taking him up towards London. There is the way in which the best of all the channels into the river is the one least used, because it would make ships go out of their way. Ships come into the Thames either from the north or from the south, so they save time, which is money, by skirting either coast, but the main mid channel only the Dutchmen use when they have occasion to come up London River; I approve them.

XXX

From *Miniatures of French History*
1925

Belloc was happiest as an exponent in literature as a miniaturist, and this book shows Belloc the historian at his best.

During this year Belloc and his wife went to Brussels where he met Cardinal Mercier, Archbishop of Malines. He recalls in a letter to Mrs Asquith that it was two years ago when he read Don Quixote which she had given him, 'the best present ever a man had. Perhaps the only book I have ever really read'. In March he gave a lecture at Louvain. on 'Thomastic economics', and in the same month his Mother died. 'For the last thirty-five years she lived in her own way, quite contented on the tiny income which survived the wreck of our fortune and seeing all whom she desired to see and in absolute peace and plentitude. Her death was consonant with this. It is rare indeed that such long happiness and such a quiet passage out of this detestable world is granted,'[1] he wrote to Mrs Frank Collins.

He dined with Max Beerbohm, who he thought grew 'nicer and nicer as he grows old' and on one of his rare visits to the theatre he went to see The Farmer's Wife which he thoroughly enjoyed.

In May he went to Tunis, and en route he visited Palermo and Cefalu. At Carthage he tells Mrs Raymond Asquith that he went to the Museum of the White Fathers 'that stele of the Priestess of Ashtaroth which moves me to the depths of my being'[2] and that Cherchell was 'the ante-chamber of Heaven and the vestibule of Paradise'.[3]

[1] *Belloc Letters*, ed. Speaight, p. 162.
[2] *Belloc Letters*, ed. Speaight, p. 166.
[3] *Belloc Letters*, ed. Speaight, p. 167.

The Crowning of the Capetian

(Sunday, July 3, AD *987)*

Let any one who would understand the fortunes of the French wander for days in the wooded valleys of the Oise. There great forests still clothe the low rounded hills which border the widenings of the slow river, where it saunters through its pasturages and its marsh, with tall, delicate aspens in solemn lines to mark its passage. It is a flat river floor of half a league across, and about it the great woods of Compiègne and of Coucy, and all the others that still bear the name of their towns or castles, make a sheet of trees. That sheet of trees may have been a wider thing in the old days, but it remains for any one who will visit it (and it is a countryside that will harbour a man for as long as he will, so broad is it and so deep) the memory of that landscape in which the fortunes of his country changed and re-arose.

But, in particular, the forest of Coucy and the depths of the tall trunks understand how the lords hunted there when the Emperor was still the Emperor, and before France was once again France. See how there still remain in fragments the lines of the Roman roads that led from town to town; all the towns that make up this countryside. Consider Paris, one hard day's ride away, two or three days' marches. Remember Laon on its impregnable horse-shoe hill upon the edge of those woods, overlooking the plains to the east and the north, and forming a bulwark and a stronghold for the last of the blood of Charlemagne.

Then, in your mind, see westward and southward the open land, Normandy and Anjou, the Island of France, the gardens of Touraine, Nevers, the high Morvan, the Champagne, crammed with Latinity, and the valleys of the Allier, of the Cher, and of the Vienne, leading upwards and southwards into those dead mountains of the centre which are the frontier against the south. Remember also the good lands that flank Brittany, and that make an approach and a barrier at once for that jealous, silent land. Do all this, and you will understand what happened when the Carolingians fell, and when, in one moment, a new line of kings that stood for Gaul rearisen was accepted and crowned in the person of its ancestor.

France would be. The Germanies learning the Faith, and informed by the French, were still the Germanies: barbaric, lacking in stone and in letters; lacking in roads. The Latin speech had not followed in them the Latin rule, and the Church which had made them human had hardly welded them into Christendom. It was not possible that Gaul should any longer be confused with these, unless, indeed, they would consent to be ruled from Gaul. That, in their new-found faith and culture, they would not consent to. Yet the imperial line and the old name of Charlemagne, now wasted for nearly two hundred years, pretended to control the issue. But France knew itself again—that is, Gaul knew itself again, through the confusion of how many centuries; and a symbol must be found for France. The line of Charlemagne was exhausted. It could present for claimant to universal rule over the Germanies, as over Gaul, as over Italy, nothing that men respected, no one whom soldiers followed.

But in Gaul itself was a family and a man.

That Robert who had died at Brissarthe, and who had come, no man knew whence, but who was so strong, and who was called 'The Strong', had founded lineage. It was a man of his blood who had held Paris against the Normans. Men of his blood had claimed the crown and kingship once, and had been a part of the Empire, and had yet dropped the claim. But their great estate of land had grown and grown. Their command over many soldiers had grown therewith. They spoke in the Latin tongue; they were of us. And of all of those who were of us they were the richest and, what is much more, the most captaining family of them. Of that great line Hugh was now the man. For a hundred years his father and his father's father and his father before him had been the true masters of those good river valleys, the Loire, and the Seine, and the Oise. If there was to be government, he, Hugh, must come.

Rheims of the Champagne, the town where Clovis, five hundred years before, had accepted the Faith and made a unity for Gaul, had in this moment for its great archbishop one Adalberon, a man very subtle, and more learned than subtle; stronger in will than either in his learning or in his subtlety, and perceiving future things.

In those days there was between men a division. The great were very great. The mass of men were hardly free, and were all very small. The slaves that had worked for Roman lords in generations now half-forgotten, if they were no longer slaves, were still mean men; and the few that could ride by the day through their estates inland were great above all men—the great bishops, the great counts, the men of the palace, and the masters of the countryside.

These, then—the Empire now plainly in default, and wealthy Gaul, as it were, derelict, and the Germanies, in their barbarism, sheering off—counselled what they should do. They met in an assembly, going up the northern road from Paris to Senlis; and here there was great tumult. For each man came with his armed men about him, and confusedly they knew how mighty a thing was toward.

In that tumult it was Adalberon who spoke: 'Charles of Lower Lorraine,' he said, 'has many to speak for him, and he says that the throne should come to him by right of lineage. But there should not stand at the head of this kingdom any but he who is great. Hugh, the commander of armies, is known to you by his deeds, by his descent, and by the armed men in his troop, who are many. If you will have government, take him.'

In the further tumult that followed Adalberon persuaded, and Hugh, coming from those who had saved Paris, and who had commanded armament in Gaul for now so long, was acclaimed by the great lords as king.

When the time came for the anointing and the crowning, and for this separation of France again from what was not France, this re-seizing of the nation to itself, Noyon was the town they chose.

Little Noyon, with its vast arcaded church, strong and Roman, amid the woods of the Oise, the altar before which Charlemagne himself had been crowned. To Noyon they came in the midst of those forests of the Oise, by that strict road of the Romans which bridged the river, and which is but one of the many that there meet, as in the centre of a wheel; for the dignity of Noyon, now so forgotten, lay in this—that men could come to it easily, even in those days of difficulty and of old arts forgotten.

In Noyon, then, was Hugh crowned.

He had no name but Hugh. Since, however, men must give names to a family as well as to a man, all the generations after him have remembered what his nickname was. For he had a nickname, this soldier and lord, and from his helmet or his hood he was called Hugh Capet, the man of the head covering—the man of the head or cap. And that is why this family is called Capetian: a little cause for a great thing.

Louis XI and Charles the Bold

(January 5, 1477)

In a small room, the large grey stones of whose walls were partly hidden under tapestries, there sat at evening a man too wizened to show his full age. He was in the fifties. He might have been fifteen years younger or fifteen years older—he would have looked the same. He was simply dressed—it was winter—in warm grey clothes, and though a great fire of logs burnt in the huge open hearth of the small room, he had a thick cloak over his shoulders. He was cold, and thrust forward to the flames long, thin and somewhat grasping hands. His keen, narrow eyes, closely set together and very bright, shone in the firelight. On a large oak table to his left stood carefully ranged a mass of papers, and one great parchment which he had been consulting. But for the moment he read nothing. He muttered to himself.

One soldier was in the room, standing silent by the curtain which hid the door. Without could be heard from time to time the metallic clinking of arms and the steps of men coming and returning. At long intervals there came from distant roofs of the castle the cry of the sentry. For the rest there was no sound in that room save the crackling of the fire and the continued muttering of this man.

It was the king—Louis XI.

To his hand there upon the table, and docketed and filed minutely, stood his immediate affairs; accurately, in shelves which lined the larger rooms of the castle, and served by a great staff of clerks, was further stored the whole business of the realm.

In his childhood that realm was ruined. As a little frail child of five he had seen Joan passing through his father's palace at Bourges. In his boyhood had come the difficult reconquest; his manhood had been filled with exiles, with quarrels against his father, the reigning king, and with a long apprenticeship in intrigue.

It was his business to rebuild the realm. And for now nearly sixteen years he had plunged into that business as private men of the same sort will plunge into the accumulation of a fortune. It had absorbed him altogether, and his soul, never sane, had suffered from that absorption, much as suffer the souls of men who devote themselves in the same fashion to gold.

But his zeal was for the re-establishment of the realm. This, the unceasing pressure of a spirit which for centuries had urged and spurred the Capetian line, which had made them—some quite unconsciously, none quite consciously—the agents of a great purpose, had urged Louis continually. His task was nearly done. Only one great rival still loomed to the east of him. It was Burgundy.

All that Rhineland, all that great street from south to north, from the Alps to the Low Countries, all that belt of true French soil, and of its extension into the Germanies, was under a man—Charles the Bold—ten years younger than himself, who, building on his father's power, had dared to conceive independence. He would make a new State, breaking the vassalage with the King of France. He would leave France halved.

This man, Charles, stood against that older man, Louis, in a contrast more complete than any two rivals you can name: Louis frail, cunning, tenacious, garrulous, delighting in a millioned web of detail, patient, cruel, diseased: Charles, short but strong in the saddle, square-shouldered, violent in action, somewhat silent, his mass of thick black hair ponderous upon his enormous head, living in the midst of charges, and thinking that the world could be carried at a charge.

The last issue between these two men had come. The one was sitting here in his narrow room, in the heart of France, holding the threads which stretched to the ends of Europe. The other, in camp, pursued the siege of Nancy, and was in the act of taking that capital, destroying Lorraine: confirming his power.

As King Louis sat there, his hands and feet towards the flame, muttering to himself, and his bright, narrow eyes seeing scheme after scheme conjointly in the dancing of the fire, his mood changed and, as though he were alone, careless of the attendant, he suddenly threw himself upon his knees at the chair where he had been sitting, and raised his mutterings somewhat into prayers. He groped in his breast for an amulet and kissed it fervently, and continued in a litany name after name of those who should protect him and his race, and all his land. But the name which occurred most often in that confused torrent of intense mumbling was the name of St Martin of Tours, his neighbour, his protector, he to whom Louis the King had shown such generosity; he upon whom Louis the King had showered so much wealth, and before whom he continued to bow.

In the first light of a very cold morning the king rode out with half a dozen familiars. He was helped with difficulty not on to a horse but on to a mule. His long, thin, somewhat deformed legs with difficulty held the saddle, and he stooped forward gracelessly as he rode. No one could have told him from a chance traveller of the poorer sort. He was in grey, as always—a thick, coarse cloth— and on his head a rough, pointed hat, with a leaden medal stuck in the band of it, and on the medal, stamped, an image of Our Lady.

He rode out over the drawbridge towards Tours, in the bitterly cold mist as the day broadened. One hundred yards and more behind came the archers and the drivers of the wagons; for he had begun a journey.

The king and his little group of attendants halted for twenty minutes in the town for Mass. As he came out of Mass, he turned to the first poor inn of the market square, and ate the first short meal of the day, while the innkeeper and the serving-maid watched him in terror, and the passers-by in the streets huddled in corners, catching glimpses of him through the thick, small panes of the window.

And all during that meal he talked, and talked incessantly, to his companions, upon every point of his policy: upon the place they should visit, upon the chances of meeting the messenger whom he expected—upon all things.

They took the road again like a little company of poor pilgrims; they followed up the Loire.

They came at last to a place where the road, damp with melting snow but now lit by a pale morning sun, passed through a deep wood along the river bank, and there stood a hut which the foresters used. It was the appointed spot. The king halted, dismounted, and entered with but one companion. The rest stood without.

They had not long to wait. Another small group approached

from the west, but these were splashed with mud, broken with fatigue, their fine horses hardly carrying them, and stumbling as they went. One of them was half in armour, and seemed to be their chief. He scrambled down stiffly from his beast, almost falling as he did so, entered the hut, and knelt before the king.

The king raised him, but before he could tell his great news Louis deluged him with yet another river of talk. How were the ways? What had he met? Had he passed through Bar, or had he come round north through Argonne? Had he heard what the common people were saying in either place?

Twice the newcomer attempted to tell his news, and twice he was swamped again by that ceaseless flood of clipped, tumbling words. At last he had his moment, and he took it to tell in three phrases the enormous thing which he had carried in silence through that night and through four desperate marches before.

Charles the Bold was dead. Nancy was relieved. Lorraine was master of his own again. The imagined new State was in ruins. Louis took up the ceaseless chatter again, patting the hand of his messenger as he did so, and smiling a thin but contented smile.

His work was accomplished. His great scheme was fulfilled, and yet such a moment led him to nothing more solemn than an endless cataract of words—save for one moment, when he fell again upon his knees on the earth floor of that hut and prayed as fervently as though he had been alone. He rose again to question re-question, and to make his comments. He was exhausted before he was silent.

Meanwhile, far off in Lorraine, the battle had been brought to its conclusion, and the great duke was Dead.

It was upon Sunday, January 5, 1477, that Réne of Lorraine, coming out from his Mass in the Abbey Church of St Nicholas, had ordered his armies—some few of the lords of the Barrois, some few more from the Charolais, some from the Jura were there; but the great mass of his rank and file were a hubbub of German talk from the Alsation towns and from the Swiss mountains—ten thousand of them.

They had not far to go. Nancy was but a short two hours' march away, and there, before his capital, starving and on the edge of surrender, Lorraine knew that the way was barred by the army of Charles.

It had been bitter cold, but there was half a thaw. The ice on the Meurthe (to the right of the road as the long column went northward up the bank) was still continuous, but thin and slushy. The great masses of snow round about were melting. It was somewhat before noon that they saw, drawn up in rank upon slightly rising ground before them, the host of Charles, and in the distance behind it, two miles away, the spires of Nancy.

From a wood upon his right to the west, down to the river Meurthe upon the east, Charles had drawn his line, with his guns commanding the road whereby the columns of Lorraine should advance. Fine snow began to fall, and under the veil of that cloud Lorraine detached a mass of the Swiss to follow round secretly by the hollow lane along the woodside. So they came up, unperceived, upon the flank of the Burgundians.

But those Burgundians, Charles's men, stood in rank awaiting the shock upon their front, ignorant of the turning column. They were but five thousand all told, and against them were two men to their one. They knew not that half their enemies had thus been detached secretly to the west. Still they waited, confident in the strength of their position: waiting for the heavy armed knights of Lorraine to charge.

Even as they so stood, the Burgundians heard something which no troops will stand—the sound of attack behind their line.

It was the custom of the Swiss to sound their horns three times just before they struck, and that loud, unexpected challenge came where none thought soldiers to be—far off and behind them to their right, from the woodside.

It was in vain that Charles attempted to convert his line to the right, to face that sudden danger; it was in vain that he called for the guns to be dragged round and faced westward to the wood and the Swiss. All came too late; for all was in confusion, and already his line was dissolving. Upon such a beginning of chaos Lorraine, from the front, charged; and with that the Burgundian troops became a mob, and the action, hardly begun, turned at once into a slaughter.

Charles's cavalry, upon the left, near the river, cut itself out across the water, losing heavily, the horses stamping through the thin ice, and a remnant escaping by that ford.

Round the great Duke himself a devoted centre rallied, half of them of his nobility, but it could not stand—it was forced back in the general flood, and all the two miles of ground that afternoon (the snow had ceased, and the sun shone upon the carnage) was filled with a confused mass of massacre and of flight. The Swiss and the Germans and the French lords of the Barrois pressed on into the midst of the broken herd, right up to the walls of the town.

A mile from the city gate there ran a brook, the brook of St John. There, in the hurly-burly, Charles the Bold, Duke of Burgundy, parried right and left desperately, his lords about him, and in their midst were the enemy, ahorse and afoot, the long halberds of the Swiss, thrusting pikes, and the swing of swords.

None knew the great Duke Charles in such a confusion. They saw his rich armour, but they had no other sign; for the golden lion of Burgundy upon his helm had fallen even before the battle, and he himself, as he saw the crest tumble on his saddle bow, all those hours before, had muttered: 'An omen—*signum dei !*'

So that man, unknown to the enemy, fought hard with his visor down, A thrust took him in the left thigh, another in the back. As he reeled he cried 'Bourgoyne!' but one Claude, the Lord of Bauzemont, who was fighting there for Lorraine, hearing that cry, thrust a lance at him, not knowing whom he struck. The helm and its visor shattered. The face of the great Duke was gashed from ear to chin, and he went down. None knew who had so fallen, for all the nobles about him also were destroyed. And that was the end of Charles the Bold.

The press of the conquerors rushed up to the city gate, the Gate of St Nicholas. The starving people ran to cheer, the garrison let down the bridge beyond the town, the last remnants of Charles's force were massacred at the bridge of Bouxières.

The winter sun was setting. The force had its hold again upon all the fields. The Duke of Lorraine held festival that night—back in his own city, and all his people eating again and drinking, and rejoicing in victory.

But one thing checked his triumph: whither had Charles gone? Was he in Metz, or fled perhaps into the Germanies, or got home among his own people in the Low Countries?

All the next day, Twelfth Day, the Feast of the Kings, they searched the battlefield, heaps of naked bodies stripped by the spoilers, but none could say that they had found the great Duke. But that evening, as Lorraine rode back into Nancy, despondent and fearful, a captain brought to him a young page, one of the Colonnas of Rome, and said to him: 'This lad knew the great Duke.'

So next morning, the Tuesday, January 7th, very early, they went out among the bodies in the snow, and the Italian boy would say first of one, then of another: 'It is not he . . . it is not he.' And with him also went one who had been a maid in the service of Charles. Then, at last, they came to the strong body, lying all wounds, with its dreadful gashed face, and the mass of thick, black hair against the snow, and the Italian page cried, 'That is the Duke,' and the servant knelt down crying and sobbing, and they heard her say, 'Ha! Burgundy, my Lord! my Lord!'

René of Lorraine had that famous body lifted with reverence, and wrapped in a linen shroud, and carried with pomp into Nancy.

Thenceforward, with whatever vicissitude of come and go, the Rhine was recovered for the Gauls.

The End of Chateaubriand

(November 27, 1843–July 18, 1848)

Chateaubriand was in England. He was at 35 Berkeley Square—a very old man (he was in his seventy-fifth year), and nearer the tomb than he knew. His legs, very thin and feeble, supported him ill. His hands, gouty and knotted, trembled a little. Even his fine eyes had lost much of their brilliance. He stooped in his slow walk, but he was supported by pride. He had determined to return to England where, fifty years before, in the eagerness of his young manhood, he had first loved. For of all his unstable, self-reflecting, unrooted adventures in those affairs, two only left something permanent with him—one the parson's daughter of his youth in Bungay, and the other the strong friendship of his last hours. He returned to the country where he had been ambassador and in the height of his fame.

It was the heir of France in exile who had bidden him come, and it was certainly in loyalty to the throne—to that immemorial line, to the institution which was the soul of his country, to the Capetians—that the old man had made the journey. It was not for memories of Bungay, still less for memories of the Embassy.

It was November—the most lonely month of the year. It was the 27th of that month. Chateaubriand had already been in London three days. The young heir of France in exile, the Comte de Chambord, bade him to that house, giving him for his use all the ground floor (for the great man dared not face stairs, though he still could move), and when, the next day, the prince received, he had himself helped and carried up to the main room, where a crowded mass of curious English, of loyal or interested French, passed before the prince in exile and bowed in turn to him. At the back of that crowd the Comte de Chambord saw, standing with difficulty among the rest in the press, the figure of the man whom he had brought at such a season overseas. He moved towards him at once, vigorously and spontaneously; without care for his own position at the moment; eager to salute the man whose greatness he sincerely recognized, whose usefulness to the throne had been a tradition for that younger generation (the prince was but twenty-three), and whose name was at the moment greater than any other name in France. He took both his poor gouty hands and said Chateaubriand must not stand. He put a chair for him. He told him, without flattery, that he depended upon his presence.

There was no one in that room like him, and Chateaubriand himself complained how many French had stayed away from fear—he had also complained, without reason, that official England had shunned the exile—there was no one in that room, I say, but saw two figures supreme among them: the exile, who later might, if he would, have been king; and that old man of the laurels, who knew himself, and was known by all of them already, to be a sort of immortal—such a pen had he.

The reception was over, the blaze of candles extinguished, the old man had been helped back again to his rooms below. He took paper and, as best he could with his failing fingers, noted the points of what next day he must dictate—as next day he did—to his last friend. Next day also that long letter was written and remains to us. It has a phrase upon the Comte de Chambord, upon Henri V, which is not to be forgotten:

'The kings would have done well to have saluted this young ghost of a time outworn. They would have done well not to insult, as he passed, a traveller who had nothing to show but a broken sceptre in his hand. They laughed: they did not see that the world has grown tired of them, and that time will force them at last to take that same road as has been taken by the great royal line which protected them all and lent them a life which fails them now.'

Chateaubriand was in the rue du Bac, in those rooms on the ground floor where he was to end. The great windows opened upon a town garden, dark with trees in spite of the light of July.

His friend, Jeanne Françoise Récamier, was awaiting, herself in old age, ready to join him again.

Everything that he had been, all that had made up himself—his vivacity and changeableness of love, and tenacious hate—seemed to have departed, and he lay as though he had already fallen into the power of death, though his eyes still shone. He heard, but with difficulty. He spoke hardly at all, and then in but few, murmuring words. Over his paralysed body they had thrown a coverlet, upon which his hands lay still. He was waiting for the advent of the friend whose friendship alone remained to him of life. But she herself, who had been the most famous of beautiful women as he had been the most famous of lyrical men, had come also to the term of things; and those eyes of hers, which had held captive a generation, were now nearly blind. As he so lay, awaiting her, there returned to his weakened mind a certain phrase of his own writing not so long before, where he had spoken of human affection and had said of love that time changes our hearts as it does our complexion and our years. Nevertheless there is one exception amid all this infirmity of human things, for it does come about sometimes that in some strong soul one love lasts long enough to be transformed into a passionate friendship, to take on the qualities of duty, and almost those of virtue. Then does love lose the decadence of our nature and lives on, supported by an immortal principle.

She to whom—or rather, round whom—those words were written was brought in, a ghost of the past, as he was a ghost of the past, to sit by him as he lay there, silent and deafened, on the edge of death. There could pass very little between them. They had neither of them the strength to speak at any length: nor she in a voice which he could well hear, nor he in a voice strong enough to reach her ears. But her presence was a final consolation.

When she left him after that singular interval of communion and silence he slept a little, and the next day he knew that his end had come.

It was Sunday, July 2nd. Outside, in the streets, the noise of the popular revolt had hardly died down, and contrasted with that too great energy of sound and of young fury was this silent room opening upon the garden, and the figure lying there. He asked in a whisper for the Sacraments he who had said in a phrase which showed the man like lightning: 'No Christian believes as I do, nor is any man more sceptical than I.'

On the next day, Monday, the 3rd, his life still dragged on and diminished, yet he whispered to his nephew, who took down the words from his lips: 'I declare before God my retraction of all there may be in my writings contrary to the Faith, to good morals, and in general to the principles which are conservative of good.' And his nephew put down beneath those lines: 'Signed for my uncle, whose hand can no longer sign.' He had the declaration read to him; he tried to read it with his own failing eyes. Yet another night dragged on; but it was not until Tuesday, the 4th, that he died, and there had come back to that death-bed the friend, the old woman—Madame Récamier. Besides her there was but his nephew, his confessor, and a Sister of Charity. It wax a little after eight in the morning. The priest and the Sister of Charity were kneeling at the end of the bed; the two others stood and saw his passing.

So he died.

A fortnight later, upon Tuesday, July 18, 1848, they brought the body of Chateaubriand for burial to the place which he had chosen. That insecure, moving, intense soul of his was steeped in its own time, thinking that sublime which today we think grotesque, and which tomorrow our descendants may think sublime again. He had determined, in his passion for things both singular and glorious, in his vanity, but also in his love of greatness, upon a peculiar tomb, and it was now to receive him.

The Cathedral of Saint Malo was filled with the sailors of the place, with peasants come in from the countryside, with the clergy of the province, with all the officials of the town and even of Rennes—a vast crowd. They laid the coffin in the Chapel of the Sacred Heart, blazing with candles, and all that afternoon and all night long the crowd kept pouring in to pass by this lying-in-state and to pray, in a stream that did not end hour after hour.

On the next day, the Wednesday, after the last Mass to be said over him, the runners harnessed the horses, and the whole train set out for the rock which is an island at high tide and in which his tomb had been cut. It had been placed for him alone, and he had ordered—a last singularity—that there should be no name or inscription upon it whatsoever. As they laid him in his tomb the guns sounded a last salute, the walls of the city were covered with men and women watching that strange sight, and even the rocks to seaward and along the shore were black with people. They say that fifty thousand stood by and saw the sight.

And there he is today; and no one can say at all whether, with the passage of time, he who was at that moment the greatest of the great will become greater still, or insignificant.

XXXI

Advice to the Rich

1926

Remember that you will shortly die.

Let us hear a little less about your taxes.

Give largely, and especially to the embarrassed of your own station in life. Thus you may possibly escape Hell.

Do not be too angry with the man who goes about carrying a large model of a needle with an eye and a little toy camel in his left hand. The camel is made of india rubber and can be squeezed through the eye of the needle; but with difficulty.

Do not patronize: they are at least as good as you and most of them better.

What you are really keen on is new emotions. Try this: dress up like a poor woman and tramp it for one week seeking work (if you are a man, which I doubt, dress up like a poor man).

Spend lavishly on your pleasures. After charity it is the best use you can make of your money, but take care that they are pleasures; for most caviare is uneatable and as for most champagne . . .

Have your oysters opened
    (*a*) on the deep shell,
    (*b*) keeping all the liquour,
    (*c*) not wholly detaching them,

(*d*) immediately before you eat them. And do please remember that of the 6d you spend on each oyster 5½d is robbery: which you well deserve.

Learn about the inwards of your motor car.

Rule your children, your servants and your husband (or wife, as the case may be) or they will rule you (and that is all right in the case of husband or wife, as the case may be, but all wrong in the matter of children or servants—or beasts, for that matter).

Do not sell yourself. Poor people don't and you have no excuse; yet you are always doing it.

Do not let doctors cut you up: it is heads they win, tails you loose.

𝕯rink 𝕳earty: there is no more detestable sight than a rich teetotaller it always connotes dipsomania—a poor one is bad enough.

You are quite right to be keen on horses: the riding Englishman is the finest sort there is: but don't worship the silly beast. Worship God who made you and has long ago repented of that effort—thus may you appease Him.

When you use the word 'gentleman', use it in its exact sense of a particular English product with certain vices and certain virtues—upon the whole admirable. But don't use it as a piece of self-worship or as equivalent to 'a perfect being'.

Say what you really like and what you really don't like, and don't say you like things you don't like simply because they happen to be in the fashion.

I say it for the second time: 𝕯rink 𝕳earty.

𝕻ray for the pious donor of this advice, which he has given you freely and which is so vastly to your advantage.

XXXII

From *Short Talks with the Dead*
1926

*Despite the General Strike, this year proved a highly active one.
Belloc published six books and among them A Companion to Mr Wells'*
Outline of History. *It is among the publications of his from which we
would have liked to have drawn an extract, but in the space at our
disposal has not been possible, but the 'war' between Belloc and Wells
was a major event between two of the most powerful literary minds of
the day. They were obviously 'poles apart' in outlook, though the two
men had met and had got on quite well together, but their beliefs had no
meeting point. The fight did not end with Belloc's* A Companion to
Mr Wells' Outline of History *for Wells replied with* Mr Belloc Objects
(1926) and a still further reply from Belloc with Mr Belloc Still
Objects *(1926). Writing in June of that year to Lady Lovat he says
'H. G. Wells has written a very strong letter indeed saying that I am a
wicked man and an attacker of the innocent which is himself . . .'*

A Chinese Litany of Odd Numbers

The Nine Deplorable Social Habits

Drunkenness
Dirt
Shuffling
The Loud Voice
Scratching
Unpunctuality
Peevishness
Spitting
Repeated Jests

The Nine Admirable Social Habits

Relieving of tension
Courteous attention
Discreet mention
Tenacious retention
Assiduous recension
Wise abstention
Calculated prevention
Tactful intervention
A sense of dimension

The Nine Follies

To think oneself immortal
To think Investments Secure
To take convention for Friendship
To expect a reward for right doing
To imagine that the rich regard you as an equal
To continue to drink after you have begun saying to yourself
    that you are still sober
To write verse
To lend (or still worse, to give) money
To travel with much luggage

The Nine Rules for dealing with the Poor

    To be courteous
    To be distant
    To oppress
    To exploit
    To pay little
    To pay exactly
    To pity vaguely
    To interfere
    To denounce to the Authorities

The Nine Rules for dealing with the Rich

    To flatter
    To attend
    To remember many faces
    To love none
    To hate very few
    To attack only the defeated
    To enrich others by counsel
    To enrich oneself by all means whatsoever
    To lie

The Nine Negative Rules for Walking in the Country

    Not to fear beasts
    Not to walk without an object
    Not to become self-conscious when another approaches
    Not to hasten or linger but to adopt a dull stride
    Not to avoid trespass
    Not to avoid mud
    Not to avoid hills
    Not to brood on trouble
    Not to walk when you can ride, drive or be carried

The Nine Negative Rules for Walking in Town

    Not to talk to oneself
    Not to barge into others
    Not to swing the cane
    Not to cross the street in a reverie

SHORT TALKS WITH THE DEAD

Not to neglect a salute
Not to contest authority
Not to purchase unnecessary wares
Not to despise the evil eye of beggars
Not to leave a fallen coin lying

The Nine Jollities

To laugh
To fight
To fulfil the body
To forget
To sing
To take vengeance
To discuss
To boast
To repose

The Nine Final Things

Disappointed expectation
Irretrievable loss
Inevitable fatigue
Unanswered prayer
Unrequited service
Ineradicable doubt
Perpetual dereliction
Death
Judgement

[Here end the *Nines*]

THE SEVEN SEVENS, OR SEPTETS

The Seven Hateful Things

Scorn from a woman loved
Acute pain of the body
The memory of shame
Insult accepted from the rich
Defeat of one's country
Seasickness
Despair

265

The Seven Rare Things
  Vision
  Recovery of things past
  Good cooking
  Being loved
  Satisfaction
  Remarkable wine
  Justice

The Seven Common Things
  The mother's love
  Embarrassment
  Quarrel
  Ambition
  Disappointment
  Misunderstanding
  Appetite

The Seven Delightful Things
  Deep sleep
  Conscious vigour
  Reunion
  The Landfall
  Unexpected praise from a loved woman
  Resurrection
  Final beatitude

The Seven Medicines of the Soul
  Remorse
  Repentance
  Submission to the Divine Will
  A wide landscape
  A sublime air of music
  A firm determination to combat evil within
  Believing by an act of the will

The Seven Medicines of the Body
  Work
  Bed

Combat
Riding
Bread
Wine
Sleep

The Seven Stenches

The Traitor
The Pervert
The Cruel Man
The Sly Man
The False Teacher
The Deserter
The Politician

[Here end the *Sevens*]

THE THREE THREES OR TRIADS

The Three Oddities

The Dwarf
The Giant
The Foreigner

The Three Standbys

A Loyal Friend
A Good Wife
A Stiff Boat

The Three Perils

The World
The Flesh
The Devil

[Here end the *Threes*]

The One Thing of Both Good and Evil Effect

Honour preserved

[Here ends the *One*]

XXXIII

Extracts from *Many Cities*
1928

'Take books as you find them, and treat travel as travel. For you, when you go to a foreign country, see nothing but what you expect to see. But I am astonished at a thousand accidents, and always find things twenty-fold as great as I supposed they would be, and far more curious; the whole covered by a strange light of adventure.' Thus wrote Belloc. He was a great traveller in the truest sense of the word, and of all his travel works Many Cities *is one of the most delightful encompassing as it does his impressions of all the European countries he loved best.*

Cefalu

On the northern shore of Sicily, well westward of its midmost point, stands a rock and a town which may be taken for the type of the reconquered lands. These are the rock and the town of Cefalu.

All that coast is a procession of enormous headlands, Gibraltars of their kind thrown out against the seas, Corfano, Pellegrino and a score of others. But among them the rock of Cefalu is pre-eminent in its savage isolation, its defence, its bold challenge and the antiquity of its appeal to man. On the crags of its summit—I know not how high above the harbour, perhaps a thousand feet, perhaps twelve hundred—the first most ancient city, far older than any record, held its secure state; inexpugnable; looking down from its walls upon precipice every way. A few blocks of its enormous monuments remain and a trace of its wall. A little hook of reef, a narrow strand, provided a sufficient refuge and approach from the sea, thence a made path and steps of stone led up the sheer to the inhabited summit.

This, the first destiny of Cefalu and cause of its settlement, its place as a fortress, was renewed time and again all down its incalculable history, it certainly will reappear when the next phase of confusion and decline shall fall upon civilization. But with the Roman peace the high town was abandoned and the city stretched along the belt of shore, the sloping foot of the huge crag. The town left the summit and gathered round its little harbour, strung upon either side of the coast track which leads from the Straits of Messina to the last eastern cape of the island by Trapani. There has it since remained, clinging to the sea-fringe of its towering cube of stone, forgetting its first cyclopean foundation above.

All the ebb and flow of the East and the West have passed over it. Greece gave it its headland name. Carthage ruled it: Rome wrested it away. In the height of the Dark Ages—perhaps before the death of Charlemagne—Islam had planted a garrison here and made it an outpost in that sweeping of the Mediterranean whereby the Mohammedan and his Asia so nearly overwhelmed us. The Saracen chieftains, quarrelling among themselves, let in the Norman adventurers, the men from the Cotentin, who had set out to seize these lands a lifetime before the Crusades. It was with them that the recovery of Cefalu by the Christian West began, and from them that Cefalu received the great building and the shrine which is its mark today and has dignified it during nearly eight hundred years. For it was here that Roger of Sicily, the Norman King, driving landward in a storm, ordered to be set up in his name the church which he had vowed to build in whatever place should harbour him, if he should save his life and come to land. He devoted revenue largely to his vow, and thus it is that there stands in Sicily today a cathedral of the North, one of the very earliest to depend upon the pointed arch, large, of one kind: with superb mosaic looking not a lifetime old, but set into its cement before Richard of England sailed by with his square crimson sails to conquer Cyprus and to fail before Jerusalem.

That mosaic is as vivid a witness to history as you could find in all the South, or in any part of the recovered lands. Here is an art that was the glory of the later Empire before the generals revolted and began those disorders of the last Roman armies in which Rome was sacked, Britain lost, Africa cut off for a time and Gaul left derelict under a local commander of auxiliaries. The mosaic, with its eternal quality, remained, the characteristic of those church walls on which the Christian Emperor impressed permanent record. It is the art of Justinian as of Theodosius. It is the sign manual of that restoration of our culture which the genius of Belisarius effected in the West and which Islam came so near to destroying.

Islam swept over Sicily. Its chaos ruled. It began the massacre of the forests, the desiccation of the soil. The towns decayed, and their crafts. The Norman order and Christendom brought back a spirit not of that climate, but of the North. Yet here, in the most typically Norman of all Sicilian things, the not-Norman, the Byzantine mosaic returns, appearing again above the retreat of the Saracenic flood and set in the frame of that Ogive which means for us rather Chartres, Canterbury and Notre Dame than anything of Byzantium or of Ravenna.

All the apse is filled with it: sombre purples, a few deep reds, and innumerable squares in a sheet of glittering gold. The great subject is Christ in Judgement, the Heroic Face that dominates all the nave from above. He holds in His right hand the Open Book of record, His left is raised for acquittal or sentence. Below this head, with its not mortal proportions, are fixed upon the square space, above the altar, the lesser figures of the twelve apostles; and the whole, I say, seems to be of yesterday, or of our fathers' time at the most, so living is the surface. Yet it has looked down upon Christian men for more than seven centuries. May the evils of a coming time spare it!

Around that Head and Face, upon either side, following the border of the pointed arch of the roof (the true equilateral of the first Gothic) runs in legible, large, square script, lighter against a darker ground, the noblest motto yet found for the Judge and Redeemer and Brother of mankind. It was the sight of this motto which inspired Sargent to what is, undoubtedly, the highest, by far the highest, monument of his genius—the work in the public library of Boston, showing the fall of the old gods and centred upon such a treatment of the Crucifixion as one would have thought no modern man had it in him to create. But Sargent created it, thus inspired from Cefalu.

The motto runs thus:

> *Factus homo factor hominis factique redemptor*
> *Judico corporeus corpora corda Deus.*

An hexameter and a pentameter, with the characteristic internal rhyme of the second. And it means 'I, having been made Man, and being the Maker of Man, and the Redeemer of what I made, judge in bodily form the bodies and the hearts of man: for I am God.'

But Sargent in his masterpiece changed one word for the sake of his subject—this being not the Christ in Judgement, but the Christ crucified. He changed 'Judico' to 'Redimo'—writing 'I redeem' for 'I judge'. A transposition was necessary, also, for the sake of the metre, so that the motto to Sargent's Christ on the Cross at Boston reads:

> *Factus homo factor hominis factique redemptor*
> *Corporeus redimo corpora corda Deus.*

I think his genius to discover, and to be inspired by, such lines was as great as that which produced his painting.

Such, then, is Cefalu, crammed with the ages. It may be asked whether nothing is left here to mark their passage except this effect of the Norman married with the Imperial mosaic of Constantinople: nothing Saracenic or Greek and Roman?

I saw nothing—save fragments, on a shoulder of the hill, of a castle built there in the Middle Ages and on the bare summit against the sky a few huge boulders of the town before history.

There was not here in Cefalu that desire to fill every bare space with detail, nor that occasional hint at a pinched curve which reveals an Arabian spirit in Palermo, nor any of that perspective of crowded arches round a small, cool court which, in the Benedictine cloister of that town, reminds one oddly of the African palaces oversea. There was no delight in that excessive involution of line, that chipping of surface into fret and cusp which workmen once occupied on Saracenic walls and domes with difficulty forgot when they dealt later with the Christian shrines. In the outer lines of the cathedral, in the body of the building there is only the Northern spirit, with squat towers that might have come from Lisieux or Coutances; and within, there is that tradition of tessellated wall-picturing, a Christ that might have come from the Bosphorous.

It was very strange to observe, against the dark of the choir, a transept capital which, at a distance, seemed Corinthian, but which, close at hand, was a cluster of grotesques: monsters and monkeys. It was strange, under the eyes of such a Face as that which looked down upon us from the eastern roof, to see a baptismal font supported by the fierce leopards of the Dark Ages, the mythology of Anjou and Maine, the things men imagined during the long wars against the heathens of the North Sea, before Europe awoke to the noise and splendour of the Crusades.

Such is Cefalu: the weight of its nave and apse is prodigious above the town and against the Mediterranean. It had, before it left fame and drew apart from the story of Europe, one great memory more. It was here, I am told, that they brought the body of Frederic II, the *Stupor Mundi*, to lie in a place he would have chosen: the man who so nearly made himself an Anti-Christian master of his world: the last of the Emperors to hold, or attempt to hold, the South.

Later they took him on to Palermo, and he lies there now in his porphyry tomb. But Cefalu was nearer to his spirit.

Rocamadour

Of all that strange limestone country which forms the southern part of the central French mountain group I suppose the best known point is Rocamadour, yet travel does not reach it very largely even now, and probably such travellers as do go to it carry away with them the impression that it is unique. For the railway or the car takes them for the most part to other lands immediately, and few of them indeed go northward and eastward up into that high, half-desert country with its deep cañons and ancient mountain towns.

Yet Rocamadour is only one of perhaps half a hundred examples of the way in which man, for innumerable centuries, has used the physical character of the upper Dordogne basin; and if you wander about that part of the world on foot—which is much the best way—you will carry away the impression of one village and castle and shrine after another, clinging to precipitous crags which over-hang the waters in every valley.

To go down the Dordogne itself and make any excursion to right or left is a sufficient experience, and from such a position Rocamadour is only a few miles up a lateral valley to the south; but, as I shall say, it is not the best way. Originally Rocamadour—in historical times at least—was not a fortress but a shrine. As a fortress it would have had no very great value, for, sheerly precipitous as it is on the western side, the approach from the east is over an open plain without defensive value. In other words, Rocamadour is nothing but the jutting cape of a cliff; but the fact that it began as a shrine has made it what it is. The fact that the shrine was half-way up the precipice, beginning presumably as a hermitage, roughly sheltered by the overhanging rock, compelled the building of inns for pilgrims, and the establishment of shops for providing their necessities, and all that goes with them. They were compelled to choose the very boulders of the cliff face, clinging to them preca-riously, having steep steps for their village ways, and for their only street one very narrow levelled edge of mountain road, perhaps a third of the way up the steep.

It is this display of miniature miracles in construction and primi-tive engineering on a cliff face which lends all its character to the famous village—for village it now is, though in the Middle Ages it must rather have been a small town during the height of its fame.

The shrine is dedicated to Our Lady and has been so as far back as we can go; but a legend, historically unsupported, gives it an origin either earlier or later than the true one. As the legend runs, the Zaccheus of the Gospels wandered here after persecution in Palestine and built his hermitage half-way up the sheer side of the rock. The certain truth is, that you find a shrine widely visited, and with the name of St Amadour attached to it, just as the Dark Ages break into the light of the Middle Ages at the time of the Crusades, and that its origin is then already lost in an immense antiquity. It is possible that this antiquity stretches back for years beyond the beginnings of our civilization—or that of Rome. The heart of the shrine is a subterranean chapel—as at Chartres, and as at the Souterraine, some days away to the north; and we know how, all over Europe, the shrines of pagan antiquity were taken on by Christendom. Although we have the name, Amadour, it tells us nothing. A vague guess has been made that it corresponds with a real historical personage, St Amator, but of this there is no proof. It is to me half the fascination of Rocamadour that it goes back to the beginning of things—and beyond.

It is one of the places in Europe whose name has been revived, and such a thing is always pleasant to discover. An endless stream of pilgrims, kings, saints—among them was St Dominic, came to give thanks long after for the victory of Muret—and populace passed through it during the vigour of the Middle Ages. It dried up with the final corruption of medieval civilization. The site became deserted and half forgotten. But in our own time, just within living memory, a Bishop of Cahors revived it, and his efforts had a more far-reaching result than he had hoped for. It was as though a lamp, in which the oil was believed exhausted, being relighted, should burn with a brilliant flame. Nothing pictorial, certainly nothing descriptive in writing, can give fully the individual effect of the place. The platform in front of the three superimposed chapels, the tall building of the monastery above, plastered to the rock, the castle well towards the summit, the narrow town hanging far below, the whole thing resembling a ladder on a natural outline of broken rock against the sky rather than the work of a man.

Since the first effect of that vision is one of the most remarkable in Europe, I advise everyone who visits it to approach it in the particular manner which has been made most feasible through the advent of the railway. The approach should be across the edge of the *causse* or plateau from the east, whether you journey on foot or by car, until you come to the little hamlet called Hospitalet at the edge of the cliff. There halt a moment, and instead of going forward to the edge (as yet you see nothing) turn somewhat to the left above the highroad which runs down to its tunnel through the rock. There, before you get to the tunnel, or just above it, the valley opens before you and the precipice of Rocamadour rises against the green distant hills: a cascade of building, or a clambering of stones, one upon the shoulders of another, mingling with and fretting the sheer rock, as the details of a Gothic ruin against the sky fret the main perpendicular line of it: a sight that no one who has seen it will forget, and which no one will feel so keenly who has come upon Rocamadour from the west or north. Most of the great shrines in Europe have this natural appeal of landscape—as you may test at Chartres if, again, you come in the right way from the Beauce by the William Gate—and perhaps it is only in our own age that this appeal has been overlooked. Perhaps in some future day it will be recaptured.

XXXIV

From *Belinda*

1928

On July 20, 1928, Belloc wrote to Maurice Baring: 'I have finished Belinda—a fearful sweat—like sawing marble—but worth it. It is the only thing I ever finished in my life and the only piece of my own writing that I have liked, for more than forty years.'

Belloc was fully justified in writing thus, for this novel is charming, a timeless miniature. It tells simply of the love that Belinda, daughter of the wealthy Sir Robert Montgomery, has for the son of his impoverished neighbour, Horatio Maltravers. How the lovers are separated by a conniving rival and his lawyer friend, by the interception of their letters to each other, and how they are reunited in a château in France. It is a touching and beautifully told little tale.

'Of all', writes Robert Speaight, 'Belloc's works in prose Belinda is the most perfect, the most original, the most timeless, and therefore perhaps the most secure. It is also the most difficult to define. If we call it "pastiche", we realize at once that we have employed too light and artificial a word. Artificial in a sense it is, and no one could describe it as heavy; but deep feeling underlies the artifice and the humour has the weight of Belloc's own gravitas. The book grinds no axe and proves no point. It is a gratuitous, disinterested and quite impersonal essay in romantic irony. Small in scale and purposely conventional in subject, it still leaves an impression of grandeur; fine, not finicky; hard as a diamond and delicate as wrought iron.'[1]

Again this was a tremendous year in his literary activity. The third volume of his History of England *appeared as well as his biography of* James II, *and yet another historical work,* How the Reformation Happened. *There were essays—A* Conversation with an Angel. *and a further novel—But Soft, we are Observed.*

[1] R. Speaight: *Hilaire Belloc.*

Belinda

Winter had passed; the full trees were heavy with new leaves against the lingering sunsets of June, when Sir Robert Montgomery gave a Ball at his house, in order that Belinda might appear beneath her father's roof as the Queen of Wiltshire society. He was supported in this by a near female relative, a cousin, of austere and resolute presence, whose private means he had often supplemented, for whose worldly judgement he had a high regard, and whom he retained to accompany his daughter and advise him in his affairs.

Miss Hackman (as we have seen to be the lady's name) prepared the noble function in its every detail, and yet found time to suggest, to design, to command the ravishing *toilette* in which the débutante should conquer the admiration of all beholders. It was of a white and gauzy kind, relieved with large blue flowers of artificial construction; and while its ample but tenuous contours enhanced (if that were possible) the lure of her delightful carriage, its hue and cut proclaimed her charming innocence.

The movement of the crowded room, the hum of polite conversation, were halted to silence as the young Hostess appeared. That silence was succeeded by more eager words, till, at a signal from the band (which was conducted by M. Melchoir himself), the music of the dance arose in sensuous grandeur and the partners were set for the 'Martagnaise'. In the third figure of this graceful though foreign measure, the gentlemen, as is well known, advance in rotation, and next, just touching with uplifted hands the fingers of an opposing number, step for a moment with each lady in order, until the file is exhausted and the manoeuvre at an end. It is an occasion when those not partners in the dance yet greet for a moment, and when Beauty may be saluted (though not detained) by each admirer in turn.

XXXV

New Cautionary Tales
1930

About John,

Who lost a Fortune by Throwing Stones

JOHN VAVASSOUR
DE QUENTIN JONES

Was very fond
of throwing
stones

At Horses, People, Passing
    Trains,

But 'specially at Window-
    panes.

Like many of the Upper
            Class

    He liked the
        Sound of
            Broken
                Glass[1]

[1] A line I stole with
    subtle daring
    From Wing-Com-
    mander Maurice Baring

BELLOC

It bucked him up and made him gay:
It was his favourite form of Play.
But the Amusement cost him dear,
My children, as you now shall hear.

JOHN VAVASSOUR DE QUENTIN had
An uncle, who adored the lad:

And often chuckled; 'Wait until
You see what's left you in my will!'
Nor were the words without import,
Because this uncle did a sort
Of something in the City, which
Had made him fabulously rich.
(Although his brother, John's papa,
Was poor, as many fathers are.)

He had a lot of stocks and shares
And half a street in Buenos Aires[1]
A bank in Rio, and a line
Of Steamers to the Argentine
And options more than I can tell,
And bits of Canada as well;

[1] But this pronunciation varies.
Some people call it Bu-enos Airés.

He even had a mortgage on
The House inhabited by John.
His will, the cause of all the fuss.
Was carefully indited thus:

   'This is the last and solemn Will
Of Uncle William—known as Bill.
I do bequeath, devise and give
By Execution Mandative
The whole amount of what I've got
(It comes to a tremendous lot!)
In seizin to devolve upon
My well-beloved nephew John.

   (And here the witnesses will sign
Their names upon the dotted line.)'

BELLOC

Such was the Legal Instrument
Expressing Uncle Bill's intent.

As time went on declining Health
Transmogrified this Man of Wealth;
And it was excellently clear
That Uncle Bill's demise was near.

At last his sole idea of fun
Was sitting snoozling in the sun.

So once, when he would
  take the air,
They wheeled him in his
  Patent Chair

(By 'They', I mean his Nurse, who came
From Dorchester upon the Thame:
Miss Charming was the Nurse's name).
To where beside a little wood
A long abandoned green-house stood,
And there he sank into a doze
Of senile and inept repose.
But not for long his drowsy ease!
A stone came whizzing through the trees,
And caught him smartly in the eye.
He woke with an appalling cry,
And shrieked in agonizing tones:
'Oh! Lord! Whoever's throwing stones!'

Miss Charming, who was standing near,
Said: 'That was Master John, I fear!'

'Go, get my Ink-pot and my Quill,
My Blotter and my Famous Will.'

Miss Charming flew as
though on wings
To fetch these necessary
things,

And Uncle William ran his pen
Through 'well-beloved John', and then
Proceeded, in the place of same,
To substitute Miss Charming's name:

Who now resides in Portman Square
And is accepted everywhere.

XXXVI

On Translation (Taylorian Lecture)
1931

'*To find*', *wrote Robert Speaight*, '*Belloc's prose at its best, the reader should turn to the magnificent but little known Taylorian Lecture* On Translation, *delivered at Oxford in 1931. This was the first honour Belloc had ever received from Oxford and he felt like a boy getting the third prize for spelling, or better still, like a rosebud at her first ball on coming out.*'[1]

The lecture is given in its entirety here.

[1] Letter to the Hon. Mrs Mervyn Herbert, quoted in Speaight's *Hilaire Belloc*, p. 499.

On Translation

The art of translation is a subsidiary art, and derivative. On this account it has never been granted the dignity of original work, and has suffered too much in the general judgement of letters. This natural underestimation of its value has had the bad practical effect of lowering the standard demanded, and in some periods has almost destroyed the art altogether. The corresponding misunderstanding of its character has added to its degradation: neither its importance nor its difficulty has been grasped.

Writing men work in part for fame. Nearly all of those with any pretensions to write well—that is, to write as writing should be—take fame for a large part of their incentive; some, perhaps among the greatest, have the attainment of fame for their whole motive. If, therefore, in any department of writing it be impossible to attain fame, that department will presumably be neglected.

That insufficient fame should attach to translation is as inevitable as it is unjust. But though it be inevitable in kind we can modify it in degree and do some justice to the translator, as well as promote the end of great translation, by considering what that achievement of good translation is.

In the first place good translation is exceptionally hard of attainment (and the talent and instruction for arriving at it are correspondingly rare) because it demands what may be called a 'dual control'. The translator is working in two mediums, which two he has to be keeping abreast during every moment of his work, which both have to be present before him in equal weight and yet—what is a subtle point, but an essential one—present before him in two different ways. He has to be at the same time understanding that which he translates and producing, or as I should say actually creating, the translation in which it is to appear.

He has obviously both to know the tongue into which he translates and the tongue from which he translates, but he has also to possess a sort of shadowy tongue, the wraith of a composite language, a mysterious idiom which combines the two, acts as a bridge, and permits him to pass continuously from one to the other. Further, he must write well in the tongue into which he translates, for a translation is a bit of writing like any other and varies like any other in vernacular excellence. It is not enough that he should fully understand that which he is translating; he must also erect the new form in such a fashion that it shall be good in itself, so that any one reading it and not knowing it to be a translation should be as satisfied as though he were reading a good original.

Again, when I say that a translator must 'know' each of the two languages involved, that word 'know' signifies much more than a supposed precise meaning attaching to each term in each tongue; for not only is there no such possible exactitude of definition, but in one tongue the connotation even of a simple word simply representing a concrete object will be different from the connotation of the corresponding word in another tongue. Its historical and social connections will be different; its effect upon the rhythm of the sentence and therefore upon the emotion produced will be different —all that!

No wonder that we call translation a difficult art! No wonder that translators even of moderate value are rare, and translators of excellence as rare as poets! And with all that, I repeat, they are forbidden their full reward.

But the social importance of translation has always been great, and, as I shall hope to show, is today greater than ever. The moment one society has intercourse by commerce, policy or arms with a society of another idiom, translation is an imperative activity, you cannot carry on without it. It commands the value of treaties and of commercial contracts and of military capitulations. In a wider field, it is a condition of order between nations and therefore of peace. In a still wider field, it is the condition without which a common culture cannot exist.

And here I would particularly call attention to translation as a function of religion, for in the very nature of the case, translation has been an essential to the maintenance of religion among men, and since the religion of a community, that is, its sanctified customs in morals and action, is the determinant of that community, translation lies at the very roots of society.

For religion has about it two characters which thus compel the presence of translation. In the first place it is, or professes to be, emancipated from time, dealing with immortalities. But living languages are mortal. Therefore this original pronouncement of a religion becomes archaic (it is a part of their strength), and needs rendering into the speech men know in each succeeding age, lest the guide should fall dumb and his lantern be extinguished. In the second place Religion is of its nature universal and its application to various societies demands the rendering of its fundamental doctrines into the idiom of each in such fashion that all the renderings shall make for unity of thought, corresponding with the thought of the original.

Of such historical importance has this special function of translation been that, during the last five centuries at least, the main impetus of all translation has proceeded from it; and nearly all the great translations known to us, from the Septuagint and the Vulgate to the early English and Bohemian Bibles, to the renderings of Calvin's Institute and the innumerable vernacular explanations of Latin forms in the Roman communion, have issued from this source. It was, we may say, through religious translation, that English prose, in particular, was discovered: and largely by those translations that the modern English character was made.

As with religion, so with the external forms of culture, so with doubt, so with information. The translator is the purveyor of them all.

Now in this point of culture it is that translation acquires its special importance today. For the characteristic of our time is a singular disunion within that which is and must be essentially *one*: which had a common origin and which must have common fate: which used to be called Christendom, and is still called Europe: though the term now implies today extension over seas. This disunion proceeds from the long absence of a common philosophy, that is from the disruption of what was a common religion; and it is expressed in the department of language in a peculiar fashion which all do not appreciate but which is of profound effect upon the life of all.

And the disunion is complex: for the disunion in language between the modern groups of our common civilization is not even coincident with those groups. One social group has one official language, generally known to its citizens as a whole: thus the Italians have Tuscan, the Spaniards Castilian. A neighbour has another official tongue; and the two tongues are often so alien one to the other that in passing from one to the other you pass into a different world, as, from the world of Trent to the world of Innsbruck. Yet you cannot say of any one such group that its political personality is coincident with its language: County Clare talks English and the Masurians Polish. Because groups of languages are thus not coincident with national feeling, the tendency to create new divisions is enhanced. Were Englishmen, for instance, familiar with good translations of what was once the universal tongue of Irishmen, they would the better know the Irish mind.

Unless translation, then, be proceeding continually and over a very wide range of interests the unity of our civilization is distorted and its energies become self-destructive; but unless that work of translation is not only widely done but well done, it may actually do more harm than good.

When men were more fully conscious of our cultural unity in the west they clung to the tradition of Latin, which died hard. It is possible that this tradition will be revived, but for the moment it has lost its efficacy and we are like a group of individuals without a common bond of comprehension, with power of speech yet artificially dumb. We need translation today in Europe more than ever we needed it before. We need it materially in the satisfaction of common life, for discovery is common to all our culture and is not of one province. We need it spiritually, in the spreading and comparison of separate cultural efforts more than ever it was needed before, at any rate of recent centuries.

So much for the weight of my subject. So much for presenting the truth that translation is of very grave moment to us today. Now let us examine the nature of translation as a task, the rules which should guide it, the departments into which it falls, and conclude with the perils under which today it lies.

One may divide the task of translation into two departments, corresponding to two ends or functions. The one I would arbitrarily call that of instruction—translation used in order to convey in one tongue facts determined in another tongue; the other I would arbitrarily call literary—the translation into one tongue of spiritual effect determined in another tongue. A segregated example of the first is the translation of a textbook; a segregated example of the second is the translation of a great story or a great poem.

But here it must be remarked that the second is but a particular case of the first. In what I have called the 'translation of instruction' we are primarily concerned with exactitude of rendering; we are 'literal', our business is so to render the original that in its new form the writer of the original should have no quarrel with it but admit it to be the precise rendering of what he had written. The second, or literary form, demands the same qualities of exactitude and the same conscientious effort at rendering the original, but adds to these something indefinable which corresponds to what we call in pictorial art colour. The first sort of translation corresponds to draughtsmanship, which is no less necessary to a coloured than to an uncoloured picture; the second corresponds to the copying of a painting in which the draughtsmanship must be exactly rendered, but also the sensuous effect, harmony and contrast of hues.

Translation falls, like every literary activity, into the two main forms of prose and verse; nor is discussion of the boundary between these much to the purpose. More important is it to recognize the diversity of origin which differentiates the two. For prose appeals through the reason, verse through the emotions: the one to the Intelligent the other to the Appetitive in Man.

And this is true even in the department of persuasion (whereby men are governed). For when you would persuade by the use of the reason, the more strictly prosaic your prose the more thorough your achievement. But when you would persuade by the emotions, which is the commoner and easier way but the less enduring in its results, you must inevitably—though you believe yourself to be writing prose—bring in that admixture of something other which is the property of the poet. And before you know where you are your prose has taken on the colours of rhetoric.

This is true even of narrative, where narrative is intended to work upon the heart rather than the head. All great emotional narrative, however sober in appearance, is essentially rhetorical at heart. I admit this little digression with a useful purpose, which is to show how there must be two attitudes towards translation, corresponding to the two media with which we are dealing; for when we are translating prose, or when we are translating verse and its penumbra of rhetoric, we must use a separate fashion for each.

Because the matter to be translated is thus diverse at its origin, and branches out into further diversities within each group, therefore the rules which we seek to establish for right translation are general and particular: the general rules applying to all translation, the particular to translation of particular kinds.

Of general rules there would seem to be three, two positive and fairly obvious; one negative, not so immediately evident, and therefore more often transgressed.

The two positive rules are:

(1) That the translation should be into the language of the translator.

(2) But that the translated language must be possessed as perfectly as possible by the translator—*short of confusion in his mind*.

(3) The third or negative rule I take to be as follows:

The translator must be emancipated from mechanical restriction, of which the two chief forms are:

(*a*) The restriction of space.

(*b*) The restriction of form.

Let me develop these brief sentences.

First, as to translation being at its best in the language of the translator:

The end of translation is the production of a work in a certain language. If I translate the 'Song of Roland' into English my object is to produce an English epic—whether in verse or in rhetoric may be later discussed. If a man translate a German statistical summary into French he has the object of producing a French statistical summary. The importance of this rule increases with the subtlety or the spiritual magnitude or the high individuality of the work to be translated. It is better that a German statistical table should be rendered into French by a Frenchman, but it is essential that a Frenchman and not an Englishman or a German should attempt a French rendering of Shakespeare's plays.

There enters into this the admitted truth that what is not wholly conscious in us decides the larger part of our action. We possess our native tongue in an intimate fashion which permits us to use it coincidently with thought. All men who pride themselves upon facility and exactitude in a particular idiom know the peril of thinking in terms of another idiom, lest the purity of their text be modified and its value therefore lessened. The French writer who became famous under the assumed name of Anatole France refused to learn any foreign living tongue (though it was to his advantage that he knew the classics) lest his style in French should suffer: at least, that was the excuse he gave for his ignorance, and it may well have been a true one. Obviously the translator cannot enjoy privileged ignorance of this kind; he must know something of another tongue or he could not translate at all. But it seems equally obvious that unless there is one medium which is native to him and in which he writes well, he cannot translate save into that medium; for only in a man's own language can a man write generously and continuously, in a manner worthy of his powers, and make a permanent thing.

The rule that the translated language must be possessed as perfectly as possible may seem so obvious as not to be worth setting down: but I think that if we consider certain of its implications we shall see that it needs to be both stated and considered.

In the first place let us note that this second rule is somewhat less important than the first.

It is true that misconceptions of the original language will mar a translation, and it is even true that in particular cases where the essence of the subject turns perhaps upon a single phrase an error may destroy the value of the whole. But normally the original language is sufficiently possessed by the translator for his task, or he would not have undertaken it; and normally one or two errors in the brute meaning of the original will do no more than put blemishes upon a translation. But if the translator wields his *own* instrument badly, is not a good writer in his *own* language, then the translation *must* be bad throughout, however well the original may be known. One might put it in another way by saying that occasional errors in the meaning of the original will generally have no more than a mechanical effect, while an insufficient use of the language into which the translation is made is of organic importance, affecting the very tissue of a work and affecting it throughout.

The possession of a foreign idiom must extend to much more than the possession of what are called literal meanings; and here let me digress upon an essential point which would alone be matter for more than one lecture such as this. *There are, properly speaking, no such things as identical equivalents*; it is a point we came across at the beginning of these remarks and I would like to deal with it here more thoroughly.

The reason there are no such things as exact equivalents between two terms in two different languages lies in two characters of the Word. First each word, however simply used, is used with multiplicity of meaning. Secondly, the history of a word, its use in the prose and verse of the language to which it belongs, its sound-value in that language, its connection in the mind of the cultured reader of that language with its use in certain masterpieces and remembered phrases, and in general all the atmosphere of its being, make it one thing in one language from what it is in another even where the use being made of it is similar. To take one of the simplest examples: the word 'terre' in French, the word 'land' in English.

The word 'terre' in French may be variously translated by the words Land, Soil, Ground, Earth—to give only four of its distinct meanings. Thus of sailors at sea, making a landfall, 'C'est bien la terre' means 'It is certainly land'. 'C'est de la bonne terre' means 'It is good soil'. The fine sharp musical phrase, 'Les Rois de la terre' in the 'Marseillaise' means 'The Kings of all the earth' and 'Il mit pied à terre' means 'He put foot to ground'. In the plural 'ses terres' used of a magnate means not 'his lands' but 'his land' or 'his estate'—and so on.

The difficulty is a familiar one. The ambiguities produced by it are difficulties against which even the most elementary translator is on guard. But what must also be remarked and what is equally important when one is attempting the rendering of any great matter —great through its literary form or its message—is the atmosphere of the word. The word 'terre' in French is a long and powerful syllable, becoming two syllables on occasion. It can be given a mystical value to which the English word 'earth' alone corresponds and no other of its supposed equivalents. It is a more profound word in a peasant society than in an urban society. There is more still; it connotes very vaguely but quite certainly in one language one type of landscape, in another another. And there is more, it has been used by the poets and the great prose writers in different ways in the two languages, and this historical difference marks its effect whenever it is used.

In the same way certain words are common or even touch upon the ludicrous in one language whose apparent literal equivalent has no such atmosphere about it. There is the classic instance of the word 'handkerchief' in *Othello*, which, translated by the French word 'Mouchoir', interrupted the tragedy with loud laughter. Or again, the simplest word may suggest abuse or anger or repulsion in one tongue and not in another. One may say that the word 'vache' means 'cow', but the very sound of that long vowel 'vache' has led to its use as a term of odium peculiarly violent and comic only on account of its violence. There is an old and excellent French joke about a Parisian lady who saw a charming little calf and said, 'Quel malheur que ça devient vache!' One cannot translate that by saying 'How sad that it should grow into a cow', because cow suggests something absurd but certainly not something fierce and angry; it is not an opprobrious term. Now so much does this word 'vache' have this other connotation in French that it is the common popular insult to a policeman and is a motive for imprisonment. It is one of the favourite challenges thrown down by young and eager revolutionaries to ordered society.

Next note that there are, in the more modern developments of European languages, and especially in those which have a great mass of colloquial literature, a number of terms for which there is certainly no equivalent at all, even approximate. The English word 'cad' has grown up almost within my memory. Men somewhat senior to me could tell me of a time in their own youth when it had nothing of the signification it has now. It is the peculiar product of an aristocratic society, and you can no more translate the word 'cad' into French than you can translate the word 'gentleman' into French, at least not by a single word. Nor, for that matter, can you translate the word 'scholar'; nor can you translate into English the French word 'goujat', or the French word 'frondeur'.

I should exceed the limits of the time allowed me if I were to dilate further upon this theme, for it is almost inexhaustible. Everywhere it leads on to the conclusion that the thorough possession of the original language is essential to the translator, and the more perfect his possession of it *with the one reservation I made* the better for his task. Let me give one example of how a single error may vitiate a whole piece of important rendering. As everybody knows, Rousseau's *Social Contract*, one of the greatest as well as one of the most effective books ever written, turns upon the conception of the General Will, and upon the author's rightness or wrongness in characterizing the General Will the value of falsity of his thesis depends. Now early in the great essay occurs the phrase, 'La volonté générale et toujours droite'. I remember an occasion when during the attempted translation of the work an Englishman was about to publish the phrase under the form, 'The general will is always right': a phrase which is not only patently nonsensical and would put Rousseau out of court at once, but is also at issue with what goes before and what comes after. 'La volonté générale est toujours droite' means, 'The general will is always direct'; a very sound remark which has been put in another form by the moderns who say, 'Le peuple est toujours simpliste'. And there again, what is the English for 'simpliste'? You need a whole phrase to translate it.

I have said that the possession of the original tongue as perfectly as possible *subject to certain qualification* was obviously an advantage. That qualification it will be remembered was, 'short of confusion'.

Too great a familiarity with a foreign idiom may render a man confused between that foreign idiom and his own. It may make him at times run the two together within his mind, diluting and marring each with the properties of the other. When this happens you get very bad translation indeed; and we all must have noticed that it does happen over and over again nowadays in the writings of those rare scholars who are really steeped in a foreign idiom, or at any rate in its spirit if not its vocabulary. There is a certain degree of familiarity with German which makes an Englishman, especially in the theological field, incomprehensible. There is a certain degree of familiarity with French which makes the English sentence professing to translate a French one unnatural and slightly ridiculous. Such confusion must be avoided in translation even at the price of some less perfect knowledge of the original language, lest being steeped in the foreign tongue one falls in one's own tongue into unusual order, odd neologisms, and metaphorical phrases the force of which are a commonplace to the foreigner but with us a grotesque novelty.

In this connection it may well be asked whether a bilingual person has ever been known to make a good translation. I can recall no case and to this I ascribe what is surely true, and if true, lamentable—that we have no sufficient rendering of the Welsh classics into English. For that there is such a thing as Welsh classical stuff, and that Welsh rhetoric and historical tradition have been so finely put as to move Welshmen profoundly we can all testify. But the trouble is that the Englishman born who knows Welsh well is sadly to seek, and while there have been scholarly men who thought in Welsh but talked in English familiarly, they were not apt for the task precisely because they did not think in English. It is other with the effect of some ancient Irish matter, which has been the better translated because the translator was spiritually in deep sympathy with the Irish tongue but had from childhood been trained to use English.

We may ask ourselves, however, whether an occasional touch of the foreign atmosphere in the translation of a foreign thing be of advantage or no: whether a slight Gallicism here and there in the rendering of a French essay is to the advantage of the English version, and vice versa, an Anglicism in some such work as the admirable modern translation of the works of Kipling into French.

It is perhaps a matter of taste, but for my part I should reply in the negative. I should say that any hint of foreignness in the translated version is a blemish; I should keep to my canon that the translated thing should read like a first-class native thing. And here, by the way, let me give an example which covers all the ground, showing both what a translation should be in its excellence and how little fame a good translation earns for the genius capable of it—I mean that work which I am afraid not one man in a thousand has heard of, the anonymous 'Devil on Two Sticks', the translated *Asmodée* of Lesage.

What fortunes the book has had I know not; possibly the translator (presumably obscure) will be known to those with more scholarship than I. In the two editions which I have, one of them a first edition, no name of a translator appears. It is one of the best books, not only in the language as an English book but as a translation, and it shows what wages one may expect who undertakes this trade. The wages of literature anyhow are pretty bad; they come next, I think, in order of disappointment to the wages of sin: but of all literary wages as paid in fame the very lowest are the wages of the translator; and I suppose that is why translation has today almost been given up in despair.

I gave for my third rule a negative one: translation must be emancipated from mechanical troubles, of which the two chief are:

(*a*) Space.

(*b*) The set form of the original.

The attempt to keep the scale of the translation exactly parallel to the scale of the original is fatal. Nearly always must a translation be of greater length than the original. Nor is the reason hard to find. Unless you could get a more or less satisfactory equivalent—and we have seen how hard *that* is—you are compelled to expand. In each idiomatic term a whole phrase is packed, and the term must be unpacked if we would put its meaning into our own tongue, when there is no general close corresponding single term by which to express it.

This is particularly true of translation from almost any other language into English, for English has less inflexion than the generality of languages. We have to express continually by relatives and the addition of adverbs ideas which are contained within the very structure of the foreign word. The cases in which there is any direct necessity, or at least serious advantage, in attempting to maintain the scale of the original, are rare. In those cases it may perhaps be inevitable or advantageous to torture the translation somewhat and fit it into its unnatural mould of a precise limit in length, but the translation is always the worse for it.

This negative rule applies with particular strength to verse. What difficulties lie in the translation of verse I shall discuss later, but in connection with the particular point with which we are now dealing it is especially to be remarked that a desperate effort at translating one line by one line or one page by one page will ruin the result. To show what I mean I will delay my example until I come to talk of the translation of verse, and will there quote Mr G. K. Chesterton's remarkable translation of Du Bellay's famous sonnet:

Heureux qui comme Ulysse.

As of space, so of set form. You need not translate the sonnet by a sonnet, nor even the chapter by a chapter, still less the paragraph, by a paragraph. In each, for the true rendering of the spirit, you need a native form in the place of a foreign one. For example, Victor Hugo suffers very much in English translation by the preservation of the short paragraph which was natural to the French fiction of his time, and has always been unnatural to ours. He becomes grotesque in English where in French he is sublime, not only by the rendering of his short paragraph into a medium unsuited to it, but by the rendering of the very brief epigrammatic sentence or question into an idiom where it is unnatural. The same is particularly true of Michelet, whose glorious rhythms can be and are rendered puerile by insufficient translation. Thus, of the great Girondin's singing, 'Quelle était cette voix?—'C'était la Révolution même', I would not translate, 'What was that voice?' 'It was the Revolution itself'. That seems to me, in English, grotesque. I prefer, 'One might have said, on hearing such a voice, that one had heard the Revolution itself in song.'

In general I should say that, apart from these two mechanical restrictions of space and set form, all mechanical restrictions should be avoided in translation. The translator should be emancipated from them under the same spirit which emancipates the writer in any other form from mechanical restraint. By which I do not mean that having chosen a form you must not maintain that form; having sat down to write a translation as a sonnet you must not run to fifteen lines, having sat down to write an epitaph you must not produce a little biography. All creative work must be fitted to a frame. But what I mean is that creative work adjusted to a scale not native to itself but borrowed from some other thing is marred, and so is translation marred when the translator erroneously believes it must be perpetually referred to the shape and scale of the original.

So much for the three general rules which, as they appear to me, should govern the business of translation.

Now what particular rules attach to the two particular departments of prose and verse?

In the translation of prose I find these special points:

(1) The translator should, I think, not plod on, sentence by sentence, still less word by word, but always 'block out' his work. When I say 'block out' I mean that he should read over his material at large to grasp it as a whole in the original before he undertakes the translation, and after that, when the translation is under way, he should take it at least section by section, paragraph by paragraph, and ask himself before each what the whole sense is which he has to render, what the effect of the unit as a whole may be, before reproducing it in another tongue.

In connection with this occurs a necessary warning upon the use of the dictionary. However well a man may possess the original tongue from which he is translating into his own, there will arise— unless he be completely bilingual, which I have called a drawback to translation—occasions when it is necessary to verify the exact meaning of a particular word, and for that service the dictionary is essential. It is equally necessary that the best book of reference, of which there is not usually more than one, be used. But to rely upon the dictionary continuously is fatal. It argues either an insufficient knowledge of the original, or an insufficient confidence in oneself, which, for translation as for any other creative work, is an evil. If you are fairly certain from your experience that a particular meaning is intended do not fear to give that meaning although the dictionary has it not; for remember that all dictionaries are made by translators and that every translator is like yourself, an imperfect being. Your own experience, when you are sure of it, is a sufficient guide.

(2) It is of high importance to render idiom by idiom; and idioms of their nature demand translation into another form from that of the original. The Greek exclamation, 'By the Dog!' is in literal English merely comic. An Englishman does not ejaculate, 'By the Dog!' as a natural emphasis and ornament to conversation, although the worship of the dog is a religion which the Englishman holds and the Greek did not. I should propose here a transposition of letters, and I suggest that the harmless phrase, 'By God!' is much nearer to 'By the Dog!' than anything else you could get. It is the same thing with the idiom of the question, both rhetorical and definitive, and with the idiom of the historic present.

Thus in translation from French into English we must remember that the French use of the question not for purposes of inquiry but for the regulation of the prose is not native to the English tongue, and the same is true of the French historic present. Whole pages of French matter will be written in the historic present which, if they reappear in an English form, should be thrown into the past. The most sober of French historians will continue in paragraph after paragraph to represent an action in the historic present, and the prose will follow quite naturally. The effect in the original will not be strained. Put the same into English and you get at once an exaggerated effect. So with the question, rhetorical or definitive. The ample use of the rhetorical question is native to ordinary French prose, not to English. It is also native to French prose to define a proposition by putting the data of it first into question form. It is not native to English to do this. It is rather native to English to put the data into statement form. Thus for a French phrase such as 'Que demanda-t-il? Demanda-t-il une solution financière ou une solution politique? Il demanda bien une solution financière, mais une solution financière subordonnée à la solution politique', I should not write in English, 'Yet what was his aim? Was he considering a financial or a political solution?' etc. I should rather say, 'The solution he was seeking was essentially political, and in so far as there was a financial element in it, this was subordinate to his political aim.'

In this same connection of idiom you have a multitude of points, of which I will select only this: the sentence without a verb. It is native to French idiom: it is not native to English. The sentence without a verb can be, and sometimes should be, used in English, but rarely and with great discretion. It is forceful only because it is unusual; in French it is ubiquitous.

(3) You must, in rendering a foreign phrase, render intention by intention. A neglect of this rule leads to absurd results. The intention of a phrase in one language may be less emphatic than the form of the phrase, or it may be more emphatic. It always leans a little one way or the other, and when you are rendering a foreign phrase into your own tongue you must consider whether the usual form it takes in your own tongue exaggerates on the one side or the other. Thus a French political writer speaking of some law of which he disapproves will say: 'Voila ce qui a perdu le pays.' Should you translate this into 'That is what destroyed the country', you quite miss the original intention. The French exaggerated phrase was not intended to say that the country was destroyed by the law; obviously it was not destroyed: it means, 'was hurt', 'was weakened'. The corresponding English phrase would be normally too low pitched rather than too high pitched, and one would rather say, 'This law had grievous consequences for the country.' Conversely, there are many French phrases which are the other way about, which say less than they mean where the English one says more. An excellent example is the journalistic and Parliamentary form, 'parfaitement incorrect', which does not mean 'quite inexact' but rather 'utterly false'. It is a very strong expression indeed, put in studiedly pale terms. When an Englishman says 'you can't believe a word he says'—which is manifestly nonsense on the side of over-emphasis, yet a very common phrase—a Frenchman would probably put it: 'On ne peut guère toujours le croire.' I should not wonder if the

tradition of the Duel had something to do with this under-pitching of the personal statement.

In this effort to render intention by intention it is often necessary to conform to the idiom of one's own tongue by adding some word not in the original. For instance, I would translate La Rochefoucauld's excellent remark on funerals something after this fashion: 'I like a funeral, for I come away from it saying to myself, "I have got rid of another of them, anyhow".' The word 'anyhow' is not in the original; I think the English form needs it to express the savour of the French.

(4) When we translate prose in these late modern times of ours, following upon so many centuries of varying use in words, we must be very much upon our guard against words of similar form in the two languages, that one from which we are translating and that one into which we are translating; and we must equally be upon our guard against taking an early meaning to be the same as the later meaning of the same word. Both dangers have a similar source. Each proceeds from the fact that with the passage of time a word changes in meaning while retaining its form. There has been no more fruitful source of historical error (not only in constitutional discussion but in what is more important, theological discussion) than this. Fustel de Coulanges did great service when he pointed out that the word '*cum*' meant quite a different thing in a Merovingian document from what it would have meant in a classical one. 'Rex *cum* proceribus' did not mean, for Dagobert, 'The King *together* with his magnates'—as the man familiar only with classical Latin would think it meant; it meant rather, 'The King *in the presence* of his magnates.' It in no way connoted the necessity of assent by the magnates. The Merovingian king was heir to the Roman Emperors, not to tribal chiefs. Similarly, in all the mass of discussion upon the Eucharist, the verb 'repraesentare', given a modern meaning, not only vitiates but contradicts the earlier use; which earlier use did not connote a symbol but the exact opposite, the actual transference of the thing named.

In translation from the Teutonic languages into English the danger takes one form, in translating from the Latin languages another. A word similar in spelling, nearly identical or even actually identical, may, as we all know, have a very different meaning in English from what it has in the original German. And the danger is all the greater because, in the case of the Teutonic languages, those English words which are of Teutonic derivation are at the very core of the speech. The use of 'bitter' during the war is a good example. The odiously un-English term 'Bitter fighting' nearly passed into the language. But it is in translating from the Latin languages and particularly from French that the warning must be most emphasized. There are hosts and regiments of words, most of them branching out from the Renaissance, others of earlier origin, but all entering directly or indirectly from Latin, which are similar or identical in spelling and which, if rendered as equivalents, make a translation wholly false.

Examples will occur to every one. One of the most obvious is the word 'déception', which in French means today a disappointment, in English a deceit. Another less known one and one most important to remember in daily work is the criss-cross of 'magistrate' and 'judge'. In French the former word stands for the greater office, in English the lesser one. I cannot help recalling an instance of this danger which we had immediately after the Great War. A politician —English-speaking but not, I am glad to say, English—was roused to indignation by the presence in a French document of the word 'demande', which he thought equivalent to his own familiar word, 'demand': an error comparable to mistaking a salutation for a blow.

(5) Transmute boldly: render the sense by the corresponding sense without troubling over the verbal difficulties in your way. Where such rendering of sense by corresponding sense involves considerable amplification, do not hesitate to amplify for fear of being verbose. For instance, if you come across the French word 'constater', which in point of fact you do in nearly all official documents with which you may have to deal, you must always replace it by a full English sentence, even so ample as, 'We note without further comment', or 'We note for purposes of future reference', or in another connection, 'We desire to put on record'. In the same way there are whole French phrases which should justly be put into a shorter form in English. Take such a sentence as this, 'Il y avait dans cet homme je ne sais quoi de suffisance'. The right translation of this would not be: 'There was in this man I know not what of self-sufficiency'; the right translation is rather, more briefly, 'There was a touch of complacency about him'. Sometimes, even often, a whole passage must be thus transmuted, a whole paragraph thrown

into a new form, if we would justly render the sense of the original; and the general rule should stand that, after having grasped as exactly as possible all that the original stands for, with the proportion between its various parts, the distinction between what is emphasized and what is left on a lower plane, we should say to ourselves, not 'How shall I make this foreigner talk English?', but 'What would an Englishman have said to express this same?' *That* is translation. *That* is the very essence of the art: the resurrection of an alien thing in a native body; not the dressing of it up in native clothes but the giving to it of native flesh and blood.

(6) Lastly, I would add this epigrammatic counsel: never embellish. You may indeed embellish if you are desiring to produce a work of art of your own, careless of what happens to the vile body which you are adapting, just as you may melt down some silver spoons and fashion with the material an elaborate cup. But if your object be sincere translation never yield to the sometimes considerable temptation of making the new thing (in your own eyes) better than the old. It is a counsel of perfection, and I grant that had it always been observed some of the best work done by man would never have appeared, for some of the best work done by man has been struck out in the rendering, or at any rate after a first reading, of some foreign thing by the reader who was inspired to make something better in his own language. But that is not translation. It is as much an error in *translation* as the converse error of rendering what was noble in the original into something base.

I might here, had I the space, digress upon the very interesting question whether the translation of some dull foreign writer be not the master-test of the translators' art. I mean the translation of a dull foreigner so that his original insufficiency shall appear in the new form. There is a pleasing irony about the subject. I leave it with regret, in the hope of returning to it elsewhere.

For the translation of verse and rhetoric three main rules suggest themselves to me:

First, that translation must here be almost wholly occupied with spiritual effect; next, the consequence of this, that verse should normally be translated not into verse but into prose; and lastly, a negative rule, that one should abandon the effort to translate the untranslatable.

(1) As to spiritual effect—especially in rhetoric—there is of

course no rule for obtaining it in its myriad forms, but there is the rule of making it one's supreme object; and a triumph it is to achieve that object and rarely is it achieved. Great rhetoric and verse, which in its highest form we call in modern English *poetry*, has upon the mind of man an unmistakable effect, separate in its quality of emotion from all other. It is that effect which the translator must attempt, half despairing, to reproduce: or at any rate it is that effect to which he must approach. Unless he bring in something at least of that magic he has not translated at all. A translation even of good verse, let alone of poetry, which does not convey something of the thrill, which does not grasp something of the poignancy proper to the original, is as it were the negative of translation, it is a minus quantity, it is worse than nothing. For instance,

τῷ Δ' ἅμα τεσσαράκοντα μέλαιναι νῆες ἕποντο.

translate this, 'He was followed by 40 black ships', and you had much better have spent your time playing Patience. But translate it, '40 dark ships followed him', and you are some miles behind—but still in the wake—of the fleets that sailed to Troy.

(2) It is, I say, from this truth that there follows the injunction to translate *as a rule* verse into prose and not into verse. I know that the very greatest renderings of the most famous poems have commonly been themselves in verse. Yet I think that is to be regretted. Let me take an example and a justly famous one. These lines:

Τῆλε Δ' ἀπὸ κρατὸς χέε Δέοματα οιγαλόεντα
"Αμπυκα, κεκρύφαλόν τ', ἠΔὲ πλεκτὴν ἀναΔέομην
ΚρήΔεμνόν Θ', ὅ ῥά οἱ Δῶκε χρυοέη 'ΑφροΔίτη
"Ηματι τῷ ὅτε μιν κορυθαίολος ἠγάγεθ' "Εκτωρ
'Εκ Δόμον 'Ηετίωνος . . . (*Iliad* X, 467–71).

It would require scholarship which I do not possess to decide upon the exactitude of translation from the Homeric poems. But it requires no more than a sense of English, which I claim to possess, and a love of the original, which I also feel, to judge whether this be not as excellent an abbreviated rendering as was ever given. It is, in my ears at least, better than anything that has been done in verse that I ever read, in those efforts men have made to put the original hexameters into English lines.

'. . . and from her head dropped the net and the wreath and the diadem which golden Aphrodité gave her on the day when Hector of the glancing helm took her from the house of Eëtion [to be his bride.]' I do not think this effect would have been produced in verse. Chapman does not produce it, grandeur though he has, nor Pope, the common criticism of whose obviously un-Greek method has always seemed to me beside the mark. Pope was a great poet and Chapman a great translator, but a little book which I shall treasure all my life called Church's Stories from Homer does the trick better than either of them.

The rule of not translating verse into verse is indeed a hard commandment. For verse inspires by its rhythm, and the temptation to reproduce the effect in rhythmical form under the air of one's own tongue is very strong. Moreover, I must admit that, especially with short things of precise form, the temptation has been yielded to with advantage, often with real success; and sometimes I think with a success which would not have been achieved in any other way. This is particularly true of epigram, as for instance the epigram of Anacreon:

> Love's self is sad, love's lack is sadder still,
> But love unloved, oh that's the greatest ill.

A translation rather of verse than of poetry. But no one has sufficiently put into verse what may certainly be put into solemn prose, the loveliest of the laments from the Anthology, Meleager's Δάκρυα σοὶ καὶ νέρθε (vii. 476).

That sometimes even a whole sonnet can be retranslated into sonnet form we know from the high success of Du Bellay, some of whose greatest work was an adaptation from the Italian (and that in its turn from the Latin), and oddly enough it was Du Bellay himself who gave the opportunity for one of the finest exceptions in this line, I mean Mr G. K. Chesterton's translation of the famous sonnet upon 'Liré' which, as a model of what can be done in this fashion, I will take the liberty of reading to you now, first reading Du Bellay's fourteen lines and then those of his English compeer.

(*Then the lecturer read the two sonnets, French and English.*)

If I may introduce the personal note I will admit that in that translation of the 'Song of Roland' which I fear I shall not live to complete but which I most desire to accomplish as a task, and which of course I have undertaken in prose, I could not forbid myself the admission of verse here and there, so powerfully was I possessed by the lyric form of the original. Thus I cannot but translate:

> Hauts sont li puys et tenebreuses et grants
> Et dans li vals sont les eaues courants.
>
> High are the hills, and huge, and dim with cloud,
> Down in the deeps the living streams are loud.

And again:

> Ami Roland, prud'homme, jouvente bele.
>
> Roland, my friend, young gentlemen and brave.

No, one cannot kill the desire to render verse by verse. But one must not let it run away with one, and one must preserve the canon that in general and especially for the longer flights and more especially for the epics, verse should be rendered into prose.

(3) I added, 'Do not try to translate the untranslatable'. The negative commandment is perhaps the hardest of all. Were it too much impressed upon men no good flash of poetic translation would ever be struck out. But it is true that if you find a thing quite untranslatable, if you discover your effort to be wholly unworthy of the original, it is far better for two good reasons to burn it than to let it stand. The two good reasons are, first, that by publishing it you traduce the poet; and second, that you commit that unforgivable crime of making a fool of yourself. I defy any man to translate into English verse or prose the perfection of Gauthier:

> . . . et par la petitesse
> De ses mains, elle etait Andalouse, et contesse.

I would conclude with a certain unhappy warning for what threatens translation as a whole in our time. I would not like to end without that warning, because it is very much needed and the evil in connection with which I make it is increasing every day.

Translation—of a sort—swarms today on a scale unknown to the past. Our popular press is filled with renderings of things said and written by men of other speech, and though we do not sufficiently translate foreign books into English, at least, not the best foreign books, yet of this work also there is a very great deal. That is because the time in which we live is one in which all men read—whether for their good or their ill let others determine.

Now the time in which we live is not only one in which this mass of translation is continually going on, but also one in which it is worse done than ever it was done before. It is worse done today than it was yesterday, and it looks as though it would be worse done tomorrow even than it is today. The bad results of such a state of affairs are manifest. In our own particular province, which is but one of many, the province of the English-speaking world, bad translation not only cuts us off from our peers and fellows in a common civilization but what is worse, ministers to isolated pride. For who shall believe that there is great work done in any other tongue than his own if whatever appears in a foreign tongue is put before him inadequately?

The cause of this rapid deterioration in translation is not only the huge inflation of reading which today we suffer or enjoy, but also what is in the very blood of our time, the commercial spirit: the motive of gain. And coupled with this the vast increase of what may be called the 'intellectual proletariat', of whom we may say that their intellectual quality is relative, but their proletarian quality positive and certain.

Under this combination arises a state of affairs where thousands think they know enough of a foreign tongue to translate into their own, and where those thousands are equally confident that, because they can write in one sense, they can write in another. Every one is taught to write, and most think that the setting down of words on paper is a sufficient definition of the art of writing. Hence a sort of translation can be had for next to nothing. Hence does the owner of a newspaper—and even the editor thereof, who is commonly a better educated man—accept almost anything by way of translation; hence does the publisher make out his costs for a translation upon a lower scale than he would ever allow for even the meanest of original work. There are places called Translation Bureaux where you can take any piece of French, German, Russian, or Japanese (but not, I am glad to say, Latin), and get an English rendering of it neatly type-written in a few hours. And the spirit of the translation bureau is upon the whole trade. There is only one remedy, and like the remedy for every department of our modern disease, it must be slight in its effect and probably fail if it be attempted; that remedy is to create a social consciousness of what translation means; to aim —at least in important cases—at real translation, and with that object to pay translation at better rates and to give that other half of the writer's wages, which is fame, to the translator as well as to the original writer.

Failing this, you have to depend upon the chance labour of love, such as the late Scott Moncrieff's work or the excerpts recently published by Mr Maurice Baring. Now the proportion that such work, done from enthusiasm and with the enjoyment of leisure, bears to what might be and ought to be done is almost negligible. We must pay translation better and we must praise it more; or pay the penalty of further isolation and of further self-sufficiency—at the end of which is the death of our culture. For no province of Europe can stand alone.

XXXVII

From *A Conversation with a Cat*

1931

Belloc was still continuing to publish a great variety of works. The year 1931 was noteworthy for his Taylorian Lecture, On Translation, *and apart from the above named book of no less than thirty-nine essays, he completed his fourth volume of* History of England; *a biography of* Cranmer; *an Introduction and Commentary on Murray Allison's* Travel Notes on a Holiday in France; *and his famous poem* In Praise of Wine, *which Belloc dedicated to Duff Cooper. For a man of sixty-one this was an extraordinary achievement*

A Conversation with a Cat

The other day I went into the bar of a railway station and, taking a glass of beer, I sat down at a little table by myself to meditate upon the necessary but tragic isolation of the human soul. I began my meditation by consoling myself with the truth that something in common runs through all nature, but I went on to consider that this cut no ice, and that the heart needed something more. I might by long research have discovered some third term a little less hackneyed than these two, when fate, or some good influence or accident, or the ocean and my fostering star, sent me a tawny, silky, long-haired cat.

If it be true that nations have the cats they deserve, then the English people deserve well in cats, for there are none so prosperous or so friendly in the world. But even for an English cat this cat was exceptionally friendly and fine—especially friendly. It leapt at one graceful bound into my lap, nestled there, put out an engaging right front paw to touch my arm with a pretty timidity by way of introduction, rolled up at me an eye of bright but innocent affection, and then smiled a secret smile of approval.

No man could be so timid after such an approach as not to make some manner of response. So did I. I even took the liberty of stroking Amathea (for by that name did I receive this vision), and though I began this gesture in a respectful fashion, after the best models of polite deportment with strangers, I was soon lending it some warmth, for I was touched to find that I had a friend; yes, even here, at the ends of the tubes in sw.99. I proceeded (as is right) from caress to speech, and said, 'Amathea, most beautiful of cats, why have you deigned to single me out for so much favour? Did you recognize in me a friend to all that breathes, or were you yourself suffering from loneliness (though I take it you are near your own dear home), or is there pity in the hearts of animals as there is in the hearts of some humans? What, then, was your motive? Or am I, indeed, foolish to ask, and not rather to take whatever good comes to me in whatever way from the gods?'

To these questions Amathea answered with a loud purring noise, expressing with closed eyes of ecstasy her delight in the encounter.

'I am more than flattered, Amathea,' said I, by way of answer;
'I am consoled. I did not know that there was in the world anything
breathing and moving, let alone one so tawny-perfect, who would
give companionship for its own sake and seek out, through deep
feeling, some one companion out of all living kind. If you do not
address me in words I know the reason and I commend it; for in
words lie the seeds of all dissension, and love at its most profound
is silent. At least, I read that in a book, Amathea; yes, only the other
day. But I confess that the book told me nothing of those gestures
which are better than words, or of that caress which I continue to
bestow upon you with all the gratitude of my poor heart.'

To this Amathea made a slight gesture of acknowledgement—not
disdainful—wagging her head a little, and then settling it down in
deep content.

'Oh, beautiful-haired Amathea, many have praised you before
you found me to praise you, and many will praise you, some in your
own tongue, when I am no longer held in the bonds of your presence.
But none will praise you more sincerely. For there is not a man
living who knows better than I that the four charms of a cat lie in its
closed eyes, its long and lovely hair, its silence, and even its affected
love.'

But at the word affected Amathea raised her head, looked up at
me tenderly, once more put forth her paw to touch my arm, and
then settled down again to a purring beatitude.

'*You* are secure,' said I sadly; 'mortality is not before you. There
is in your complacency no foreknowledge of death nor even of
separation. And for that reason, Cat, I welcome you the more. For
if there has been given to your kind this repose in common living,
why, then, we men also may find it by following your example and
not considering too much what may be to come and not remembering too much what has been and will never return. Also, I thank
you, for this, Amathea, my sweet Euplokamos' (for I was becoming
a little familiar through an acquaintance of a full five minutes and
from the absence of all recalcitrance), 'that you have reminded me
of my youth, and in a sort of shadowy way, a momentary way, have
restored it to me. For there is an age, a blessed youthful age (O My
Cat) even with the miserable race of men, when all things are
consonant with the life of the body, when sleep is regular and long
and deep, when enmities are either unknown or a subject for

rejoicing and when the whole of being is lapped in hope as you are now lapped on my lap, Amathea. Yes, we also, we of the doomed race, know peace. But whereas you possess it from blind kittenhood to that last dark day so mercifully short with you, we grasp it only for a very little while. But I would not sadden you by the mortal plaint. That would be treason indeed, and a vile return for your goodness. What! When you have chosen me out of seven London millions upon whom to confer the tender solace of the heart, when you have proclaimed yourself so suddenly to be my dear, shall I introduce you to the sufferings of those of whom you know nothing save that they feed you, house you and pass you by? At least you do not take us for gods, as do the dogs, and the more am I humbly beholden to you for this little service of recognition—and something more.'

Amathea slowly raised herself upon her four feet, arched her back, yawned, looked up at me with a smile sweeter than ever and then went round and round, preparing for herself a new couch upon my coat, whereon she settled and began once more to purr in settled ecstasy.

Already had I made sure that a rooted and anchored affection had come to me from out the emptiness and nothingness of the world and was to feed my soul henceforward; already had I changed the mood of long years and felt a conversion towards the life of things, an appreciation, a cousinship with the created light—and all that through one new link of loving kindness—when whatever it is that dashes the cup of bliss from the lips of mortal man (Tupper) up and dashed it good and hard. It was the Ancient Enemy who put the fatal sentence into my heart, for we are the playthings of the greater powers, and surely some of them are evil.

'You will never leave me, Amathea,' I said; 'I will respect your sleep and we will sit here together through all uncounted time, I holding you in my arms and you dreaming of the fields of Paradise. Nor shall anything part us, Amathea; you are my cat and I am your human. Now and onwards into the fullness of peace.'

Then it was that Amathea lifted herself once more, and with delicate, discreet, unweighted movement of perfect limbs leapt lightly to the floor as lovely as a wave. She walked slowly away from me without so much as looking back over her shoulder; she had another purpose in her mind; and as she so gracefully and so

majestically neared the door which she was seeking, a short, unpleasant man standing at the bar said, 'Puss, Puss, Puss!' and
stooped to scratch her gently behind the ear. With what a wealth of
singular affection, pure and profound, did she not gaze up at him,
and then rub herself against his leg in token and external expression
of a sacramental friendship that should never die.

On Jonathan Swift

A solid piece of comfort in the times through which we have to live
is the permanence of Swift. He alone of the great prose masters
survives on one level, in spite of hostile or indifferent or enthusiastic
mood; and that although our literary moods have fallen into chaos.

There is no writer of English for whom modern England should
be less sympathetic; and (save in his case) it would seem that grave
modern lack of sympathy, though it does not kill the reputation
of a name, kills the reading of that to which the famous name was
signed.

Pope is an example. It may be fairly said that for one who reads
Pope today among educated men, there were fifty in Pope's own
day. Swift should be far less sympathetic than Pope. He was
essentially a satirist, and the modern reader does not only fail to
understand satire, but withdraws from it as from an unpleasant
experience. He is not only bewildered by it; he actually dislikes it.
Again, that which Swift satirized has passed. It is no good pointing
out that a man who exposes the vileness of human nature has an
eternal theme. In the concrete the things he made fools of are no
longer known. For instance, his chief butt is the courtier, because
in his day a simulation of power still attached to monarchy, and it
was not even certain that monarchy might not return. Today the
courtier has disappeared. The politician has taken his place; and all
the anger of Swift against the courtier is anger against what is to us
a void, and all his indignation against the courtier is wasted effort.
Yet his satire on the dead courtier survives, and suggests what we
might write today (had we a Swift) upon the moribund Parliamentary Politician.

Again, Swift is perpetually harping on Ireland. He was born in
Ireland; and may be called spiritually, through all the middle and

later part of his life, a sort of 'native but naturalized' Irishman. Now, of Ireland our readers of today may properly be said to know nothing. They know less of the place and temper than they do of those of France, let alone Italy, which many of us do half-understand. Yet his writing upon that foreign country, and in the air of that foreign country, actively survives.

Nor is this all. The very Ireland with which he is concerned and which he takes for granted, alien to the reader because it is Ireland, is doubly alien because his was a phase of Irish history which has melted into nothingness. Swift wrote for and about and to a governing alien minority. In his eyes the mass of the Irish are submerged (presumably) for ever. The Dublin which we find in Swift is a Dublin of his Protestant co-religionists, and down to the street hawkers and up to the bishops it is of, for, and to a Protestant world that he writes. One may fairly say that nothing else exists for him in his surroundings, save as a very vague background or mass which can never actively count or be vocal again. Put Swift into Catholic Ireland today, and he might think himself in another planet—especially in Dublin. Yet what he has to say is of the same power as it was when he was saying it more than two hundred years ago.

It is perhaps still more remarkable that he survives in spite of iconoclasm. He survives in spite of his ceaseless onslaught upon that which is for us an idol. Whether we know it or not, all our history and three-quarters of our literature is Whig. Its heroes are Whig heroes; its villains are those whom Whiggery made out to be villains. Swift's whole temper is anti-Whig, and, though he changed masters, his best work was done against that political theory, against its exponents and its beneficiaries. I can read unendingly, and I hope many others can and do, *The Public Spirit of the Whigs*. A modern writer who should today so thrust himself against what had become the fixed historical tradition of the country would be neglected for a crank. Swift is accepted.

Now, why does the great master so survive? Let us begin with a few negatives. It is not because he wrote one immensely popular book which can be bowdlerized for children, and enjoy the immortality which a good child's book enjoys from generation to generation. If Swift had never written of giants and of dwarfs, he would be just as famous, and would perhaps be read today as much as he is. He is certain of a strong reading public for the future indefinitely.

Obviously, this is not because he conforms to any national doctrine of our time. Thus the great modern doctrine of the impeccability of lawyers which sceptics have assailed but which still has great strength, was not so much as conceivable to Swift. He writes of the legal profession as one might write of poisoning, and of lawyers as of base scoundrels. His attachment to dogmatic religion is equally alien to us, and his contempt for that sort of free thought which is everywhere in our drawing-rooms. He defends the creed, and he defends it with that intellectual scepticism which is in the unintelligence of today almost forgotten.

Nor does his strength lie in the national talent for portrait painting. There is no 'character' in all Swift. Even in the immortal *Tale of a Tub* Lord Peter himself is hardly a living person, and his two brothers are still less individual. In such a lack of power to portray the individual, Swift is unique. The whole flood of English letters, from a century before his time right down to our own, is a crowd of living men. In Swift there is not one. Why, then, is the position of Swift unchanging?

I think I should say, in answer to this question, that the chief cause of Swift's immovability is Style. The word is abused; but rightly used it is significant. Swift excelled in, he survives by, style in prose.

It was one of the most just among the many just pronouncements of Lord Chesterfield, in his *Letters to His Son*, that Swift should be taken as the model of English prose. For hardness, sufficiency and exactitude he has no peer and no rival. His prose is without the least suspicion of rhetoric, and its rhythms are so broken, and at the same time so concealed, that I doubt if he was himself aware of them. On nine pages out of ten they cannot be analysed at all. But since prose style is excellent in proportion as it is lucid, Swift is first. There never was a man who could say what he had to say more clearly, nor with a better certitude that every reader of every class would immediately understand him.

It is strange that this virtue is apparent in the same degree with the first of his sentences and with the last: stranger because the end of Jonathan Swift, as he himself prophesied, was a tragic mental decay. Now when madness or imbecility is the nature of a writer's exit from this world (and such an exit is a frequent penalty exacted by the dreadful trade of letters), we expect, and commonly we find, as the years advance, an inclination to confusion. It was so with Pascal, whose exit was of that kind. I think we may admit that it was in some degree true of Ruskin. There is no trace of it in Swift. He writes up to the end as sharply and with as hard an edge as in his early manhood—and during the tragic years he writes no more.

It is to be noted that in this admirable prose there are no mannerisms; and that in itself helps to account for the similarity of it in each lustre of his writing life. For it is the mark of age that a writer's mannerisms, if he has any (and nearly all writers have), increase upon him. A mannerism is a vehicle; it saves effort both in thought and in construction; it is commonly praised by flatterers who are the guides of writers as they grow old. Also mannerisms are a label by which the man who desires reputation knows that he can be recognized. Further, they ensure a public; for the public, having grown used to expect a mannerism, is satisfied on finding it again. Swift has not such a thing as a mannerism about him. And yet if anyone present you with a short paragraph of his you will know it at once for Swift's. No one else wrote like that. No one since Swift has written like that. No one before Swift wrote like that.

And there is this last thing to be said about him (which is true of so very few), that his writing never grows old. Young men not yet born will read it, as I read it when it broke upon me in a wealth of delight more than forty years ago. The generations will recognize and salute it in turn, as I do now. For, to tell you the truth, I finished *The Public Spirit of the Whigs* only a fortnight ago, it being perhaps my twentieth or my hundredth reading of it. And I am now setting off home to read it again.

On Thinking

Canon Dimnet of Cambrai lately wrote a little book upon the *Art of Thinking*. He wrote it, I believe, in the English tongue; but whether it be a translation or from his own pen (which is the more likely, for he writes English like an Englishman), it is a book without the mark of a foreign origin; and perhaps he chose English for his medium on the consideration that thinking had often been condemned during the last century and even lately in the English tongue as a solvent of judgement and instinctive power. I desire to take the title of this book for a text, and to affirm that the business of Thinking has been somewhat underestimated of late: I desire to proclaim its modest value: to urge its use (in moderation, of course), and to say, even though I must say it timidly, a word in its favour. Come, let me take up the unpopular side, play the devil's advocate, and write a cautious brief in defence of this half-forgotten exercise, Thinking.

It was said some months ago by a witty Englishman, in praise of his own people, on returning from some foreign conference or other, that there was written up in flaming red letters upon the cliffs of Dover, for all returning men to read:

Thou shalt not Think. Thought is the foe of action. Therefore by Thinking men and nations perish.

It is a precept which has been repeated in various forms a thousand times. I doubt its soundness. It still seems to me that Thinking must have some good about it, and that those who decry Thinking are misled by an abuse of terms: an ambiguity. For the word 'thinking' is used of musing, as when we say of a man run over by a motor car that he was plunged in thought: and it is used of doubt, as when one says: 'I don't think the earth is flat: I know it'; it is used of vain illusion, as of Algernon, who thought himself the hell of a fellow; but it should more properly be used of discernment, so that by thought we see clearly the consequence of things, and by intelligence decide affairs and reach success in conclusions.

I have noticed not infrequently upon my rambles through this world that men (my brethren and similars) would order animals about: great strong animals, such as horned beeves, fierce dogs, and nervous horses; and that they were able so to do (it seemed to me) was due to their superior power of Thought. Observing this result, I have ever felt a certain anxiety lest, if we give up Thinking altogether, we may not become the prey of other nations more exercised in the practice.

Then, also, I have noticed that fame (which we all desire) is not unattached to this art of Thinking. Of close and clear thinkers there occur to me—Euclid, Descartes, Aquinas, even Cicero, and no one can say that they will be easily forgotten. Newton, by the way, should be added, and Locke, and John Stuart Mill; three prominent men who seem to have rebelled against the patriotic order emblazoned upon the cliffs of Dover.

But, talking of patriotism, there have been other rebels. For instance, not only was political economy founded here in England, where we are told no man should be allowed to Think, but the inferences and deductions of geology as well; for the beginnings of Geology are English. Then there is the whole science and practice of the Law, wherein I admit men will continually protest they prefer good honest sense to thinking, but wherein also I notice there is quite a lot of Thinking done, sometimes a little too finely.

Then there are all those of the delicate professions, if I may use that term. I mean, the careers in which men advance by a certain light dexterity in appreciation of others and by the laying of subtle plans. Such are promoters, share-shufflers, big-business men, money dealers, sharpers, those of the three-card trick and the great army of snatchers and lifters. Which of them would survive if he did not think—rapidly, clearly, continually?

When, therefore, I hear the phrase that what is of importance to mortals is character, not intellect, I am so moved that I fall into verse—a thing habitual with versifiers when their emotions are stirred—and on this very matter have I composed a short epic, the first lines of which I will now humbly put before you, reminding you, however, that they are copyright, and reserving the sequel that I may sell it again later:

> I knew a man who used to say
> (Not once, but twenty times a day)
> That in the turmoil and the strife—
> His very phrase—of human life,
> The thing of ultimate effect
> Was character: not intellect.
> He therefore was at constant pains
> To atrophy his puny brains,
> And registered success in this
> Beyond the dreams of avarice.

The epic goes on to describe his career, how, when he had become completely imbecile, he was selected for the highest posts in the land, and died—for even such men must die at last—saturated with glory, rolling in money and a model for all of us.

But this poem, I must warn you, was by way of satire, or something the opposite of what it plainly states. It was malicious. It was not to be taken literally, for within my own great soul I knew well that some measure of intellect was essential, even to public life, let alone to the running of a whelk stall.

I fancy that those who decry the ancient and honourable practice of Thinking are mixing it up with two things very different, which are called Deduction from Insufficient Premises, and Deduction from False Premises; or perhaps they are mixing it up with Argufying—which of all the detestable habits of man is perhaps the most intolerable—unless, indeed, it be set to work upon matters wholly undiscoverable, wherein it is a very tolerable pastime. Indeed, you may note that men in their cups generally talk metaphysics. And this, let me tell you, is not particularly true of the over-educated, but of all men whatsoever. It was but the other day I heard two men, with no pretence to any excess of culture, shouting at each other in the bar of an inn close against the shores of the Southern Sea, and one of them kept on saying, 'How d'you know that what you saw *was* Bill's ketch, anyhow?' And the other kept on replying, 'Why, it stands to reason that if I saw the thing it was there.' Wherein was developed all the quarrel of Kant and the sceptics with the peripatetics, and of sophists with common sense from the beginning of time; also the dear little fuss about phenomena.

And as for Thinking interfering with action, that is using one word in two senses. It is not Thinking that interferes with action; Thinking decides action. It is hesitation in Thought that interferes with action; it is paralysis in Thought that interferes with action, like that weariness of the mind wherein a tune goes on buzzing in one's head. The man who keeps on saying, 'Shall I? Shall I not?' is not Thinking, he is cutting the nerve of Thought. And even if Thinking have no practical value (though I stoutly maintain it has), at the least it is an absorbing exercise, bridging over those empty moments when we have neither scandal to talk against our neighbours, nor money to filch from them, nor vapid books to read.

Therefore do I think that I shall continue to think; and whether you think I think right in so thinking I care not, for I think so.

XXXVIII

'Heroic Poem in Praise of Wine'

1931

*Of Belloc's serious verse, this poem is the best-known. It was com-
pleted in 1928 and appeared originally in the* London Mercury.
*which was edited by J. C. Squire. Most critics are agreed that in
its qualities no better poem in heroic couplets is to be found in contemporary verse. It is in praise of what Belloc most treasured in life—
the open-air—the sea—the world in which he travelled—and with
always at hand a flask of wine.*

Heroic Poem in Praise of Wine

TO DUFF COOPER

To exalt, enthrone, establish and defend,
To welcome home mankind's mysterious friend:
Wine, true begetter of all arts that be;
Wine, privilege of the completely free;
Wine the recorder; wine the sagely strong;
Wine, bright avenger of sly-dealing wrong,
Awake, Ausonian Muse, and sing the vineyard song!

Sing how the Charioteer from Asia came,
And on his front the little dancing flame
Which marked the God-head. Sing the Panther-team,
The gilded Thyrsus twirling, and the gleam
Of cymbals through the darkness. Sing the drums.
He comes: the young renewer of Hellas comes!
The Seas await him. Those Aegean Seas
Roll from the dawning, ponderous, ill at ease,
In lifts of lead, whose cresting hardly breaks
To ghostly foam, when suddenly there awakes
A mountain glory inland. All the skies
Are luminous; and amid the sea bird cries
The mariner hears a morning breeze arise.
Then goes the Pageant forward. The sea-way
Silvers the feet of that august array
Trailing above the waters, through the airs;
And as they pass a wind before them bears
The quickening word, the influence magical.
The Islands have received it, marble-tall;
The long shores of the mainland. Something fills
The warm Euboean combes, the sacred hills
Of Aulis and of Argos. Still they move
Touching the City walls, the Temple grove,
Till, far upon the horizon-glint, a gleam
Of light, of trembling light, revealed they seem

HEROIC POEM IN PRAISE OF WINE

Turned to a cloud, but to a cloud that shines,
And everywhere as they pass, the Vines! The Vines!
The Vines, the conquering Vines! And the Vine breathes
Her savour through the upland, empty heaths
Of treeless wastes; the Vines have come to where
The dark Pelasgian steep defends the lair
Of the wolf's hiding; to the empty fields
By Aufidus, the dry campaign that yields
No harvest for the husbandman, but now
Shall bear a nobler foison than the plough;
To where, festooned along the tall elm trees,
Tendrils are mirrored in Tyrrhenian seas;
To where the South awaits them; even to where
Stark, African, informed of burning air,
Upturned to Heaven the broad Hipponian plain
Extends luxurious and invites the main.
Guelma's a mother: barren Thapsa breeds;
And northward in the valleys, next the meads
That sleep by misty river banks, the Vines
Have struck to spread below the solemn pines.
The Vines are on the roof-trees. All the Shrines
And Homes of men are consecrate with Vines.

And now the task of that triumphant day
Has reached to victory. In the reddening ray
With all his train, from hard Iberian lands
Fulfilled, apparent, that Creator stands
Halted on Atlas. Far beneath him, far,
The strength of Ocean darkening and the star
Beyond all shores. There is a silence made.
It glorifies: and the gigantic shade
Of Hercules adores him from the West.
Dead Lucre: burnt Ambition: Wine is best.

But what are these that from the outer murk
Of dense mephitic vapours creeping lurk
To breathe foul airs from that corrupted well
Which oozes slime along the floor of Hell?
These are the stricken palsied brood of sin

BELLOC

In whose vile veins, poor, poisonous and thin,
Decoctions of embittered hatreds crawl:
These are the Water-Drinkers, cursed all!
On what gin-sodden Hags, what flaccid sires
Bred these White Slugs from what exhaust desires?
In what close prison's horror were their wiles
Watched by what tyrant power with evil smiles;
Or in what caverns, blocked from grace and air
Received they, then, the mandates of despair?
What! Must our race, our tragic race, that roam
All exiled from our first, and final, home:
That in one moment of temptation lost
Our heritage, and now wander, hunger-tost
Beyond the Gates (still speaking with our eyes
For ever of remembered Paradise),
Must we with every gift accepted, still,
With every joy, receive attendant ill?
Must some lewd evil follow all our good
And muttering dog our brief beatitude?

A primal doom, inexorable, wise,
Permitted, ordered, even these to rise.
Even in the shadow of so bright a Lord
Must swarm and propagate the filthy horde
Debased, accursed I say, abhorrent and abhorred.
Accursed and curse-bestowing. For whosoe'er
Shall suffer their contagion, everywhere
Falls from the estate of man and finds his end
To the mere beverage of the beast condemned.
For such as these in vain the Rhine has rolled
Imperial centuries by hills of gold;
For such as these the flashing Rhone shall rage
In vain its lightning through the Hermitage
Or level-browed divine Touraine receive
The tribute of her vintages at eve.
For such as these Burgundian heats in vain
Swell the rich slope or load the empurpled plain.
Bootless for such as these the mighty task
Of bottling God the Father in a flask

HEROIC POEM IN PRAISE OF WINE

And leading all Creation down distilled
To one small arden sphere immensely filled.
With memories empty, with experience null,
With vapid eye-balls meaningless and dull
They pass unblest through the unfruitful light;
And when we open the bronze doors of Night,
When we in high carousal, we, reclined,
Spur up to Heaven the still ascending mind,
Pass with the all inspiring, to and fro,
The torch of genius and the Muse's glow,
They, lifeless, stare at vacancy alone
Or plan mean traffic, or repeat their moan.
We, when repose demands us, welcomed are
In young white arms, like our great Exemplar
Who, wearied with creation, takes his rest
And sinks to sleep on Ariadne's breast.
They through the darkness into darkness press
Despised, abandoned and companionless.
And when the course of either's sleep has run
We leap to life like heralds of the sun;
We from the couch in roseate mornings gay
Salute as equals the exultant day
While they, the unworthy, unrewarded, they
The dank despisers of the Vine, arise
To watch grey dawns and mourn indifferent skies.

Forget them! Form the Dionysian ring
And pulse the ground, and Io, Io, sing.

Father Lenaean, to whom our strength belongs,
Our loves, our wars, our laughter and our songs,
Remember our inheritance, who praise
Your glory in these last unhappy days
When beauty sickens and a muddied robe
Of baseness fouls the universal globe.
Though all the Gods indignant and their train
Abandon ruined man, do thou remain!
By thee the vesture of our life was made,
The Embattled Gate, the lordly Colonnade,

323

The woven fabric's gracious hues, the sound
Of trumpets, and the quivering fountain-round,
And, indestructible, the Arch, and, high,
The Shaft of Stone that stands against the sky,
And, last, the guardian-genius of them, Rhyme,
Come from beyond the world to conquer time:
All these are thine, Lenaean.
By thee do seers the inward light discern;
By thee the statue lives, the Gods return;
By thee the thunder and the falling foam
Of loud Acquoria's torrent call to Rome;
Alba rejoices in a thousand springs,
Gensano laughs, and Orvieto sings . . .
But, Ah! With Orvieto, with that name
Of dark, Etrurian, subterranean flame
The years dissolve. I am standing in that hour
Of majesty Septembral, and the power
Which swells the clusters when the nights are still
With autumn stars on Orvieto hill.

Had these been mine, Ausonian Muse, to know
The large contented oxen heaving slow;
To count my sheaves at harvest; so to spend
Perfected days in peace until the end;
With every evening's dust of gold to hear
The bells upon the pasture height, the clear
Full horn of herdsmen gathering in the kine
To ancient byres in hamlets Appenine,
And crown abundant age with generous ease:
Had these, Ausonian Muse, had these, had these . . .

But since I would not, since I could not stay,
Let me remember even in this my day
How, when the ephemeral vision's lure is past
All, all, must face their Passion at the last.

Was there not one that did to Heaven complain
How, driving through the midnight and the rain,
He struck, the Atlantic seethe and surge before,

HEROIC POEM IN PRAISE OF WINE

Wrecked in the North along a lonely shore
To make the lights of home and hear his name no more.
Was there not one that from a desperate field
Rode with no guerdon but a rifted shield;
A name disherited; a broken sword;
Wounds unrenowned; battle beneath no Lord;
Strong blows, but on the void, and toil without reward.

When from the waste of such long labour done
I too must leave the grape-enobling sun
And like the vineyard worker take my way
Down the long shadows of declining day,
Bend on the sombre plain my clouded sight
And leave the mountain to the advancing night,
Come to the term of all that was mine own
With nothingness before me, and alone;
Then to what hope of answer shall I turn?
Comrade-Commander whom I dared not earn,
What said You then to trembling friends and few?
'A moment, and I drink it with you new:
But in my Father's Kingdom.' So, my Friend.
Let not Your cup desert me in the end.
But when the hour of mine adventure's near
Just and benignant, let my youth appear
Bearing a Chalice, open, golden, wide,
With benediction graven on its side.
So touch my dying lip: so bridge that deep:
So pledge my waking from the gift of sleep,
And, sacramental, raise me the Divine:
Strong brother in God and last companion, Wine.

XXXIX

Napoleon

1932

Belloc was not happy with this study of Napoleon and indeed would not allow it to be translated into French. Yet Belloc's opinion on Napoleon must be of perennial interest. Especially interesting is the account we give here of Napoleon's youth.

The Annealing

On April 21, 1779, the little Italian boy, the little Corsican, Napoleone di Buonaparte, only nine years old, was leaving the school at Autun to be sent to Brienne in Champagne. He had been brought over to France by his father but a few months before.

He cried a little, but very little, at leaving behind him in Autun his elder brother Joseph—who cried much more profusely—and so went out all alone in his tininess, conducted by an old Captain whom he had never seen. He was cut off from all that he had known.

The child was very short even for his years, too frail and thin, with big serious grey eyes in a face extremely pale, olive of the south, and long dark hair not abundant.

He was delayed somewhat on the journey, but delivered at the grey severe barrack-like building of the monks at Brienne by the middle of May; and thenceforward for five and a half years he was to know nothing else but those gaunt rooms, long empty corridors, the sad large playground court, the lessons of his masters and the noise and tumult of his hundred schoolfellows, from whom his temperament kept him apart.

The place was not a prison, though the little cubicles in which each child slept were fastened from outside at night and though the furnishing was pitifully simple. They took walks in the country round, and he remembered the landscape years after. He remembered also with pleasure the avenue of lime-trees which belonged to the College: but his soul was imprisoned and thrown back upon itself. He was in an isolation as complete as can fall even upon childhood. He remembered Corsica, the sun, the strong scent of the brushwood on the hills, the droning heat of the summers and the great wooded mountains falling into deep bays of warm sea. He remembered his companions of the little town, all speaking as he spoke and all of his own kind, and his brothers and sisters playing noisily at large in the big spare room that had been especially dismantled for them and their games. He was desperate for his home —and here he had only before him the northern skies of Champagne and the rolling empty fields of that plain, its chalky dust; no line of hills to be a companion for him against the sky—and for human beings aliens all around.

Children cannot—and would not if they could—express what sufferings impose on them. The more does their mood take root and become instinctive because it is not contemplated or analysed. So it was with this child, and the cutting of him apart from intercourse with his kind.

In such isolation there was emphasized in him the Corsican patriotism which, even so very young, he had taken in on every side from the moment when he could see or hear or understand the speech of men. He already knew, in this his tenth year, that he was odd and in his origin despicable or absurd—at any rate to his equals and to the older boys around him. He had already learnt to talk French well enough, but the French were for him foreigners and hated; his homesickness added to the hatred, and in spite of the new language which was becoming his own he could only think of himself as 'Napoleone'—the name by which they had known him at home and which was his very self to him. Yet that name, with its foreign sound, only earned him the jeers of those about him. He built a wall between himself and them and within it passed those years of intense feeling which give to the whole of life coming after its form and trend. The particular exaltation which in childhood and on into youth he retained for the Corsican cause and for the name of Paoli left him in early manhood; but what never left him, what was to mark him to his death, was that outer armour, that segregation from human souls about him, which this childhood and its sequel made.

Luckily for him he could fight, therefore he was not bullied; and, also luckily for him, he had inherited with his mother's blood a profound tenacity apparent even then, in childhood. Luckily for him, there arose in him during these case-hardening years, a third quality—intellectual energy, intense, increasing. 'Energy,' said he later, when he was grown a man, and in so many definitions struck out the very core of truth, 'is the well-spring of intelligence.' From the first days when the nuns had taught him his baby arithmetic in Ajaccio he had thought in terms of numbers and of forms, and now as he approached and entered his teens mathematics were his delight. But he had this great advantage over the most part of minds so directed, that he added to the vividness of his imagination the seeds of a literary aptitude which he could not as yet suspect. Also he read all that he could lay his hands upon and was thus being formed (though they gave him woefully little Latin and no Greek) in the tradition of the ancients. In common with all of his time he devoured Plutarch, in good French translation. Without knowing it, he responded at once to style—style, whereby thought and doctrine live in the minds of men. Later, in the height of his glory, he marvelled inwardly at Corneille, responding like an equal to the marble and the bronze. Being thus sensitive, and always in all his waking moments on the defensive, his solace was reverie; and, since he combined this aloofness with courage, he seemed incapable of gaiety in those years when, to a southern, gaiety should have been most spontaneous, seemed also indifferent to the little common pleasures of boyhood. They nick-named him 'Spartan'.

In all those years of homesickness and dereliction which did but knead strength in him as he slowly and insufficiently grew in body, he had no air from home. As he approached his fifteenth birthday he was already grown to such stature as he would have; legend has belittled it, but short he was always to remain, almost exactly five foot seven in English measure. But his frame was still so spare and lean—it was to remain so until close upon his thirtieth year—that it seemed less than it was, and only that fixed prolonged regard and the evident control behind it preserved him from contempt, though there was also this, which had come with his teens and which added a dignity to what as yet had little dignity, the fullness of the oval of his face and the perfect strength and roundness of the chin, above which those close fine lips—his mother's lips—speaking but little, not smiling as yet, grave, seeming incapable of irony, witnessed to a sharp edge of character.

One break there was and only one, and it came late in this same fifteenth year. On the Midsummer's Day of 1784 his father, Charles Buonaparte, passed through Brienne. It was the first time since the child had come there more than five years before. He brought with him the younger brother Lucien to place him also in the school, a boy of nine, vivacious, alert, intelligent, active, ready to mix with all and full of good humour, as also of will. He brought with him, further, two other children, Corsican girls of his own rank, daughters of friends, one of them the sister of that Casabianca who was destined for the navy and who was to fall at the Nile. They were on their way to the school for the daughters of the gentry at St Cyr.

Charles Buonaparte was on his way to Paris to demand certain government grants for Corsica, but he was coming also and mainly to seek the doctors, for the illness was already upon him—that cancer in the stomach—which was to kill him within a year.

Young Napoleone was sent for to the parlour, and for some brief moments the boy had the air of his childhood and of his home about him. It was an experience of the most violent kind, and the only one with any touch in it of consolation. The father spoke to him of all home affairs, treating him as though he were (what he should have been) the eldest son, and speaking of the one who was indeed the eldest, Joseph, as though seeking for advice from this serious lad whose judgement he valued. For Joseph was not satisfactory. He had been destined for the Church where the important friends who protected Charles Buonaparte would have given him preferment, for it was urgent in the narrow circumstances of the family that the boys and especially the eldest should be well placed; but Joseph would not go the way he was bid. Not from stubbornness, but from its opposite—spiritual indolence. He would not even think of the learned arms, he wanted the infantry, where a man could just live and do nothing. The father and the son talked together at length on that problem, and then, after so short a visit, Charles Buonaparte was gone, and the boy never saw his father again.

His time at Brienne, wherein he had learned so little, was coming to its end. He particularly desired that on leaving he should himself be directed towards the navy; it was esteemed the senior service, it gave an opportunity for action and promotion beyond any branch of the army and was at that moment especially favoured— even fashionable; for the time was full of the naval success which had ensured the independence of the United States of America, wherein the French fleet had played a capital role; it seemed certain that further action against England—still the superior power at sea —was bound to come and give him every opportunity.

What decided him reluctantly to abandon the plan was the objection of his mother. She thought the dangers too great, and as second best there remained to him a chance (though it seemed at first a small one) of a commission in the Artillery.

The French Artillery was at this moment the first in Europe. It had a very proud tradition, and was already reacting against the technical form by which it was counted as one of the Regiments of the Line—the 64th. It was the learned arm; his talents suited him for it, and the position it would give him appealed to him. His little brother Lucien was not without effect upon him at this moment. Though he was but a child he had heard what it was to be a gunner, and Napoleone listened to what he had to say. Thus, it was that the gunner who was to be the most famous of all gunners in history entered the career.

But, as I say, the chances were small. He must go first to the military school in Paris, it was unlikely that coming from Brienne and with no special protection he would obtain his commission save after some long delay—if then. But among those who taught him (he remembered them all in after life) there should be noted in particular one figure: that of an odd tall man, rubicund, not over reliable, who for the purposes of the school (though not in orders) went about in a cassock: one Pichegru, who years after was to plot against Napoleon's life and to lose his own in so doing.

It was midway through his school days that there came to Napoleone what often comes to boys of that age (his twelfth to thirteenth year) at least to boys of the Catholic culture and surrounded by an unescapable routine of religious practice—the failure of religious faith.

That this should not have come to him in the eighties of the eighteenth century at such a place and time would have been astonishing enough—that it did come to him was normal to the circumstances. It was the moment when the mind of Europe and more especially the mind of France had moved furthest from Catholicism, and had most forgotten that creative influence whence all our civilization, through the long centuries of its formation, had proceeded.

The decline had been rapid and universal. It had been the more complete because all the externals still stood. It is always so. When the clothing, the trappings of a failing thing, the mechanism, the social habit of its expression, are destroyed, there remains no grievance against it: men cannot and do not accuse it of oppression or false claims. They are more moved to pity and to inquiry. They wonder whether, after all, the thing be as insignificant as it appears. But if the externals are maintained when the life seems to have departed from within, there is a strong reaction against them; they do not justify themselves; they have the effect of a perpetual coercion—and whatever affection remained for the living Thing to which these forms were the adjuncts is destroyed by detestation of unrealities imposed. Now at Brienne, in the hands of the monks, the Royal school and wholly official, all the mechanism of a religion which educated men had lost continued unchanged. There was daily Mass; there was a fixed, regular and frequent forced date for Confession; the routine of religion was kept mechanically at work. The more did that routine contrast with the ambient spirit of the time.

The little boy had been fervent enough as a child. His preparation for his first Communion he always remembered and that day stood out for him all his life; but when the first active use of reason came it found no food on which to exercise itself so far as religion was concerned. To all the questions upon the Unseen no answer was given but dusty affirmation, often insincere. It was so in bulk with the training of youth, the youth of the gentry at least, throughout that world of the 1780s in France. For things to have fallen otherwise with the boy Napoleone there would have been needed either some strong association of ideas by which the things he loved were so interwoven with the spirit of the Faith that to abandon it was to abandon them, or else something in the child himself utterly original and of a different stuff from the generation to which it belonged. Normally, as things were then, the loss of Faith must come to Napoleone just in those years, especially as he was cut off from his home. Nothing he loved was connected directly and vitally with the formal religion about him. It did not represent to him his country nor those things which he had been taught to admire, nor the practice, the example and daily effect of a personality whom he revered or would follow. And as for that strong eccentric quality which sometimes launches an individual into conflict with all the spirit of his time, Napoleon was never of that kind. He was wholly of his time, and though made upon a scale far greater than his contemporaries, he was of the same texture, the same stuff. The errors he made were their errors, the enthusiasms he had were their enthusiasms, the things he took for granted were the general postulates of the day. The older boys among his comrades talked as all then talked in the current sceptical speech of their fathers. They were what he would himself become. There was no contrasting example to make him pause, and even the imposed ritual was perfunctory, hurried, not vital.

It is significant that among the community in whose charge he was there came defections when, later, the Revolution set men free to break their vows. The brother of the Principal was notorious for his unfrocked career when once the new laws had given him licence to break his vows openly. Napoleon, had not looking back on his childhood in that place, any remembrance of holiness, and hardly any remembrance of strong intelligent belief. But on this point it must be remembered that the lad who lost his Faith in his thirteenth year retained that underlying foundation which is only rejected by a conscious deliberate effort and never disappears unless there has been bred in the character, by some accident or some ill-doing, a positive hatred of that which it has lost.

Such hatred Napoleon never felt either in youth or in manhood, therefore the foundations remained.

The things he said upon the matter of religion were often merely political, commonly superficial either in praise or in blame, and in saying them he was but talking the language of his contemporaries, the only language he knew. But that mind of his was too profoundly rooted in the soil out of which he had come not to nourish him throughout his life, and that is why towards the close of it we shall find religion again apparent—uncertainly, and only at the very close but increasingly, until in the final hour, while consciousness still remained. He always rebuked Atheism. A cynical denial disgusted him, and when, at his coronation there was a question of his receiving the Sacraments, he made no objection to Confession, but as to Communicating he hesitated and said gravely: 'No! It would be hypocrisy.' He was at the last, when he came to die, in full Communion again.

This eclipse of religion coming in the critical moment of adolescence served to increase his isolation from his kind. For though he was thus to be at one with the general philosophy around him, he was left unprovided with a motive for approaching his fellows. He was divorced from spiritual curiosity and left indifferent to, and disdainful of, what might be passing in other minds.

Such is the story of Napoleon's first annealing, of that process which continued on and on for years until the time came when, a very young man so formed by isolation, he was to emerge suddenly, equipped for greatness, and to become famous in a moment during the business of Vendémiaire.

It was in the month of October, 1784, a little before the beginning of the new scholastic year, that five of the boys (of whom Napoleone was one) left Brienne for Paris, where he was to enter the École Militaire, the fine great building—something of a palace in its aspect—which fronts the Champs de Mars and is neighbour to the Invalides.

The monk in charge of the boys brought them up north by water; it was the cheapest carriage and not much slower than a coach: a great barge with an awning, towed down the rivers, filled with country-folk, plying twice a week, did the journey; so upon October 19, 1784, Buonaparte being then two months past his fifteenth birthday, the lumbering vessel came creaking alongside the wharf of the eastern end of Paris, where the Rue St Pol came out on to the quays. The monk in charge gave the lads their dinner in a modest eating-house upon the southern side, and then, by nightfall, handed over his charge to the authorities of the Military School.

For the first time Napoleon knew Paris, and for the first time he came in contact with that world of great wealth, of fixed aristocratic tradition and privilege which was then so near its end.

The experience was to affect him deeply. He was at once proud of his own noble birth (but it was a very small nobility) and offended by the airs of superior rank. The paradox is not only common but, one may say, universal. He was a gentleman, sensitive beyond degree to his claim, the more tenacious of it because that gentility of his had been so very petty and provincial a thing, carried on upon the narrowest and most uncertain of incomes in the newly annexed island on the remote extremity of the realm. Here, in the École Militaire, dressed in a uniform which was already the uniform of the King, mixing with others who like himself were maintained by royal favour and at the King's expense, but also, and as familiarly with young fellows of the wealthiest and most ancient families who, unlike himself, were paid for (and luxuriously) by their own people, he felt and suffered what is felt and suffered by every educated man who is poor and experiences the social contrast immediately and at first hand.

But there was more in the effect of this first mixing of his with aristocracy: the young fellow was—for a time—sincerely and at heart what was later to be called 'Jacobin'. He had caught the passion for equality. Nor was it a personal feeling alone, it was a common doctrine in which he felt himself to be supported by all he had read and known. Rousseau at second hand had already begun to work upon him, though Rousseau did no more than put forward with all the power of verbal mastery what the mind of his time had come to believe.

There were but a few months of this life. They were not unhappy ones, save that he did feel sharply the loss of his father when he heard of Charles Buonaparte's death in Montpellier in the spring of the next year.

The military air was all about him: it suited him and formed him. The classes were summoned by a roll of drums, sentinels were at the gates, and the gentlemen cadets were divided into companies with certain of their own number set over them as officers.

His new studies, which were serious especially on the mathematical side, absorbed him, and there was a life and reality about the place, a spaciousness for the intelligence, and in spite of the simplicity of the quarters a grandeur about his surroundings which suited him well enough. The table, for instance, was of a different kind from what he had known at the dreary provincial college in Champagne, and the architecture of the building, its decoration, its furniture and the conversation of those about him—all was of a new and larger sort, and great Paris was all around.

During those ten months therefore (for that was all the time he spent within those walls) he was not cut off as he had been in the earlier years; he would not have seemed to a spectator isolated as he had then been; yet the process of annealing continued, for he was still silent, awkward enough, still unsmiling and still taking refuge in long reveries. He still felt that gulf between himself and his fellows which had opened from the first days of his miserable homesickness as a shivering child in Autumn, when his father went away and left him there. He still retained the old childish enthusiasm for Corsica and all his Corsican patriotism, the alien feeling;

though it was declining under the influence of the Capital. As for the Italian language, he had lost it altogether and was wholly French-speaking.

As it had seemed improbable that he would leave Brienne as early as he did, or be received so young into the École Militaire, so it now seemed improbable that he would fulfil his ambition to be given an early commission and so join the artillery. It would come sooner or later, but probably he would have to wait. He was one of twenty-five whose names were down for that arm, but he soon stood fairly high among them in the mathematical science, at which he worked feverishly, and when, of the twenty-five, eighteen were selected and put to a *viva voce* before the great Laplace—at the very end of the sojourn of his at the School, in the September of 1785—he succeeded.

We have no record of the questions or of the effect that Napoleon made upon the man who was then the greatest in Europe at his trade, but we know something of the scene: the large hall in the École Militaire with its ornamented curtained windows, the two big slates set up for the chalk diagrams of the students, the benches rising in tiers so that all the students would be seen at once by the examiner, and Laplace in his black broadcloth sitting there with a shade over his weak eyes asking his questions in turn. Four gentlemen cadets passed out from that examination to their commission, Napoleon third on the list.

By the end of October he was gazetted as a Second Lieutenant with an order drafting him into the regiment of La Fère, in garrison at Valence. By the last day of the month he was on his way south, and was a soldier.

Even so, he was to live on in austerity, in great poverty and great pride and in isolation still. Not as the child, who had felt all around him to be hostile, but as a young man who, save for one or two deep friendships, felt most of what was around him to be indifferent at the best, and for the most part inferior to himself.

XL

Cromwell

1934

In a letter to Miss Pauline Cotton[1] on Cromwell, Belloc wrote: 'a man on whom the official history has lied more freely than on anybody else. He came of a gigantically wealthy family and was connected by marriage and blood with about a dozen millionaires of his day. It is great fun to see how bewildered he was by finding that it was necessary that he should take on the boredom of government which he didn't like one little bit. He was a great cry-baby, always breaking out into a loud Boo-Hoo upon every occasion that lent itself to sentimentality.'

He had already contributed Cromwell to Benn's sixpenny paperbacks in 1927. Unlike many of his other historical studies this was a book that pleased him, though of course his interpretation of the man is unconventional.

[1] Speaight: *Belloc,* p. 425.

Growth of Character

Character grows from circumstance acting on that which is within. What circumstance, in the formative years and in early manhood, acted upon what inward material here, in this cadet of a great but new fortune?

First, of course, the New Religion. We shall see it at work. He will suffer Conversion in his agonies. He will wrestle with God. He will be of the Elect. Beyond that, certain things favourable and unfavourable: an early and happy marriage saving from nervous ruin a very young man who still suffered for years from that horror of darkness where the soul is abandoned and evil calls from the abyss—and the pretty modern name for that is 'depression'. Next a bitter humiliation, never forgotten: the loss of the house that had made his family great. Next a good life in the fields, on a horse and with his beasts; the delight in children; some consideration of friends; the whole remote and obscure. Luckily for him an ample income, plenty of backing. Then common entry into public life such as comes to scores of his kind. Underneath all this, quite concealed from his own soul and all around it, was a soldier made for soldiering: fitted throughout with all the capacities for that trade. Only when that trade was, by an accident of life, thrust upon him, did he know what he was. It was a special dispensation. Henceforward he felt himself guided everywhere by the direct intervention of heaven almost to the end—but not quite to the end.

The years of Cromwell's youth and early manhood, up to his twenty-ninth year when he first entered public life, have no interest to general history: they have the highest particular interest in the question how such a man came to be.

His worshippers, who have collected every scrap of information and tradition available, have discovered very little about him; but that little has at least one value, it is consonant with what followed and therefore explains the man.

Here we must remember an historical principle which the men of the nineteenth century nearly always lacked when they spoke of Cromwell, as had those of the eighteenth century and later seventeenth before them. The principle is that we must accept evidence neither helped nor hindered by affection or hate. It was inevitable that a man who had had so extraordinary a part thrust upon him for such a few concentrated years should become a demi-god or a demon in the national story. For the hundred odd years and more during which he was the national Bad Man any wisp of tradition, any fragment of evidence which made him ridiculous or wicked was eagerly seized and established—and plenty of guess-work followed upon the same lines. After the turnover between the end of the eighteenth century and 1830 the influence of the new Non-conformist mercantile fortunes, of the Whig policy in triumphant defence against Rousseau, it was the opposite; nothing that was remembered, nothing that was proved—of the few things that are remembered or proved upon those early years of Cromwell—was accepted if it were derogatory to him; or, if accepted, it was explained, often absurdly, in his favour.

Carlyle does not (of course) even attempt to weigh the evidence; but it is unfortunately the same with men better balanced than Carlyle. They follow each other throughout the period immediately before our own in a long string of denials, refusing any story, tradition or even known fact which did not conform to their imaginary picture of one whom they had now set up to worship—just as he had been set up by their fathers to be condemned. When the fact was too prominent and too well attested to be thus passed over it was given a favourable interpretation at all costs.

But Cromwell remains the same man, whether he be made to play the one exaggerated part or the other, and the right way to treat the very meagre evidence upon the earlier years—from his birth in 1599 to his presence in the Long Parliament of 1641—is to judge it by its agreement with the mass of things we know of him in later life, that is, from 1641 to his death in 1658. These last years were less than one-third of the whole—seventeen out of fifty-nine—but if we find the mature acts consonant with the acts or moods of youth on which there is even only vague tradition we are justified in accepting that tradition, whether it proceed from an enemy or a friend.

The traditions and statements, certain or half certain, help us to understand that character, for they belong to the formative period of his development. After the Parliament of 1628, when he was already a man approaching thirty, that character can develop no longer; his life changed and the curve of his career developed out of all knowledge—but the man himself was fixed before his thirtieth year, as very nearly all men are. . . .

The first thing to note about that childhood and the adolescence which followed it is the intense nervousness of temperament apparent in them. That also was a characteristic which followed Cromwell to the end.

I use the word 'nervousness' with some hesitation, for it is ambiguous and might convey a false impression of timidity. I use it in the sense of a mind at tension, a gift of visual imagination which may fall suddenly into an extreme, an inability to repose, mortal fears, a liability to sudden anger, and a source of energy.

There is here a very marked contrast between the two chief military figures in modern English history—Cromwell himself and Marlborough. Marlborough was the most stolid of men. Save for the passion Sarah Jennings inspired—an emotion which completely mastered him—he was the most indifferent of men. Cromwell was all the other way. The violence of his emotions is apparent from the beginning to the end; it fastens upon him in the matter of religion as it would upon similar a man today in the matter of patriotism or of some political or economic creed—Communism for instance. It shows itself in floods of tears which he cannot restrain even at awkward moments and into which he falls quite naturally even when he is exciting himself by an argument which he himself knows to be insincere. It is a very great error to think such characters lacking in tenacity. It is an even worse error to think them lacking in judgement. There is no necessary connection between violence of feeling and instability, nor any between such violence and confusion of thought. They are often found in combination but they do not grow from a common root.

This leading mark in the Protector's spirit, half morbid, and nourished by what was defective in the material part of him, runs through all his life. As a child he sees a great shadow opening the curtains of his bed, and is convinced that the vision communicates to him great things upon his future. For such an extravagance his father had him whipped; without result, for he remained convinced that the apparition was real, and he could not keep the memory of it to himself.

He had, as he grew older, alternative fits of horseplay and despair. Fantasies upon, or beyond, the borders of what is sane haunted him in his early manhood. Of one of these manias we have certain and curious record through not a sufficient description of its character. We only know that it had something to do with the Town Cross of Huntingdon, and that he saw in or about that inanimate object horrors beyond this world. The medical profession catalogued him in early manhood under the term '*melancholicus*', which meant, in the technical language of the day, what we call today in a similar case, 'melancholia'. And to that diagnosis of '*melancholicus*' there was added the adverb '*valde*' ('very') to emphasize it; he was looked upon as a very bad case. A modern critic would see illusion also in his confidence that repeated revelations were granted to him throughout his life; while the other symptom, the terrors, also reappear at the end—as naturally they would when the strength of the body began to fail. It is all of a piece with his exceeding anxiety in the matter of Government, leading to bewilderment and exasperation. This I say must be put first because it conditions all the rest. That intensity of nervous structure is allied to the rapidity of his decisions in the field, to the clarity of his vision and is the main source of his drive.

But we must also note, side by side with this nervous character, what is very rare in that connection—an absence of extravagance in sensual appetite or, at least, of indulgence therein during the main part of his career. Such a temperament may have led him to debauch in early youth—he seems to accuse himself of that and there are traditions of it—but whether it did or not he was of a plain straightforward conduct in these affairs throughout all the significant years of his life; there was never a vibrant man of eminent public activity so simply devoted to his home and so certainly satisfied with his marriage. He gave example of what is meant, in any sane and just definition, by the word chastity.

There is not a sign of extravagance or irregularity from the day of his early marriage at twenty-two to his death close on sixty, nor do his innumerable enemies record anything of the kind. There are indeed two belated stories of natural children. One, a girl, the mother of that Mrs Hartopp who lived in the eighteenth century, the other a son. The first can be easily proved a confusion between the supposed bastard and Cromwell's legitimate daughter, Bridget. The other is no more than a silly imaginary romance—and a dull one—brought out in France. To estimate Oliver we must bear continually in mind this sobriety of sex in alliance with such fervour of fancy and exaltation of nerves.

Closely mixed with and proceeding from that exaltation of nerves in him must be noted once more his consuming religion. Not that it comes next in importance—it is first in importance by far, the chief element in Cromwell's character. That high potential of emotion which would, as I have said, under other circumstances have been directed to some other object was, in this early seventeenth century and in the particular case of Cromwell himself, directed to transcendental doctrine and worship. . . .

Young Cromwell in early boyhood received this Calvinist or Puritan spirit, in part no doubt from his parents, in part from the group of townsmen in Huntingdon with whom they were connected; but especially from the man whose natural place it was to give him his first training—Doctor Beard. This Beard was at the head of the Grammar School at Huntingdon; he was a Puritan Churchman, not without learning and with a reputation which extended far. He had written books upon his side of the controversy, notably one upon the common theme that the Pope was anti-Christ; he was a man engrossed in such things.

Beard's influence upon Cromwell was strong and continuous, and Oliver's interest in him long survived boyhood; it was apparent years after in middle life when Beard was an elderly man, and continued till his death. But there was another influence of great moment—of how great moment we know not by direct testimony but by its effect—and that was the appearance, as Cromwell was reaching puberty when the most vivid impressions are received, of what has ever since been known as the 'English Bible'.

The Authorized Version was but the last of some few vernacular renderings upon the Protestant side; the rhythms of its most famous rhetoric came from a lifetime earlier; its diction was already somewhat archaic—and the more impressive—so that it established itself during the course of a very few years as a verbal inspiration and literal authority throughout all that section of Englishmen for whom it was designed. It was destined at long last—by the end of the eighteenth century—to give its colour to the whole nation. It was as the Mohammedans say of the Koran, 'The Book'. Of all the cases in which the power of The Word has shown itself in the formation of societies this is perhaps the chief. Its high phrases acted like the music of armies; men drank of it and were set on fire.

Now that Book was first at work, I say, raising its earliest ferment in Oliver, just during those years when great verse or great rhythmic rhetoric most strongly seizes and stamps itself upon a mind. The new English Bible would have reached the household at Huntingdon when he was between thirteen and fourteen; he had it in his ears week by week and most probably daily, year after year, all through his early manhood. The influence was so violent that it produced in him (as in thousands of his contemporaries and scores of his social equals) that special vocabulary which seems to us grotesque but which soon became to them native. The strange names of half-savage Orientals, the metaphors drawn from the climate of Syria or the life of the desert, the characters of little highland tribes in Syria—three thousand miles away from England in distance, three thousand years in time—became in that group so thoroughly adopted that to this day men think of them as English. As for Oliver, the thing possessed him and spoke through his lips his whole life long.

Though a character is formed by thirty, though Cromwell was all this, the man on fire with the new Scripture and the man reading it in an atmosphere of Election and Conversion, yet the effect continued to develop in him. It was perhaps at its height shortly before he appears fully upon the stage, some four years before the outbreak of the Civil War, when he was nearly forty.

Here enters an element negative but all-important, too often missed, even omitted—the corresponding fear and hatred of the Catholic Church, and, consequently, the immediate readiness to act with every violence against it. . . .

Already half formed by such influences, there came upon Cromwell two things which matured him.

The first was his father's death, which took place early in his nineteenth year, while he was still a freshman at Cambridge of just over a year's standing. Most of the large income was left for his mother to manage, but he was now the head of the younger branch, and soon to have considerable interests in his own hands.

The second, three years after, was his early marriage, which moderated his dangers of temperament. That marriage was serenely successful. The high career to come owes to Mrs Oliver a debt which history has not paid because it remains so silent upon her, as she also was silent, preferring her home. History should be written in the recollection of such women, for they are creative as the talked-of women are not.

It was such a marriage as the Williams all made; one into their own wealthy world. She was the daughter of a rich and knighted London merchant called 'Bourcher' or 'Bourchier'; and the family of Oliver's millionaire uncle-by-marriage, the Hampdens, seems to have made the match. Her first four children were born to him while he still lived in that largest of the Huntingdon homes, himself the most prominent of the younger townsmen. For seven years he thus lived on his paternal land; they were not years in which he had peace—it was at their close, not their beginning, that his worst morbidities were noticed. But they were years in which his home and his wife kept him sane.

It was a simple, exactly consonant marriage with a woman of his own rank; it was fruitful, giving him a number of children to whom, as to his wife, he was devoted. That marriage, then, was the saving of Oliver.

It did not give him good equilibrium, it did not furnish him with full ballast, he was subject to violence, impulse and superstition all his life; but it calmed him sufficiently, and it gave him a certain background of happiness—as great a measure of that as a man of such temper could have. He had in his home a foundation all his life, and this is the more certain because his home obtrudes so little on to the outward story of his life. The strongest emotion in that very emotional man was his intense love of his children, of his family, his roof. Of most laymen who did great things while the Christian tradition of marriage still endured, it seems true that they were either very happily married or very unhappily, and that an inward state so nurtured provided them with reserves of power, or goaded them to external effort. For Cromwell his good marriage was a spiritual fortune.

Cromwell had another strong affection which puts him in the tradition of famous Englishmen—patriotism. But this was so much interwoven in his case (as in most others) with self-sufficiency that it is only half affection, the other half being something which you may call, according to your mood, vanity or pride. Such men see their country in themselves, and themselves in their country. And if to this natural emotion there be added a sense of divine election, which extends to both the nation and the man, then the nation is as naturally 'The Chosen Race' just as the man himself is 'The Chosen Individual'.

In the particular case of Cromwell, under the influence of that religion in him, there was a further selection, whereby his own sort in Protestantism were also specially chosen. But it must be remarked that, within the general boundaries of Protestant feeling, Cromwell was not fanatical, still less exclusive. His demand for independence in Protestant worship, his instinctive dislike of a fixed and still more of an imposed Protestant liturgy were abiding and obviously sincere. It was on this account (though the explanation may seem paradoxical) that he repeatedly showed sympathy with men who preferred organization in their evangelical worship, so long as it was *they* who chose such organization and so long as there was no forcing of it upon others. But all this toleration was granted, of course, only under the condition that the tolerated accept the main tenets of his own creed—the nullity of man's good works; the infallible witness of the English Bible as interpreted by the reader thereof; the ethical code which the Puritan takes for granted, not only in its commandments but in the order of precedence which he gives to its commandments. Cromwell cannot but believe that all men agree with him in their hearts and that therefore men with a different code or a different emphasis are, in proportion to their difference, liars and the enemies of God.

Seeing the false character that has been erected of Cromwell in order to glorify him spiritually, the sort of hagiography with which he has been surrounded, especially by men of the last generation, the errors in this laudation must be exposed. There are to be found among his actions, treasons, betrayals, falsehoods, acts of abominable cruelty, and false pretensions of motive. There are also certainly to be found acts, such as the pursuit of the King to his death, which it is difficult not to call crimes, because their motive is personal. But these do not make him black. They do not form one whole body of evil intention which would make us call him (as did Clarendon, who watched him closely) a bad man. The test is that whenever Oliver does something evil it is the yielding to a special temptation. The sin or turpitude is not part of a whole system of conduct springing from an evil root.

I have spoken and shall have frequent occasion to speak of the accusation of ambition brought against him. If there is one thing certain about the moral character of Cromwell, to the man who reads fully upon him and remembers his reading impartially, it is that he was not ambitious. Such a verdict would have sounded nonsense even to those who read widely a hundred years ago: Lingard, who must perpetually be quoted as the founder of modern English history, the forgotten quarry from which all the mid nine-teenth century historians dug their material, makes ambition the key to Cromwell's character.

It was not so. He lived to be over forty-five without making any effort at fame or power; and no man ever develops the desire for them long after youth has passed.

An immense fame came to him—he was not at all certain how—and almost unchecked personal power. Therefore was it taken for granted that he had sought both. As for fame, he takes no trouble to record his very remarkable achievements or to have them re-corded; in his own accounts he frequently passes them by, and the man is plainly so absorbed in other emotions, principally religious, that there is no room for anything of the kind. As to power, it ought to be evident that he actually dreaded it, that its exercise was for him a task, and a task uncongenial. He had never been trained to exercise it in all the years of his formation; there is no complaint from any victim of it in all those years; and they are years, remem-ber, prolonged far beyond the ordinary in the story of famous men —they reach right into middle age.

If ever Shakespeare's phrase of greatness being 'thrust upon' a man applied, it applies to Cromwell's political domination. As for glory, the great concomitant and attraction of power, he did not know what it meant. And if it could have been explained to him it would have seemed to him folly. He could never hear the music of it, nor were his surroundings such as to give him the least concep-tion of that emotion. Someone had to govern a distracted and ex-hausted England. The only instrument to hand was military, and Cromwell's only experience of getting things done was getting them done as a soldier. He had been contented enough before he was compelled to control, he would have remained contented all his life—and much more contented—if he had never been compelled to order anything beyond his own household. . . .

No one guessed—no one could dream, he himself cannot have remotely imagined it—that there lurked under all this a special supreme gift, a unique genius for cavalry.

Cromwell taking up soldiering discovered himself to be what he was. He entered fully into his own nature for the first time. The rapidity of the transition was as remarkable as its thoroughness. It is a great error that men after a certain age take on no new faculties; the seed must have been there, of course, but the plant may pierce very late. It has been seen even in the faculty of verse; it has been seen in commerce, in the management of a great business or in any great organization; men who had hitherto led one kind of life and exercised one set of activities, performed well enough but without remark one set of tasks, suddenly show supreme ability in another, and aptitudes which no one has suspected.

It is true that Cromwell had had in him certain talents apparent and in exercise during his civilian days which were of just the sort most necessary to the soldier; he had lucidity, he was tenacious, his energy was abundant, but what no one could know and what he did not know himself was the answer to this question—Could he manage men?

He certainly in the event proved thet he could not manage men in the political sense of management; but the qualities required for the management of men as soldiers are very different from those required for civil government: they are the qualities of command. Command contains an element of persuasion, but its strength lies much more in limitation than in approach—by which I mean that the faculty of command lies much more in commanding thoroughly and knowing the limits beyond which you must not go, than it does in the gradualness of your advance to control over that which it is your business to order.

But command has in it something much more than this. The faculty of command is a mysterious gift which you may perceive such and such men to be endowed with in various degrees. At first sight one observing Oliver Cromwell in his civilian days would have said that this, the highest of military qualities, had been denied him.

He was harsh, he was quarrelsome and even explosive, he would suddenly blurt out his thoughts at inconvenient times and even in moments when he weakened himself by so doing. . . .

Politically he was unstable, as when he manoeuvred back and forth in his attitude towards the discontents of the Army during the quarrel with Parliament, but in the actual military function of command he never wavered. No one under his orders had to complain of contradiction, of vacillation. He acted always at once with authority, and his violence did not here detract from the plentitude of his effect, as it does when one is concerned with equals and debaters. When Cromwell was in the face of lawyers, that violence appeared futile and certainly lessened him in their eyes, as we have seen it did in those of Hyde before the outbreak of war. But it went well enough with sudden decisions shouted from the saddle, with immediate judgements directing, checking, converting a charge.

Note further that Cromwell increased prodigiously in his capacity to 'form and to inform', that is, to mould by order from without, and to quicken by the spirit from within, the men whom he was to bind into an instrument of war.

There is no truer word than the old Greek, 'You become a carpenter by doing carpenter's work.' Cromwell's genius grew in the active exercise of it, and this was the more plainly seen because it grew by successive steps, from a smaller to a greater model. He begins with the training of a troop, the teaching of that small body while he himself was learning at the same time: he was a good horsemaster, he could judge their control of their mounts, he could advise as well as dictate, and he immediately discovered that out of the material afforded him (and at first largely chosen by him; the sons of yeomen for the most part it would seem), he could make with his own hands a first-rate unit in but a few weeks.

It was in a way an advantage (though paradoxical) that the period between the beginning of their training and their first active service was so short. But for the particular ordeal with which he and they were to be faced a long period of peace training or of service different from that in which were about to engage would have been a disadvantage.

From those first moments of the war Cromwell from the outset has become something new: he has been a soldier more than the others. He was already a soldier altogether, and soldiering will be his trade from now to the end. We must always think of him in that fashion: most of the rest of him was striking and plays its part, but this military spirit is the soul in him which quickens all the rest. He was doing his own work; he was at home; in his own skin. I say again, had all Cromwell's other qualities, not connected with soldiering, been other than what they were, had he been profoundly Catholic or cynically indifferent to any creed, had he been as sensual as he was controlled, ambitious, greedy for gain—or any other thing which he was not—yet still he would have been a soldier, a mounted soldier and supreme in that capacity: 'forming and informing'.

XLI

From *Characters of the Reformation*
1936

Characters of the Reformation *gave Belloc the fullest opportunity of airing his pet historical theory that the Roman Catholic Church is Europe and Europe the Church. Thus the Catholic Church was split asunder when Henry VIII divorced Catherine of Aragon and married Anne Boleyn. He began making public these arguments in 1920 when he published* Europe and the Faith.

Henry VIII

Now let me describe the character of this young fellow, upon whom so much was to depend. His leading characteristic was an inability to withstand impulse; he was passionate for having his own way—which is almost the opposite of having strength of will. He was easily dominated, always being managed by one person or another in succession, from this beginning of his life to the end of it, but being managed—not bullied or directly controlled.

It is exceedingly important to understand this chief point about him because a misjudgement of it has warped much the greater part of historical appreciation upon him. Because he was a big man who blustered and had fits of rage and was exaggeratedly eager to follow appetite and whim he has been given the false appearance of a powerful figure. Power he had, but it was only the political power which the mood of the time gave to whoever might be monarch. He had no personal power of character. He did not control others by their respect for his tenacity, still less by any feeling that he was wise and just and still less by any feeling that he was of strong fibre.

On the contrary, all those who managed him, one after the other—except his wife—despised him, and soon came to carry on as though they could do what they liked on condition that they flattered him. They managed public affairs while he followed his appetites or private interests. That was true of the whole series of those who 'ran' him: Wolsey, Anne Boleyn, Thomas Cromwell, and, at the end, his brother-in-law Seymour. The only exception was that admirable wife of his who, through the simplicity of her character and her strong affection as well as from her sense of duty, treated him with respect. But her influence over him was, perhaps on that very account, soon lost.

As might be expected with a nature of this kind, he revolted against each manager one after the other. He felt he was being 'run' by each in turn, grew peevish about it, had explosions of anger and would in a fit of passion get rid of them. Getting rid of them often meant, under the despotic conditions of that day, putting them to death. That is how he suddenly broke with Wolsey, that is how he broke with Anne Boleyn, that is how he broke with Thomas Cromwell—who had all three done what they willed with him, acting independently of him, showing their contempt for him in private and ultimately rousing his fury. Every woman (except his first wife Catherine) with whom he had to deal treated him pretty soon with contempt, and that is a most significant test of a man's value.

He excelled during all the early part of his life in physical exercises; he was a first-rate rider, a good wrestler, a good shot, and until disease had quite wreacked his physique he could endure a good deal of fatigue. A big red-headed, broad-faced man with a sparse beard, somewhat pale eyes set far apart in a face at first ruddy, later rather pasty. He had an exaggerated fear of death and, what was inexcusable in a King of his generation, he would never risk his body in battle. He was terrified of epidemics, which were frequent in the crowded, ill-drained towns of that epoch, and he took precautions, often absurd, to avoid any chance of infection. There were moments when the fear of death was a positive monomania with him.

He was exceedingly intelligent, and well trained in theology, to which he had first been directed when, as a boy, it was not thought that he would ever be King and he was destined by his father to become ultimately Archbishop of Canterbury. He was also well-read, could speak several foreign languages, and could speak and even think in French, as was the custom in the better-instructed upper class of his time in all western countries and especially in England. It must be remembered that within a hundred years of his birth the English upper class spoke French only, English had only recently become the common tongue.

But though he was intelligent, in the sense of being able to follow a logical process clearly or to draw up a consecutive plan or to analyse intellectual propositions such as are presented by theological or political discussion, he was a bad judge of men. He could see indeed well enough that this man or that was working hard and producing results, but he blundered badly whenever he tried to frame a foreign policy for himself; also he was very hesitant—perhaps because he half consciously recognized his incompetence in dealing with a complicated situation.

He would put off decision, advance towards a certain end and then draw back, half determining to give up objects towards which he was bent, and the main lines of action during his reign were always undertaken by somebody else.

It was Wolsey who conducted his early foreign policy entirely; it was Cromwell who later worked his breach with Rome; it was Seymour who, at the end of his life, determined what sort of will he should leave and how the succession to his throne should be arranged. He was emotional after a fashion, and especially sensitive to music; he was even a good practical musician himself and something of a poet and he composed a few songs which are not without merit, as well as other set pieces of harmony, notably two Masses to which are given his name but which are perhaps from his own hand.

He was very vain—vain of his looks, and of his athletics in early life; exceedingly touchy about his dignity and his majesty as a King. His feelings were here in comic contrast with the way in which he was always being got the better of by other people, until the moment when the regular explosion against their control arrived. It was this vanity which made him fall a victim to more than one woman, but it also prevented his being completely infatuated by them save in the one case of Anne Boleyn.

Was he industrious? The answer to this question must be as carefully sized as the answer to that other question we have already dealt with, the question of his strength. Just as he was certainly not really strong, so he was not really industrious in the sense of troubling himself to master a subject or a policy concentrated application. He could never force himself to do things, he was much too much the slave of appetite and caprice for that. Yet one may call him industrious in the more superficial sense of the word, of getting through 'agenda' and attending to what was put before him as a monarch. There is a vast mass of papers, many drawn up with his own hand, a great deal of annotation of documents with which he he had to deal, which prove this quality in him. One cannot use for him the word 'lazy'. He did not simply leave all work to other people and forget it in amusements, but he had not in this any more than in other matters that control of himself, that grasp over his own activities, that power of compelling himself to do what he felt to be tedious which is the mark of true industry; he did not *work* in the full sense of the word; he never got into the depth of anything he undertook to study or became the possessor of it.

Next we must specially insist upon the effect which time had upon his character—time and disease combined. At some date which we cannot exactly determine but certainly early in his life, probably well before his twenty-fourth year, he contracted syphilis. Thenceforward he gradually became a man deteriorating more and more in body and mind; he long retained his physical activity and to the end his mental activity, but he was more warped on the spiritual side until at last he became something of a monster—callous to the sufferings of others and capable of almost any cruelty in action. While on the physical side his health went all to pieces especially towards the end. For years the chief symptom of his troubles was a running ulcer in the leg, and for the last quarter of his reign he had become so huge, unwieldly and corrupt in person that he could hardly move. In the final years, though he was only a little over fifty, he had to be trundled about and his enormous bulk lifted in and out of a chair. At last he could not even sign his name; it had to be done for him with a stamp. But even to the very end he retained that sort of energy which takes its expression in violence.

He had, as might be imagined, very little power of self-restraint, and he never seems to have understood when this lack of control passed the bounds of common decency. Thus he would cry absurdly, almost like a child, especially when he was in a fit of passion or when he felt he had been made ridiculous.

Two last things must be mentioned about him, the first of which is very generally appreciated, the second of which is too often forgotten. The first is that his extreme selfishness, which grew upon him with the years, as selfishness always does in selfish men, probably passed at last the boundary of sanity, and this showed itself especially in the horrible acts of cruelty in the last part of his career. There had been plenty of cruelty in him when his character first began to deteriorate after Catherine lost her influence over him and after his disease had begun to work; but there were other political or personal reasons for it, while later it was often merely wanton and he would express, in the orders he gave, a sort of hellish savagery and greed of suffering and gloat over the agonies of his victims—such as those of the unfortunate Friar Forest whom he had roasted over a slow fire—and he mixed up horrors of this sort with the idea of grandeur. He seemed to think that they enhanced his stature in the eyes of his contemporaries and subjects. He came at last to rule by terror, and the extravagance of his later policy—such as the expedition to Boulogne—his sudden changes and his violent laws and edicts showed a crazy lack of balance.

But the second characteristic, most incongruous with such a character but undoubtedly present, was a strong attachment to the religious traditions in which he had been brought up. This was the only fixed thing in him approaching a principle. He destroyed or allowed to be destroyed the monastic institutions, which are the bulwark of the Church; he quarrelled and broke with the Papacy, which is the principle of unity in the Church (though in his time a principle confused and often debated); but he did have a fixed emotional attachment to the practices of the Faith, and he never got out of what may be called the atmosphere of these practices. He had a constant devotion to the Sacrament of the Altar and no little of his severity appeared in his treatment of anyone who denied the Real Presence. He insisted on the celibacy of the clergy, on the maintenance of full ritual in the liturgy and all ecclesiastical discipline under the episcopacy, which he formally maintained.

I have said that this side of him may appear incongruous with all the rest, and it is certainly strange in our modern eyes, but it is not so difficult to understand if we put ourselves in the position of his office and his time. He was sincere in these feelings, but his sincerity was reinforced by his vanity and by his constant insistence upon his political power. He thought of heresy under its aspect of rebellion, he disliked its variety and its anarchic quality because he lived by centralized despotism which he had inherited as a sixteenth-century king, and that very emotionalism which led him to his excesses of all kinds was capable of reinforcing him in those personal habits of worship which did not clash with his political objects.

There, as it seems to me, is the outline of the man. There is his character as a whole in all its lack of proportion and, as he developed its grotesqueness. None could be better suited to produce the ill effects which it did produce. If the evil powers had had to choose their instrument, assigning to it the right proportions of violence and weakness, incomprehension, passion and the rest, they could hardly have framed a tool more serviceable to their hands than that which did—without full intention—effect the main tragedy in the modern history of Europe.

Anne Boleyn

Anne Boleyn is the pivot figure of the English Reformation. It was through her that the political and social phenomenon called Protestant England came into the world.

She was not, of course, the cause of the movement, still less the cause of its final result. Innumerable causes converged toward that. But the movement would not have been launched, would not have been directed towards the goal which it ultimately reached, had not Anne Boleyn so completely dominated the King of England as to compel him ultimately to break with the unity of Christendom; and though Henry remained deeply attached to the Catholic doctrine and practice until his death, once he had broken with unity—that is, with the Papacy—there was a breach in the dyke and the flood was ready to pour through.

Not only was Anne Boleyn not the cause of the great affair, but still less was she the inspirer of it. Least of all the actors, with the exception perhaps of Henry himself, was she filled with any conscious intention of effecting such a result. The personality to whom must be given that role of inspirer, the mind which planned the origins of that great change and made it likely to succeed through economic as well as religious policy, was the mind of Thomas Cromwell.

Anne, then, was neither the cause nor the inspirer of the first movement away from Catholicism. But she is what I have called her, the pivot figure. It is because she was what she was, and did what she did, that England is what England is today.

It is, therefore, of the first importance to history to understand what this woman really was and the real place of her action in the whole scheme of the time. From her day to our own it has been taken for granted by all national tradition and by every historian that she lay at the origins of the English Reformation, but latterly there has arisen an effort to weaken or question this sound tradition and to explain in other ways the quarrel between Henry and Rome and the ultimate effect of it. This effort at supplanting true history by false is part of the general scepticism of our time, which is usually ready to accept anything new because new falsehoods sound more picturesque as a rule than well-worn truths. But there is here a more powerful motive, to make the origins of the change of religion in England look a little less ignoble than they really are. That is why Professor Pollard, for instance, who is the chief authority on the details of the period in England, tries to maintain the fantastic theory that Henry's attempt to get rid of his wife was not connected with Anne Boleyn, but with larger reasons of State, and that he had had the policy of getting rid of Catherine of Aragon in mind for many years before he met Anne Boleyn. The idea is not only fantastic, but desperate; it has no chance of being accepted out of England, and I do not think it will be accepted even in England save by those who are very hard up for material in the whitewashing of Henry VIII's character.

No, Anne remains and will always remain at the origins of the catastrophe. It behoves us therefore to understand her and her effect as best we can.

Anne Boleyn was a Howard. That is the first thing to grasp in connection with her, and it is all the more important to grasp it because historians have failed to stress as strongly as they should have stressed this capital feature in her position. She was a Howard through her mother, who was the daughter of that old Duke of Norfolk, the victor of Flodden, and who was the sister of his son Thomas, third Duke of Norfolk, who played a great part throughout the whole of Henry VIII's reign.

The Howards were semi-royal. They had a somewhat different character from all the other great English nobles, although the family was not remarkably old, and the reason of this particular character of theirs was that they stood for a younger branch of the Plantagenet family, which was the true blood royal of England. The greatest of the Plantagenet kings, Edward I, one of the chief figures of the height of the Middle Ages, the contemporary of St Louis, and of Alphonse of Castile, and of St Dominic, had a young son, Thomas, generally called Thomas of Brotherton. He gave him vast estates, the title of Norfolk and the hereditary post of Earl Marshal of England—that is, head of the English armed forces.

The family of this Thomas soon ended in an heiress, who married a Mowbray, whereupon her husband took on the title of Earl Marshal and all the tradition of the younger Plantagenet branch.

The Mowbrays again soon ended in an heiress, who married a wealthy private gentleman of legal descent, but one already possessed of land in East Anglia. This private gentleman was called Howard, and his son took over the tradition of Thomas of Brotherton and of the Plantagenet younger line. He was hereditary Earl Marshal of England through this marriage, and he was made Duke of Norfolk—the title of Duke being at that time of quasi-royal significance and only given to those who were of royal blood or represented a branch of it. In Anne Boleyn's time the Howard marriage into the Blood Royal was already more than a century old.

This Howard who thus became Duke of Norfolk only acquired his title thirty years before Henry VIII came to the throne, and, though they were not, under the name of Howard and through the male line, of any great importance, they were very important as representing the continued tradition of the Earl Marshalship and the younger Plantagenet blood and as having a Dukedom with its connotation of connection with the Crown.

This first Duke of Norfolk had fought against Henry VIII's father, and his title had been taken away from him, but it was restored to his son—the one who was victor at Flodden, as I have said—who was called the second Duke of Norfolk; and it was inherited by his son, again Thomas, third Duke of Norfolk, the uncle of Anne Boleyn.

So Anne Boleyn comes to the court of Henry VIII under the introduction and auspices of the Howard connection.

Her father, Sir Thomas Boleyn, was a very wealthy man, nothing like the equal of his wife socially, but of considerable family importance through *his* mother, of the Irish family of Ormonde. On his father's side he was descended from big merchants in the City of London. He had considerable talent, especially as a diplomatist, and was used by the Government on many occasions.

Now that we have understood who Anne Boleyn was in the high society of England at the time, the next thing to understand is her age, appearance and character.

Oddly enough (considering what a great position she held even before captivating Henry) we are not quite certain of the date of her birth. It would take up too much space to marshal all the arguments here which have been advanced for various dates; the one most generally given, 1507, is almost certainly wrong. I myself incline to 1502 or 1503; at any rate it was earlier rather than later. The point is of importance, because her age has a good deal to do with our understanding of the way in which she intrigued and of her capacity for fulfilling her ambition. If she were born in 1507, she would be only eighteen when Henry began to understand that he could not have her unless he married her, and she would only be fourteen when she is first talked of as mixed up in an affair. That is why 1507 seems to me an impossible date, for men were already claiming to be her lovers as early as 1521. On the other hand, if she were eighteen in 1521 and over twenty when she began to make it clear to Henry that he must marry her and that she would not be his mistress, the whole state of affairs becomes explicable.

Anyhow we may take it that round about the year 1525 this young woman was something between twenty and twenty-three years of age and had thoroughly captured the King. She was about the court both as the daughter of her important official father and as an attendant upon the Queen Catherine, but also in another connection which it is important though unpleasant to recollect, because it helps to explain Henry's action. Her younger sister Mary had already been the mistress of Henry VIII in very early youth, and he had got rid of her by marrying her off to one of his gentlemen. (She is usually called the older sister, but this is a mistake.)

Anne's appearance was singular. She carried herself rather badly, was flat-chested and round-shouldered. She had a very thin neck, with the Adam's apple prominent and large—to which it was thought she owed her really fine contralto voice. She also had very long dark glossy hair and powerful black eyes. Beautiful in any ordinary sense of the word she certainly was not. But she had a strange and not healthy power of fascination, at least over certain types of men. She was slightly deformed. The little finger of one hand was double. Those who would flatter her called it 'two nails'. People on the other tack roundly said that she had two little fingers. It was a defect which she was always at pains to conceal as best she could.

She used her fascination calculatedly and coldly, and she so used it from a very early age. When she may have been anything between her sixteenth and her eighteenth year—more probably about eighteen—in the year 1521 she so caught and entangled the heir of the greatest non-royal family in England, the Percys of Northumberland, that he was hopelessly in her power. He remained till his death full of that memory, long after he had had to give her up; for when she found she had a chance of higher game she got rid of him at once.

Meanwhile she had had a second string to her bow, even at that early period, in another conquest of hers, Wyatt, a gentleman closely connected with Henry, not a pleasant character and one who later, I think, traduced her, pretending that she had been his mistress as quite a young girl. I do not think this is true, because of what we know of Wyatt's character and what we know of her own, which was frigid and determined to make the most of every opportunity. There was nothing impulsive about her. She would not have ruined her chances by yielding to a man in Wyatt's position.

It was probably as early as this time, 1521, that the King, who was then a man of thirty, began to consider her. He probably also had about that time, and certainly immediately afterwards, given up living with his legitimate wife, Catherine, although there was no outward semblance of any breach between them. He had already had other adventures, and that illegitimate son borne to him by Elizabeth Blount, a lady who had been an old playmate of his in early youth. We have seen also how he had taken Anne's sister Mary for a mistress and discarded her. I have said that this point should especially be borne in mind, because it helps to explain the way in which Anne, who seems to have had much more will-power than her sister, attracted him. He was evidently drawn to the family type.

We must presume, of course, that Henry at this early stage did not intend marriage. He sent sharp orders that the engagement with young Percy should be put to an end and used Wolsey as his agent in so doing. Some think, however, that he was thus acting as early as 1521 rather with the idea of making a marriage for Anne as heiress of the Ormondes and thus using her politically. Whether this were so or no, at any rate soon after he intended to make her his mistress.

We have no documents; we can only judge by the nature of the case and by what followed. But it is fairly clear that some time before, or in the very early part of 1525, when Henry was thirty-four years of age, and Anne well over twenty, perhaps as much as twenty-three, there was some arrangement between them, and that Anne had already given Henry to understand that she would not be his mistress, but would envisage marriage if he could get rid of Catherine. In that year her father was raised to the peerage and given a new and more prominent position, and in that year we have also large gifts from Henry to Anne, and Henry interfering with her movements and saying where she is to stop.

It does not follow that Henry had thus early accepted the idea of marrying Anne. He probably still thought she would become his mistress at last. To attempt the repudiation of Catherine, the niece of the Emperor of Germany and the King of Spain, the most prominent woman in the greatest family in Europe, would be a very serious business indeed, and Henry's hesitating and uncertain character would hardly come to a decision at once in the matter.

In the summer of 1526 he had taken the first steps towards getting the marriage with Catherine annulled, upon the plea that the original dispensation for marrying his deceased brother's wife was invalid. In 1527 he took open steps in this direction and for the divorce, as it was called, though of course it was an effort at annulment and not at divorce in the modern sense of the term—for in those days when everybody was Catholic divorce in the modern sense was not conceivable. And thenceforward for five years Anne tyrannized over him more and more, until the unfortunate man was hardly sane in regard to her. She could do what she willed with him and drove him at her discretion to the most impossible public actions. In order to get her, he began that worrying of the Pope which ended at last in the complete breach with Rome.

What exactly the relations were between them during this interval we can guess rather than prove, though even our guess must be of a tentative character, as it is also of a displeasing one. Displeasing though it be, it is necessary to have some precision in the matter, because unless we appreciate the relations of these two, we shall not understand the complete subjection into which Henry fell.

She would not allow him complete satisfaction until she was virtually certain—every obstacle having been removed by the death of the old, very Catholic and saintly Archbishop Warham—that even if the Papal court did not grant annulment, Henry would take the matter into his own hands and marry her.

She thus began to live with Henry as though she were already married to him, somewhere about September or October of the year 1532. Before Christmas of that year she was with child. Her chaplain, Cranmer, had been marked down for the Archbishopric of Canterbury; he was enthroned in the March of 1533, pronounced the marriage between Henry and Catherine null and void, proclaimed Anne to be the legitimate wife of Henry immediately after, and crowned her Queen in Westminster a few days after the sentence. Her child, who grew up to be Queen Elizabeth, was born in the September of that year.

Now began the process which may be observed in parallel cases in all times and places, including our own day. It was a case such as many of us have come across in our own observation. Henry having been driven pretty well off his head by this woman's pertinacious handling of him and refusal for so many years to surrender herself completely to him, was, now that he obtained satisfaction, changed in her regard.

She had a bitter tongue, not without wit, using the French language, in which she was trained and in which she thought as well as spoke. She ridiculed Henry behind his back, and he got to hear of it. Her fine voice in singing had ceased to attract him—perhaps it had also deteriorated. She had accumulated enemies by her violent fits of temper, which she had never restrained in her angers with Henry himself. So it was not only the weariness of Henry with her, but also active irritation against her, which began to change her fortunes. He was tired of her, he began to dislike her, soon he hated her; and if they still carried on, it was only because Henry hoped that she would give him an heir, a boy.

She probably would have done so but for his brutality, for a miscarriage which she suffered early in 1536 was by herself ascribed to his infidelity and roughness to her. She said she had been so pulled down by the whole business that her health had suffered: and we must remember in this connection that Henry himself had long been suffering from venereal disease.

At any rate, a miscarriage she had, and what with his disappointment and his increasing loathing, Henry was determined to be rid of her. His character had deteriorated rapidly; moreover he was superstitious, and seems to have got it into his head that she had bewitched him. An indictment was framed against her, the validity of which I will discuss in a moment. She was accused of adultery with various people, including a couple of gentlemen about the court, one of the royal musicians, of lower birth, and even with her own brother.

Thomas Cromwell, then all-powerful, master of things spiritual and temporal in England, as the King's vice-regent over his new schismatic church, and the King's lieutenant in civil affairs was as determined as Henry upon her death, for it would get rid of a rival. Henry had already determined who should succeed her, a certain Jane Seymour, daughter of a small landed gentleman in Wiltshire, whose sons were employed at court, while Jane herself was, as Anne had been, about the Court as a maid of honour.

Henry and Cromwell used Cranmer to ruin Anne, by frightening and threatening her after a pretended friendship, and Cranmer's action was the more base considering that his whole advancement and position were solely due to his having been a creature of the Boleyns and their chaplain. The wretched woman fell into an hysterical condition at the approach of death; she was left uncertain whether she would be burned or decapitated. On Friday, May 19, 1536, she was beheaded with a sword within the precincts of the Tower of London, by the headsman from Calais, specially brought over for the execution.

Was she guilty of the misconduct ascribed to her? It is one of the most fiercely debated points in English history. Standing as she does at the origins of the Reformation, the favourers of that movement have been hot in her defence. On the other hand, those who desire to exculpate Henry as much as they can exculpate that detestable character, like to believe her guilty, while for the defenders of the old Religion nothing was too bad to be put down to Anne.

The accusations, especially that of incest, seem so monstrous that their very enormity is an argument in her favour. On the other hand, she was certainly unscrupulous in affairs of this kind, and she seems to have been quite unbalanced in the last year or two of her life. Some who have medical experience in these matters maintain that she suffered from a particular irresponsibility, which makes the charges credible enough. I have myself always inclined to accept them. But many good students of the period with whom I have discussed the matter are divided, and some urge the strong argument that the two gentlemen concerned did not confess, while the musician, who did, confessed only under threat of torture. Anyhow, they were all put to death as well as herself.

Catherine had died before her. Henry's marriage with Jane Seymour which took place immediately after Anne's death was therefore quite legitimate in the eyes of the Church, and quite probably there would have been a reconciliation with Rome had it not been for Thomas Cromwell's having already launched the policy of confiscating Church property, beginning with the monasteries, a policy which created a vested interest of great power against re-union.

Anne's fatal action, therefore, had come just sufficiently late to start the ball of the Reformation rolling. She had not intended it, she had intended only to fulfil a petty and personal policy, in which she triumphed only to bring about her own destruction. But she will remain for ever, in spite of lack of intention, the origin of that long movement which ended by the complete change of the English mind and character and the supplanting after a troubled and heavily contested struggle lasting over a hundred and fifty years, of the old Catholic England by the new and modern Protestant one.

XLII

The Child is Born

(first published in *The Universe*, Advent, 1936)

1936

The Child is Born

In the midwinter and the turning of the year to new things, Christendom has fixed the Mass of the Incarnation: of the divine birth, the renewal, the recovery of mankind.

Those who sneer at our origins tell us that the long dark Pagan time, which ended in a dawn, made this season also sacred to the Nativity of the Light. Let them learn that we glory in such coincidences. All those groping instinctive worships, symbols and imaginations, with which our Fathers sought to mitigate human despair, are the advent of the Faith. The Faith put substance suddenly into those shadows, and the forms of myth became alive with reality. The Child was born.

The Child is born; it is the Mass of Nativity, and the growth begins of That by which mankind is to be saved.

So long as Christendom held in one body and was quickened by a universal life—so long as our western world, the leader and teacher of the globe, was Catholic—the season was one of recognition and mere happiness. A Guest had arrived and was to be received with general ecstasy. All men were brethren in the feast for all were hosts and subjects of that Guest. After the promise of this holy night, the sun which rose would shine for ever. Such a spirit inhabited Christmas and the Twelve Days.

But can a secure rejoicing be the spirit of Christmas today? Hardly. Within the household of the Faith it remains undimmed,

365

but without these walls, in the growing murk of the modern world, it is fading or has gone. For long, even those who had abandoned unity (and, at last, all doctrine) retained some savour of the thing. It was weakened, lessened and diffused into a vague kindliness, the cherishing of human ties and a sort of sentimental pretence to forget mortality for a while. Later, even that vague reminiscence grew tenuous. Now at last, in our very time, for millions, increasing in number, the faint vestiges of Christmas glory are disappearing: have disappeared. The old despair returns.

What, then, is the command issued at Christmas to us of the Faith? It is our pride and boast that we have stood the siege and that, within our fortress, the Feast retains its splendour of reality. If we only look inwards we may have the same business with Christmas and the Epiphanal uprising as has been the practice of all our blood for fifteen hundred years.

But what if we look outwards? From our walls we survey twilit and ever darkening plains whereon the great mass of men sink back from the high order which the Faith had erected, into chaos. The shades, as they spread, grow confused by an extending cloud wherein men clash at random stumbling through fruitless effort and envenomed with mutual hatreds, following uncertain lights that drift and fail again, float tenuously for a moment in the thick night air and lead no whither. The host has become a herd. Its blind energies move towards its own destruction.

It would seem that in such a peril the command we receive at Christmas is to recover the world—if that may be—before it shall be lost. The ancient joy, the unchanging beauty, of the Twelve Days and their music we may cherish for our own heritage; but that does not redeem those who feel them not any more, nor can conceive them. Yet it is the spring of growth, the entry into life, this season of the Twelve Days; and the command issuing from it is that we restore the world: for, lacking extension of the Faith, even the mere material body of the modern world is doomed.

This task to which, in the crisis of such new but final evils, we are summoned has about it little of festivity and nothing of repose. Each of those who obey must prepare himself for an encounter. He will not carry with him the warmth and brightness of the Stable. He will enter the darkness and the mist. He will himself be enveloped by them and will be struck by the mortal chill. He will live an enemy among enemies, and very probably alone. Such trials are the conditions of his challenge, the essence of the cause he serves.

No one of those who undertake this task today will live to experience triumph. Those who are granted the supreme gift of perseverance will still be disappointed. They shall not see victory nor be present (on earth at least) to hear the cry: *Vincit Regit Imperat.*

But the Child is born and shall command us through what will have the semblance of a losing fight. That air of failure and those temptations to abandon the effort shall be our guarantees, our witnesses to divine inspiration. The ever-wavering line can only advance at the cost of such wounds, and they that are the victims of them are, even as they renew their suffering, victors.

We shall be told that, from the outset, the cause is hopeless and the battle already lost before it is begun.

What weapons are provided us with which to attack the spreading evil? What common ordering have we? What accepted tactic which can even doubtfully reassure us? We cannot but be starved by impoverishment, abandoned to neglect, left unheard: we must act isolated and alone without companions, and, as intelligence and instruction decline, our high message has a lesser and a lesser audience. How, against these odds, can we do anything at all?

Long ago such a war was waged and won. The heathen was thrust back and Christendom was established: the struggle was desperate and long but hopeful and united, and it was concluded—or seemed concluded—on our own terms. The Catholic Faith at last illumined all Europe. But the settlement did not endure. Four hundred years ago it was menaced. Unity, by which alone a thing is what it is, suffered shipwreck and the fragments drifted apart into the welter before which, today, we stand appalled.

The old victory was won upon a rising curve. But a summit was passed, and now for long the curve has been falling. We have lost ground unceasingly for generations and are still losing ground. What prospect can there be of reversing such a tide?

To all of which questions, and many more (and worse) to come, the answer is the proclamation of this season: The Child is born.

XLIII

A Letter to Duff Cooper

1937

Belloc had visited the Spanish Civil War battlefields in 1936—quite obviously he was pro-Franco and he even had an interview with him. In 1937 he had gone to America reluctantly. He wrote to J. B. Morton from New York: 'My one consolation for the dreadful business of lingering on here like a lost soul in Purgatory, at the end of the strain of all this lecturing, is that I have avoided London during this foul period. However, one can avoid London without going to New York. What is the betting that the rearmament programme breaks down before it is completed? I have a growing impression that it will do so, the burden is too great. But we shall see.'[1]

He sailed home at the end of May.

[1] Morton: *Belloc*, p. 152.

To Duff Cooper

Would you like to hear about America? It's only 2 years since I was here last, but the further drift from Europe is marked, even in that short time: I suppose the Spanish war has helped to bewilder them still more and perhaps it dawns upon them that Europe is complicated and difficult to understand. Also they are less and less wanting to understand or to be interested in Europe. Their own problems are absorbing enough and a place full of separate nationalities is beyond them.

The power of propaganda here—especially of unplanned, instinctive propaganda—is very great. It is less than it was but it is still much the most effective force from the outside. All that they know of the old world—and even of the past—comes to them through the English language. Such a single medium distorts, but it is all to the advantage of the people who control the medium. Outside a small clique the English version of European affairs is accepted as a matter of course.

The leaning towards the Reds in Spain is very pronounced. The Franco side does not get much of a hearing. The whole thing is looked on by the proletariat of the big towns here as a quarrel of capitalist and wage-slave—*except* where the proletariat (as largely here, and still more in Boston) is Catholic. The Catholic body—which, with its penumbra, is perhaps a sixth of the nation—is solidly for Franco, but it hardly knows why it is so, and can't explain the position to the others. The close and long association of ideas between continental Catholicism and the counter-Revolution is quite unfamiliar to them. Of the French they know nothing and what they saw of them in the war makes them more distant than ever.

Another curious development is the Anti-Nazi feeling. This is very strong even here in New York where the huge Jewish population—less than $\frac{1}{3}$ now but more than $\frac{1}{4}$—makes for a fairly strong (and blind) anti-semitic passion. The Germany of today is more and more disliked because it is regarded by the masses as repressing the effort of the wage earner to emancipate himself, and by the more or less educated, with political tradition, as the enemy of their traditions. I doubt whether any incident, however violent, would make American opinion move towards either Berlin or Rome. It is mercurial and takes sudden jumps, but it will hardly take such a jump as that. The whole attitude of centralized despotic power is incomprehensible to people here—and no wonder.

The issue on the Supreme Court is very much alive. I should say, as things now stand, that there is a shade of odds against Roosevelt's getting his way, but a single incident would be enough to swell a tide in his favour. If, for instance, there were another striking decision of the Court against organized labour or in favour of great accumulations a flame might break out against it. All but the mobs of the big cities have a rooted attachment to the Constitution, but the quarrel of capital and labour has got so violent that not even this might be enough to defeat Roosevelt if he were suddenly identified with a popular clamour among the urban wage earners and the Judges identified with their masters. By the time you get this things will no doubt have moved a peg or two one way or the other.

I see few people, for my work is very heavy. It entails constant and most wearing moving about between the City, my lecturing place[1] (ten miles out) and Long Island where—and where only—I can sleep in quiet. I stay in New York a night or two a week but it pulls me down—though I like the people and have good memories from the past. You know how difficult it is to get about there!— and, apart from constant gabble, I have to *write* about 2,000 words a day or more. What work, and in what an order!

[1] Fordham University.

XLIV

A Sentence from a Letter
to Lady Lovat

1938

IN THE TRAIN
December 28, 1938

By my nature I am all sceptical and sensual—so much so as hardly
to understand how others believe unseen things or do violence to
their inclinations.

XLV

A Letter to Mrs Mervyn Herbert[1]

1939

KING'S LAND
May 1, 1939

My head is clear for I have slept—at last. Thank God my conscience is also reasonably clear, and I have a day clear (please God! for one never knows) without interruption. So it is my duty to sit down and write seriously and at length of Charles II.[2] My opening chapter (the preface has already gone in). It is my duty I say: but Duty is one of the things which make me vomit—so I'll give it a miss and write to you. I wish I could talk to you instead. Talking is much better fun than writing and allows for more crisscross. However, if my health and temper hold, I shall be in Paris about 20 days hence[3] and babbling away like a shallow brook, chattering away like a flock of starlings, gabbling away like a great Crested Gabbler, which is, or ought to be, a sort of bird. By this post (but it will arrive later) I send you a photograph of my portrait in the Academy by Jimmy Gunn.[4] It made a great sensation on Private View day, and so it ought for it is a most remarkable picture of the Gorilla Type. The photograph is very big, 15 inches long I should say: so have it framed in a strong Renaissance frame of Massy Gold. Then set it up on an easel of costly wood—cedar is the

---

[1] Mrs Mervyn Herbert was married to a younger son of Lord Carnarvon whom Belloc had tutored at Oxford. He died in 1929.

[2] *Charles II* was published in 1940.

[3] Belloc first went to Brussels going on to Paris where he stayed at the British Embassy.

[4] The Gunn portrait of him was of course famous, as was another picture in which he painted Chesterton, Baring and Belloc. The Belloc portrait was on view at his Royal Academy on April 18th.

best; drape it with thick deep and dark velvet above and at the side, with golden tassels, and set it up in your drawing-room so that it thoroughly clutters up that apartment. If there isn't room for it (Here an interruption of 10 minutes to go out and shake hands with Mrs Bacon, 85, and Miss Polly, 73, the one the widow of my old local schoolmaster, Mr Bacon, who also taught all my children arithmetic and writing, and the other the local schoolmistress who ran the village school for 40 years and had for pupils all those who have served under this roof). If there is not room for it, I say, build on a large alcove projecting over the street and set it up there; or, alternatively, lease the flat opposite yours and set up a temporary special shrine for it like the Dresden Madonna at Dresden (you know the one I mean, Raphael's Madonna, by Raphael), and be sure to burn seven lamps in front of it by day and night, furnished with scented oil. A little incense would do no harm and I am all for a wreath of laurel for glory and another of bay for the muses and Apollo. But be careful to explain to the visiting crowds that it is but an image, a simulacrum, and not to be worshipped with divine honours, for that is idolatry. . . .

I long to hear about your three. But I wouldn't have you write for that is a beastly grind and God knows you have enough to do without adding the intolerable burden of correspondence. So wisely abandon all thought of it. When I arrive I will make up for it by Persiflage, Badinage, and sparkling Repartee—also witty anecdote and boring repetition thereof. I shall also ask you for meals and beg you to come and eat with me also and bring with you your three, also the 2 dogs. I look forward to seeing you again more than I can say. . . .

My hostess, I wish you all peace and rest and fruition, so much as may be in this difficult world. I want you to have 3 guardian Angels, instead of only one as at present. I will try and buy you the 2 others and bring them over when I come. They are not allowed to go by rail unaccompanied as big dogs do, and their wings take up a lot of room, but I'll manage it. Also I will bring some powder for scattering Devils and some Balm and some Mandragora (which is good for sleep) and some Attar of Roses and some Ambergris and whatnot.

XLVI

A Letter to Evan Charteris

1939

KING'S LAND
December 2, 1939

I am just back from the French front, more dead than alive and this letter will suffer from my exhaustion. I bumped about in staff cars over the roads of Lorraine until I was almost dead. Then I went to Brussels, for I had to give an address in French to the élite, including the English Ambassador and all sorts of other buddies. The audience was very rich and the strain was more than I could manage, for I do not naturally talk in French, and the curse of it is that I have an almost perfect French accent, so that whenever I give a lecture or an address in French it is like the story of the old German who talked the most perfect Elizabethan English but got everything wrong, and when he landed at Charing Cross in the old days, shouted to a Cabman, 'Ho, Varlet! To the nearest hostelry and that right speedily!' He was locked up because they thought he was mad.

You are right about Carlyle. I have always wanted to write a series, or suggest a series to a publisher, called 'Twelve Great Eunuchs of the Victorian Period', and the first of these would have been Carlyle. I do not think the war will cure the English—or British as they are now called—of their passion for Prussia. Love dies hard. Contrariwise, to what is often imagined, a strongly rooted love affair like that might last forever. Some say that when they begin dropping bombs on London (if ever) our affection for them might wane; but I doubt it. There is something about the Hun which fascinates all Dons and Schoolmasters; and the putrid stuff

[1] Maurice Baring, who was suffering from incurable paralysis agitans.

374

they call their philosophy, which is mere lambent emotionalism, fascinates Oxford and Cambridge—and Durham too, I suppose, though that is a University which I have never dwelt in. You think that shutting up the Universities would do the trick? I doubt it! The tragedy of it is that the Huns themselves do not like us, though we like them. 'Twas ever thus. Eros goes unrequited; and serve him right for being an idiot. What would completely cure the Prussians would be being beaten heavily with a cudgel once a week until they died.

P.S. Paris is quite light and one walks about fairly easily. But Nancy and the frontier towns are black as London is. What bores me more than the Black Out is ceaseless official Propaganda, unintelligent and vulgar.

I flew back from Paris a few days ago in a plane as old as Methuselah and the size and shape of a coffin. I got violent vertigo, as I always knew I should if I flew through the air in a flying machine. I shall probably never recover from that foolhardy experiment! How man can half live in the air is more than I can understand.

The Boche thinks that if he keeps us all on the *qui vive* till late February he can eat us up and that in France Communism will by that time have destroyed the power of the French. . . .

In Belgium they think they can keep out of it. The King, who is most intelligent, talked to me for an hour to that effect . . .

Write to me again as quickly as possible. My strength is running out, like sawdust out of a worn doll.

XLVII

A Letter to Evan Charteris

1940

KING'S LAND
July 5, 1940

You ask me why the French collapsed. I answer that that is a question impossible to answer upon any of the great collapses in history, for they are due to the convergence of a certain number of factors, more than half of which are unknown to the observer. Why did the English resistance to the new religion break down after a few massacres at the hands of the profiteers, including Russell? No one is more attached to his domestic observances than the Englishman, and yet he swallowed the startling innovation of the Prayer Book and the Calvinist Missioners from abroad without any serious resistance. Why did the Roman Legions suddenly disappear and a sort of horde take its place? Why did drawing and painting things as they are almost suddenly give way to pictures in which the grass is red and the faces of the human beings are distorted masks and no artist ever finished anything? Why did men in the middle of the third century suddenly stop sculpturing stone properly and start producing puerile rubbish? Compare the triumphant arch of Titus in dear old Rome with the neighbouring triumphant arch of Constantine, and I assure you, you will be startled: but then all this Apocalypse business will make it rather difficult to go to Rome for a season or two! Why did English lyric poetry, which was and still could be the summit of all the lyric poetry of the world, fade away and turn into chopped up prose? What happens is some disease at the roots, and we can never trace that.

The politicians of course, are mere mouthpieces of the banking power, and third rate mouthpieces at that. If we had begun making an Army in '35 or even in '36, or even as late as Duff's[1] resignation (which *ought* to have been a turning point, but nothing ever is a turning point under the lethargic conditions of Parliamentarism), there would have been no war. Better still, the French and the English might have been able to get into Germany in the summer of '39, or at any rate be together in attempting it now. But the bankers were quite certain that we could not afford an Army, and our decadence is such that no one dares mention that elementary fact of their error.

I am glad that they are lining the cliffs as you tell me, and I have discovered everywhere that the determination of public opinion is admirable. But what I doubt is the organization. I also think it deplorable that people talk in terms of unrealities. Of course, they have been brought up to do it all their lives and it is too late to change them, especially is it too late to change the illusion, almost universal in this country, that the possession of wealth is an excellence, like courage, or charity. If any one very rich man had said and printed what half a dozen poor men, including myself, have been saying and printing for years, *that an army was vitally necessary and that England was in peril for the lack of it,* that rich man would have been listened to. But it would seem that great wealth and wisdom are incompatible, unless the wealth be hereditary and exercised in mature surroundings.

I was going to Somerset to stop with Mary Herbert at Pixton and with her sister-in-law Elizabeth at Tetton, the two houses that receive me with so much kindness that they are like home to me. But when I heard on arriving in London and talking to people that the attack might come at any moment, I thought it better to wait here in London, pass my *Sunday Times*[2] article through, go down home to Sussex tomorrow and keep in touch with that house of mine where my daughter is with her husband and her children. The strain cannot last indefinitely. While it does, London and my house are sufficiently in connection for me to judge their situation. If I were to go away to my friends further off, as I have greatly desired to do (for it is many weeks since I saw them), I might get cut off by a Government order restricting travel. Old as I am I am still the

[1] Duff Cooper.
[2] Belloc was writing a weekly commentary on the military situation for the *Sunday Times* through the winter of 1939–40.

head of that little household and responsible for it. There must be someone to prevent misjudgement; though I have no fear of panic because my daughter is admirably level-headed, and her husband is a man of ability who was on the staff all during the last war in the Near East . . .

I went to his (Desmond MacCarthy's) new house, which is the one that Garrick used to have, on the tenth. It is a most delightful place with all the architecture in exact proportion, which is to the modern eye a revelation. It is not easy to get at because one has to go to Hampton Court and cross the river, but it is worth the trouble. I went there to see Cecilia the other day, and she was very happy and a delight to meet and to see.

P.S. I think the main factors of the French collapse were

(1) Months underground and doing nothing.
(2) Strong Communist propaganda . . .
(3) *Much the most important*—the Belgian folly in leaving the bridge of Vise open.
(4) Numbers. 60 Divisions to a 100, then 150, then 200. Extra numbers mean *sleep* and lesser numbers mean *loss of sleep*, and I believe that loss of sleep did most of the harm.

XLVIII

The End

1953

The last years were sad, and perhaps not unsurprisingly. Belloc had all his life taxed himself mentally and physically to the hilt, never ceasing to write or travel.

And then his son Peter who was in the Air Force had been on a raid and on returning to England was taken to hospital with septicaemia and died in 1941. This was a severe blow. It was in January of the following year that Belloc himself had a stroke and fell at the Reform Club. He developed pneumonia and it was thought the end had come, but his great physical strength kept him alive. In July 1950 Belloc celebrated his eightieth birthday but he was failing fast.

The fateful day came on Sunday July 12, 1953 when he fell in his study on to the fire. Luckily his daughter Eleanor Jebb heard him fall and together with her husband Julian they threw a rug round him and got him into his armchair. He drank some sherry, and as Eleanor Jebb said, 'For the first time in my life I saw his hand shake.'

The burns of themselves were not very bad but the shock had been too much for him[1] and he died four days later.

1 See Morton: *Belloc*, p. 178.

BIBLIOGRAPHY

I. BOOKS AND PAMPHLETS BY HILAIRE BELLOC

The following list of Belloc's publications is taken from *The English First Editions of Hilaire Belloc* by PATRICK CAHILL, from whom the complete text may be obtained at Lye End, St John's, Woking, Surrey, price 10s 6d. It is a fine piece of bibliographical scholarship, and should be consulted by anyone who wishes to have a full picture of Belloc's literary activity.[1]

1896 *Verses and Sonnets.* Ward & Downey.
1896 *The Bad Child's Book of Beasts.* Oxford: Alden & Co., Bocardo Press; London: Simpkin, Marshall, Hamilton, Kent & Co.
1897 *More Beasts (for Worse Children).* Edward Arnold.
1898 *The Modern Traveller.* Edward Arnold.
1899 *Danton.* James Nisbet & Co.
1899 *A Moral Alphabet.* Edward Arnold.
1899 Extracts from the Diaries and Letters of HUBERT HOWARD with a Recollection by a Friend. (Edited by H.B.). Oxford: Horace Hart.
1900 *Lambkin's Remains.* Oxford: The Proprietors of the *J.C.R.*
1900 *Paris.* Edward Arnold.
1901 *Robespierre.* James Nisbet & Co.
1902 *The Path to Rome.* George Allen.
1903 *Caliban's Guide to Letters.* Duckworth & Co.
1903 *The Great Inquiry.* Duckworth & Co.
1903 *Why Eat ?* A Broadside.
1903 *The Romance of Tristan and Iseult.* Translated from the French of J. Bédier by H.B. George Allen.
1904 *Avril.* Duckworth & Co.
1904 *Emmanuel Burden.* Methuen & Co.

---

[1] This bibliography is taken from Robert Speaight's invaluable biography of Belloc. (Hollis & Carter, 1957).

BIBLIOGRAPHY

1904   *The Old Road*. Archibald Constable & Co.

1906   *Esto Perpetua*. Duckworth & Co.

1906   *An Open Letter on the Decay of Faith*. Burns & Oates.

1906   *Sussex*. Adam & Charles Black.

1906   *Hills and the Sea*. Methuen & Co.

1907   *The Historic Thames*. J. M. Dent & Co.

1907   *Cautionary Tales for Children*. Eveleigh Nash.

1908   *The Catholic Church and Historical Truth* (Catholic Evidence Lectures, No. 3). Preston: W. Watson & Co.

1908   *On Nothing*. Methuen & Co.

1908   *Mr Clutterbuck's Election*. Eveleigh Nash.

1908   *The Eye-Witness*. Eveleigh Nash.

1908   *An Examination of Socialism*. Catholic Truth Society.

1909   *The Pyrenees*. Methuen & Co.

1909   *A Change in the Cabinet*. Methuen & Co.

1909   *Marie Antoinette*. Methuen & Co.

1909   *On Everything*. Methuen & Co.

1909   *The Church and Socialism*. Catholic Truth Society.

1910   *The Ferrer Case*. Catholic Truth Society.

1910   *On Anything*. Constable & Co.

1910   *Pongo and the Bull*. Constable & Co.

1910   *On Something*. Methuen & Co.

1910   *Verses*. Duckworth & Co.

1911   *The Party System*, by Hilaire Belloc and Cecil Chesterton. Stephen Swift.

1911   *The French Revolution*. Williams & Norgate.

1911   *The Girondin*. Thomas Nelson & Sons.

1911   *More Peers*. Stephen Swift.

1911   *Socialism and the Servile State*. A Debate between Messrs Hilaire Belloc and J. Ramsay MacDonald, MP. The South West London Federation of the Independent Labour Party.

1911   *First and Last*. Methuen & Co.

1911   *The Battle of Blenheim*. Stephen Swift & Co.

1911   *Malplaquet*. Stephen Swift and Co.

1912   *Waterloo*. Stephen Swift & Co.

1912   *The Four Men*. Thomas Nelson & Sons.

1912   *The Green Overcoat*. Bristol: J. W. Arrowsmith; London: Simpkin, Marshall, Hamilton, Kent & Co.

1912   *Turcoing*. Stephen Swift & Co.

BIBLIOGRAPHY

1912 *Warfare in England*. Williams & Norgate.

1912 *This and That*. Methuen & Co.

1912 *The Servile State*. T. N. Foulis.

1912 *The River of London*. T. N. Foulis.

1912 *Crécy*. Stephen Swift & Co.

1913 *The Stane Street*. Constable & Co.

1913 *Poitiers*. Hugh Rees.

1914 *Anti-Catholic History*. Catholic Truth Society.

1914 *The Book of the Bayeux Tapestry*. Chatto & Windus.

1915 *Land & Water Map of the War*, drawn under the direction of Hilaire Belloc. *Land & Water*.

1915 *The History of England* (in eleven volumes). Vol. XI is by H. B. Sands and Co.; New York: The Catholic Publication Society of America.

1915 *A General Sketch of the European War: The First Phase*. Thomas Nelson & Sons.

1915 *The Two Maps of Europe*. C. Arthur Pearson.

1916 *The Last Days of the French Monarchy*. Chapman & Hall.

1916 *A General Sketch of the European War: The Second Phase*. Thomas Nelson & Sons.

1916 *The Second Year of the War*. Reprinted by permission from *Land and Water*: Burrup, Mathieson & Sprague.

1918 *The Free Press*. George Allen & Unwin.

1918 *Religion and Civil Liberty*. Catholic Truth Society.

1919 *The Principles of War*, by MARSHAL FOCH. Translated by Hilaire Belloc. Chapman & Hall.

1919 *Precepts and Judgments*, by MARSHAL FOCH. Translated by Hilaire Belloc, Chapman & Hall.

1920 *The Catholic Church and the Principle of Private Property*. Catholic Truth Society.

1920 *Europe and the Faith*. Constable & Co.

1920 *The House of Commons and Monarchy*. George Allen & Unwin.

1921 *Pascal's 'Provincial Letters'*. Catholic Truth Society.

1922 *Catholic Social Reform versus Socialism*. Catholic Truth Society.

1922 *The Jews*. Constable & Co.

1922 *The Mercy of Allah*. Chatto & Windus.

1923 *On*. Methuen & Co.

1923 *The Road*. Manchester: Charles W. Hobson.

1923 *Sonnets and Verse*. Duckworth & Co.

BIBLIOGRAPHY

1923 *The Contrast*. J. W. Arrowsmith (London) Ltd.

1924 *Economics for Helen*. J. W. Arrowsmith (London) Ltd.

1924 *The Campaign of 1812*. Thomas Nelson & Sons.

1924 *The Political Effort*. True Temperance Association.

1925 *The Cruise of the 'Nona'*. Constable & Co.

1925 *A History of England:* Vol. I. Methuen & Co.

1925 *Mr Petre*. Arrowsmith.

1925 *Miniatures of French History*. Thomas Nelson & Sons.

1925 *England and the Faith*. A Reply published in the *Evening Standard* to an article by Dean Inge in the same journal. Catholic Truth Society.

1926 *The Highway and its Vehicles*. The Studio Ltd.

1926 *Short Talks with the Dead*. The Cayme Press.

1926 *Mrs Markham's New History of England*. The Cayme Press.

1926 *The Emerald*. Arrowsmith.

1926 *A Companion to Mr Wells's 'Outline of History'*. Sheed & Ward.

1926 *Mr Belloc Still Objects*. Sheed & Ward.

1927 *The Catholic Church and History*. Burns Oates & Washbourne.

1927 *A History of England*: Vol. II. Methuen & Co.

1927 *The Haunted House*. Arrowsmith.

1927 *Oliver Cromwell*. Ernest Benn.

1928 *Many Cities*. Constable and Co.

1928 *A History of England:* Vol. III. Methuen & Co.

1928 *James the Second*. Faber & Gwyer.

1928 *How the Reformation Happened*. Jonathan Cape.

1928 *But Soft—We are Observed*. Arrowsmith.

1928 *A Conversation with an Angel*. Jonathan Cape.

1928 *Belinda*. Constable & Co.

1929 *Survivals and New Arrivals*. Sheed & Ward.

1929 *Joan of Arc*. Cassell & Co.

1929 *The Missing Masterpiece*. Arrowsmith.

1930 *Richelieu*. Ernest Benn.

1930 *A Pamphlet*. (Privately printed for H.B.'s sixtieth birthday.)

1930 *Wolsey*. Cassell & Co.

1930 *The Man Who Made Gold*. Arrowsmith.

1930 *New Cautionary Tales*. Duckworth.

1931 *A Conversation with a Cat*. Cassell & Co.

1931 *On Translation*. (The Taylorian Lecture.) Oxford: The Clarendon Press.

BIBLIOGRAPHY

1931   *Essays of a Catholic.* Sheed & Ward.

1931   *A History of England:* Vol. IV. Methuen & Co.

1931   *Cranmer.* Cassell & Co.

1931   *Travel Notes on a Holiday Tour in France,* by JAMES MURRAY ALLISON, with an introduction and commentary by Hilaire Belloc. Privately printed.

1931   *The Praise of Wine.* An Heroic Poem to Duff Cooper. (1) No imprint. Presented by H.B. to his friends for Christmas, 1931. (2) *An Heroic Poem in Praise of Wine.* Peter Davies (1932).

1932   *The Postmaster-General.* Arrowsmith.

1932   *Ladies and Gentlemen.* Duckworth.

1932   *Napoleon.* Cassell & Co.

1933   *The Tactics and Strategy of the Great Duke of Marlborough.* Arrowsmith.

1933   *William the Conqueror.* Peter Davies.

1933   *Becket.* Catholic Truth Society. (Published also by Sheed & Ward (1933) in 'The English Way', a collection of essays by various authors.)

1933   *Charles the First.* Cassell & Co.

1934   *Cromwell.* Cassell & Co.

1934   *A Shorter History of England.* George G. Harrap & Co.

1935   *Milton.* Cassell & Co.

1936   *The Battle Ground.* Cassell & Co.

1936   *The County of Sussex.* Cassell & Co.

1936   *An Essay on the Restoration of Property.* The Distributist League.

1936   *Characters of the Reformation.* Sheed & Ward.

1936   *The Hedge and the Horse.* Cassell & Co.

1937   *An Essay on the Nature of Contemporary England.* Constable & Co.

1937   *The Crusade.* Cassell & Co.

1937   *The Crisis of Our Civilization.* Cassell & Co.

1938   *Sonnets and Verse.* Duckworth. New edition, with additional poems.

1938   *The Great Heresies.* Sheed & Ward.

1938   *Return to the Baltic.* Constable & Co.

1938   *The Question and the Answer.* Longmans, Green & Co.

1938   *Monarchy:* A Study of Louis XIV. Cassell & Co.

1938   *The Case of Dr Coulton.* Sheed & Ward.

1939   *On Sailing the Sea.* Methuen & Co.

1940   *The Last Rally.* Cassell & Co.

BIBLIOGRAPHY

1940   *The Catholic and the War*. Burns Oates.
1940   *On the Place of Gilbert Chesterton in English Letters*. Sheed & Ward.
1941   *The Silence of the Sea*. Cassell & Co.
1942   *Elizabethan Commentary*. Cassell & Co.
1942   *Places*. Cassell & Co.
1954   *The Verse of Hilaire Belloc*. The Nonesuch Press.
1955   *One Thing and Another*. Hollis & Carter.

II. BOOKS ABOUT HILAIRE BELLOC

1916   *Hilaire Belloc*, by C. CREIGHTON MANDELL and EDWARD SHANKS. Methuen & Co.
1945   *Hilaire Belloc*, by ROBERT HAMILTON. Douglas Organ.
1954   *Hilaire Belloc: No Alienated Man*, by FREDERICK WILHEMSEN. Sheed & Ward.
1955   *Hilaire Belloc: A Memoir*, by J. B. MORTON. Hollis & Carter.
1956   *The Young Hilaire Belloc*, by MARIE BELLOC-LOWNDES. New York: Kenedy & Sons.
1956   *Testimony to Hilaire Belloc*, by ELEANOR and REGINALD JEBB. Methuen & Co.
1957   *The Life of Hilaire Belloc* by ROBERT SPEAIGHT. Hollis & Carter.
1958   *Letters from Hilaire Belloc*. Selected and edited by ROBERT SPEAIGHT. Hollis & Carter.

A Note on the Type

The text of this book was set on the Monotype in a type face known as Plantin. Brought out in 1913 by the Monotype Corporation, Plantin was named for Christopher Plantin, a Frenchman born at Saint-Avertin. While in his middle thirties, Plantin settled in Antwerp, where he set up a printing press. In 1563, he added a foundry to the press and it was for this foundry and during the first decade of its existence that Claude Garamond, the greatest of all the French punch-cutters, designed the type on which the modern version of Plantin is based. A sturdy face, capable of standing up under the more difficult printing conditions, Plantin combines great dignity with legibility.

Binding design by Bonnie Spiegel